Praise for PTOWN

"[Manso] delivers with gusto o[...] sex, and money' subtitle."

"Unsparing, to say the least."

—*The New York Times*

"This is nonfiction, and the tales are all true, no matter how bizarre."

—*The Sunday Advocate*

"[A] blistering critique . . . [Manso's] point is a good and important one."

—Andrew Sullivan, "The Daily Dish"

"One of the touching aspects of Manso's book is how much sheer human kindness and volunteerism it documents. . . . Positive portraits of gay people are featured prominently throughout."

—Michael Hattersley, *Konch* magazine

"Peter Manso's book has done something that nothing else has been able to do. It has forced us to talk with each other about what is really happening to us."

—John Thomas, *Lip Magazine* (Life in Provincetown)

"Beautifully executed."

—*The Salem News*

"Manso has caught the intriguing angles that let him shed light on the heart of Ptown."

—*Kirkus Reviews*

"This postmodernist hybrid is a joy to read. Part local history, part travelogue, part whodunit, this book shows how a politically and culturally fashionable pressure group was able to succeed where the Puritans failed: homogenize a town that was famous for its diversity."

—Ishmael Reed, author of *Mumbo Jumbo*

BY PETER MANSO

Running Against the Machine:
The Mailer-Breslin Campaign

Faster: A Racer's Diary

The Shadow of the Moth:
A Novel of Espionage with Virginia Woolf
(with Ellen Hawkes)

Mailer: His Life and Times

Brando, the Biography

PTOWN

ART, SEX, AND MONEY
ON THE OUTER CAPE

PETER MANSO

A LISA DREW BOOK

SCRIBNER
New York   London   Toronto   Sydney   Singapore

A LISA DREW BOOK/SCRIBNER
1230 Avenue of the Americas
New York, NY 10020

First Lisa Drew/Scribner trade paperback edition 2003
SCRIBNER and design are trademarks of Macmillan Library Reference USA, Inc.,
used under license by Simon & Schuster, the publisher of this work.
A LISA DREW BOOK is a trademark of Simon & Schuster, Inc.

For information about special discounts for bulk purchases,
please contact Simon & Schuster Special Sales: 1-800-456-6798 or
business@simonandschuster.com

Set in Berling

Manufactured in the United States of America

1 3 5 7 9 10 8 6 4 2

The Library of Congress has cataloged the Scribner edition as follows:
Manso, Peter.
Ptown : art, sex, and money on the Outer Cape / Peter Manso.
p. cm.
"A Lisa Drew Book."
Includes bibliographical references (p.) and index.

1. Provincetown (Mass.)—History. 2. Provincetown (Mass.)—Social conditions.
3. Arts and society—Massachusetts—Provincetown.
4. Provincetown (Mass.)—Biography. I. Title.

F74.P96 M36 2002
974.4'92—dc21   2002066916

ISBN 0-7432-0094-2
0-7432-4311-0 (Pbk)

For Anna and Victor

AUTHOR'S NOTE

This is a work of nonfiction. All the names are real, with the exception of a few that have been changed to protect individuals from legal prosecution or other difficulties. Several other names have been changed at the principal's request. The scenes presented are all true to life. The spoken words were all told to me, and thoughts that I have attributed to characters were either described to me or seemed to flow inevitably from events and personalities whose authenticity was verified through careful research.

In the interest of making this book more readable, I have occasionally taken the liberty of departing from strict chronology so long as these changes did not alter the truth or meaning of individual events, or distort the overall story of the community of Provincetown.

CONTENTS

PTOWN

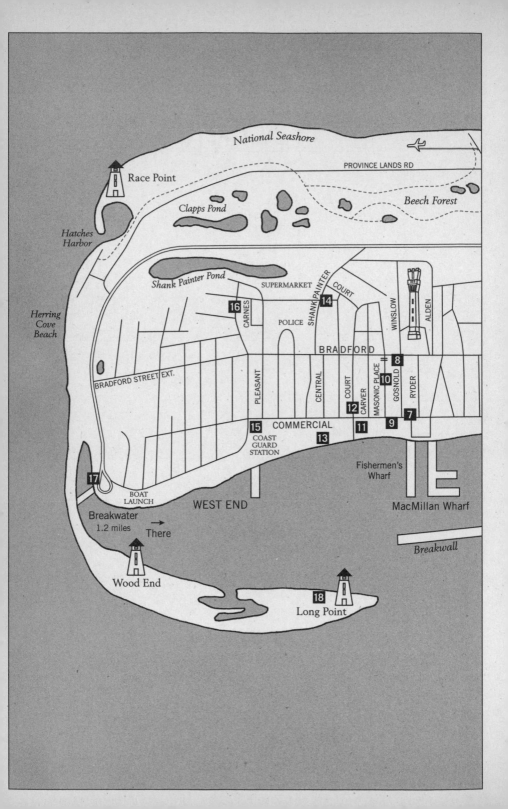

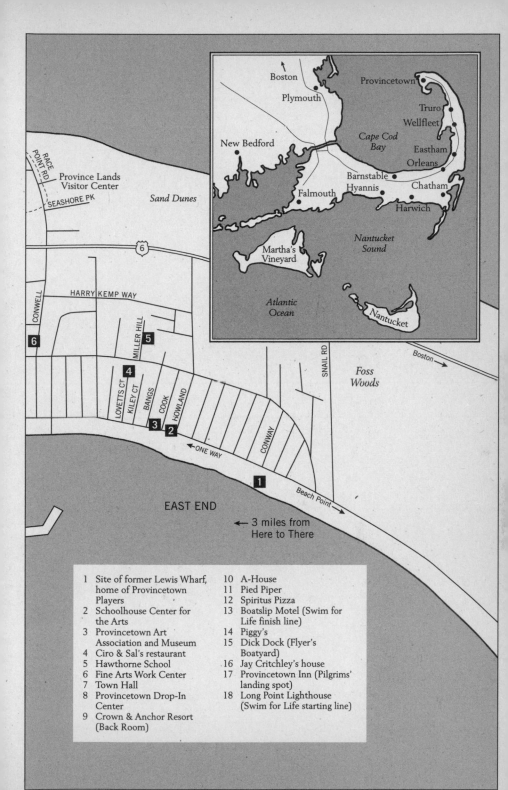

Boston

Plymouth

Provincetown

Truro

Wellfleet

New Bedford

Cape Cod
Bay

Eastham

Orleans

Barnstable

Hyannis

Chatham

Falmouth

Harwich

Nantucket
Sound

Martha's
Vineyard

Atlantic
Ocean

Nantucket

RACE POINT RD

Province Lands
Visitor Center

Sand Dunes

SEASHORE PK

6

CONWELL

HARRY KEMP WAY

MILLER HILL

6

5

4

LOVETTS CT

KILEY CT

BANGS

COOK

HOWLAND

3

2

SNAIL RD

Foss
Woods

Boston

CONWAY

← ONE WAY

1

Beach Point →

EAST END

← 3 miles from
Here to There

1   Site of former Lewis Wharf,
    home of Provincetown
    Players
2   Schoolhouse Center for
    the Arts
3   Provincetown Art
    Association and Museum
4   Ciro & Sal's restaurant
5   Hawthorne School
6   Fine Arts Work Center
7   Town Hall
8   Provincetown Drop-In
    Center
9   Crown & Anchor Resort
    (Back Room)
10 A-House
11 Pied Piper
12 Spiritus Pizza
13 Boatslip Motel (Swim for
    Life finish line)
14 Piggy's
15 Dick Dock (Flyer's
    Boatyard)
16 Jay Critchley's house
17 Provincetown Inn (Pilgrims'
    landing spot)
18 Long Point Lighthouse
    (Swim for Life starting line)

CHAPTER 1

THE HOUSE PARTY

Holding a piece of rolled sushi, flash fried in the delicate tempura batter that was the catering craze that summer, an elegant man, somewhere in his fifties, leaned over the banister and yelled down to the other guests. "Fabulous! Absolutely delicious!" He just barely saved his champagne from cascading down the spiral staircase, as he continued upward to the roof deck to take in the spectacular 360-degree view of the Provincetown night.

It would later be spoken of as the best party of the season, celebrating "The completion of 10 Cranberry Avenue, Provincetown, Massachusetts," a project that had taken the new owners, Mark Kaiser and Al Conlan, over two years and, according to most estimates, over $2 million.

The house was located in the elite Meadowview Heights subdivision, a newly developed area high above the dunes and beaches, which lay in the farthest West End. Once no one would have thought of building so far out of town. Provincetown had always been a fishing village with its homes nestled tightly around the curve of the bay and its justly celebrated "snug harbor." Most of its charm stemmed from the tiny streets and clustered bungalows. In the early 1970s, a few locals had built small homes in the area just below Meadowview, and in the early nineties, these unassuming houses had been bought up, renovated, and enlarged. The expansion, driven by dot.comers and the beneficiaries of private money, spread to Pilgrim Heights to the east and to Meadow-view, producing the high-end equivalent of suburban sprawl.

Guests had begun arriving at the housewarming promptly at the appointed hour of six P.M., a little subdued and on their best behavior. This was no makeshift barbecue, nor a mere stop on the merry-go-round of cocktails that revolved in the Provincetown bars and restaurants on a busy summer weekend.

The early gay crowd was joined by a sprinkling of straight people from town, workers mostly, including a few couples with their children. It seemed like every contractor in town had come to celebrate. The locksmith. The people who'd installed the alarm system and the ones who'd put in the elevator. The plumber. The electricians. The gay landscaper with his mostly straight crew. The stonemason who did all the work on the front stoop. People from the gas company. The guy who'd put in the irrigation system. The stereo people. Their presence was a nice touch, an acknowledgment that Mark and Al were here for real, joining the community.

Snaking his way through the early revelers and sliding outdoors onto the main deck, a tall, muscular man dressed in khakis and striped Henley approached Mark Kaiser. Mark was stealing a quiet moment for himself, staring out over the dunes, off over Herring Cove Beach and its neighbor, "*the* beach." Hidden and used as a daytime cruising area by the gay population, its location was marked by the overflowing bike racks that suddenly appeared along the road in the middle of nowhere. The sun was beginning to flirt with the horizon, colors splaying out across the sky, as though this were the tropics, not Cape Cod.

The man in the khakis whispered conspiratorially into Mark's ear, "I can't believe what you've done with this place! We've been sneaking by, trying to peek in, but you two have kept such a low profile. . . . Everyone has been talking about you, you know that. And of course the house, too."

Mark, an imposing man with broad shoulders and muscled biceps rippling under his fitted Daniel Cleary dress shirt, leaned into his guest and confided, "You know, we've had Realtors drive by and come to the door, asking to come in. 'We've heard about your house around town.' I've actually been approached by someone here tonight who asked if he could list the house if, if, if we wanted to sell . . . which, by the way, we don't. We didn't build to sell."

Mark excused himself and headed back toward the crowd gathered at the top of the stairs. Stopping at the martini bar, which had been set up in the breakfast nook beside the kitchen, he ordered a Ketel One for himself from the array of top-shelf vodkas and waited as the bartender pumped his drink into a crystal martini glass from the chrome, bar-grade liquor dispenser that measured shots. ("A toy," Mark had joked when he ordered it.) He continued to accept the guests' compliments, giving them his full attention, recommending they try the fresh vegetable pakoras in their tangy apricot sauce, or the curried beef and olive empanadas, which were being passed around on silver trays by the catering staff. For all his rapt attention to new and old friends, however, Mark was keeping an eye focused somewhere in the distance, recording everything, catching Al's eyes with a long, cool look of recognition.

Al, wearing a casual Armani summer suit over a black T-shirt, was the man behind the scenes, the breadwinner. He owned several office parks in New Jersey, an expanding real estate business he had inherited from his father. A man of few words, Al deferred to his lover when the guests offered compliments. It had been Mark who gave all his time to the project, leaving his job as a social worker and taking "early retire-ment" to work eight- and twelve-hour days, every day, on the house. Why, this party alone had taken six months to prepare. Al had insisted on the big bash; he wanted it for Mark, a celebration of their dream house.

It was the house that was the true host. Previously described by Realtors as an "expanded Cape Cod . . . angular, two floors, with addi-tions horizontal and vertical," it spread grandly over 5,400 square feet, not counting the four decks and garage. Everything led up: the graded rock path that led up to the short flight of steps that led to the front door; the steps from the second-floor entrance to the entertaining apex on the third floor, where a flowing open floor plan revealed the startling views—the marsh to the south, with the town and its broad, boat-filled harbor below; the ridge to the west; and to the north, pristine woods, dunes, and shrubbery.

The closest home was three hundred to four hundred yards away. In Provincetown, this was the equivalent of owning a small, private park.

Meadowview Heights, one of the last areas to be developed as well as the most exclusive, is a community with its own bylaws and regula- tions written into the deeds. All twenty-five of the houses on the ridge are part of the association, and a solid seventy-five to eighty percent of the owners are gay.

Al and Mark caught up with each other in their octagonal bed- room, high in the southern corner of the house. Everything was on dis- play and their bedroom was no exception. People had wandered through all evening to view the four-poster Millings Road bed, with its crisp three-hundred-thread-count Calvin Klein bedding, the two matte- black, high-tech Italo halogen lamps with long swing arms to light the bed.

Al and Mark turned and peered around the custom-made screen that separated the bed from the sitting area, as their neighbor to the west, Massimo Muntada, and his partner, Guy Pierson, entered the bedroom with an entourage of men. Massimo clutched Mark's arm, almost knocking over a shoulder-high candle stand. "I must tell you that there is an absolute fever in there," he motioned with his head toward the kitchen and living rooms. "You've done it. This is a whole new game now."

Mark lowered his head modestly, but he was smiling. Massimo continued, "Do you know that one of those Realtors, that one over there, told me that ninety-seven percent of the homes that have been sold in the last year have been bought by men? It can't possibly be true, can it? Even here in Provincetown?"

Al interrupted, to draw Mark into the cavernous closet/dressing room filled with expensive sports coats and neatly arranged trousers and whisper that they had missed the entrance, and subsequent quick exit, of David Davis, heir to the Parke-Davis pharmaceutical fortune (or Monsanto, depending on whom you're talking to). Davis was the owner of one of the most ambitious galleries in town. Several galleries actually, all under one roof, where he showed photographs and fine arts and provided space for the Narrowland Stage as well as "affordable" artists' studios.

Until recently Davis had lived in Meadowview Heights in the most expensive house in town, a big contemporary with a $25,000 lead- seamed copper roof and close to $300,000 worth of windows.

Davis rarely made appearances at events other than his own.

The pharmaceutical heir had left a modest bottle of Australian wine and an antique frame that held a small map of the dunes, rendered by an artist from the gallery. Mark placed the map on the long thin shelf that ran the length of the sitting room and housed several carefully chosen objects: a large stone angel cherub, French trompe l'oeil prints from New York, a collection of antique fans, and photos of Mark and Al and family. The map's almost pirate tone suited the tropical decor of the room. Mark tucked Davis's card into a corner of the frame.

As Al returned to the guests, Massimo continued to flatter Mark. Perched on the edge of the whirlpool tub in the master bathroom, he implored his friends to observe the $40,000 Lalique crystal sink and the whirlpool's "waterfall" fixture, which spilled water into the tub. One of his cohorts moved over to the urinal, and the automatic flush echoed softly in the room.

The house at 10 Cranberry was one of the few in the West End with a swimming pool, largely because the previous occupant had been on the zoning board and able to pull strings, or at least that was the dirt around town. The pool was the center of their summer entertaining—and Mark and Al entertained a lot. They had already booked Peter Hadley of Sumptuous Foods, a short, thinnish man in his thirties, who many regarded as the *only* caterer in town, to cater parties for them every Saturday night.

As the local families made their exodus and the night settled in around the house, the lights popped on. Carriage lights—over thirty of them, placed at every doorway—glowed with a warm, diffuse light. A string of small bulbs, the kind used on Christmas trees, were inset into the horizontal sills of the four triangular windows high on the third floor, emphasizing the breadth and grandeur of the building as a whole, drawing it out horizontally beyond its already bountiful width. Al and Mark had spent tons on the wiring after their designers had told them that you could take an average home and "kick it up a couple of notches" just by the choice of lighting.

Traditionally, Provincetown houses do not have basements, other than crude root cellars. Nor do most have a central design plan; in the majority of cases rooms have been added on, hodgepodge style, one after another over the years. This means that though many old Cape buildings are structurally sound, they are rarely efficient. They usually lack modern insulation and proper wiring, so by contemporary standards, they are primitive structures. But Provincetown's zoning makes it almost impossible to tear them down. New buildings have to conform to all kinds of regulations—upgraded setbacks, height requirements—and though it may be more expensive to renovate than to tear down, renovation gets around the rules. Mark and Al would not have been able to build a new house as high as the one they bought, and another couple who wanted to avoid the new regulations plowed upwards of $2 million into a one-thousand-square-foot fish shack at the East End, where Eugene O'Neill purportedly spent his first summer in town in 1916. After they were through, only the original roof boards remained.

In the library, Mark stopped in front of the floor-to-ceiling fireplace and contemplated the large photo mural, *The Last Jews of Radauti*, that hung to the right—a Laurence Salzman photo print, bought at the Philadelphia Museum, depicting a rabbi entering a cemetery in Poland. It was one of his favorite pieces of artwork in the house. He had bought it himself, spontaneously and emotionally, without concern for design. It was one of the few pieces they had brought with them from Jersey.

He pushed himself back up the central staircase and into the party arena. It was now after ten; the straight crowd had dispersed but other people were still arriving. The high-beamed room was filled with Sinatra.

In the perfectly appointed center kitchen area, three women in chef's jackets were into their third hour of producing a nonstop stream of sushi. The appliances were of the highest quality: a Sub-Zero refrigerator with matching backlit, see-through-door wine cooler; stainless-steel six-burner Miele range complete with salamander; yards of pink-granite countertops. This was the one area that Mark had conceded to Al, though neither cooked or even knew how. Al-the-body-builder loved sushi and loved the idea of food being prepared publicly, with the air of a live performance. The three women were perfect. They managed to keep a low profile, serving ornate and unusual varieties of the Japanese delicacy—tuna, salmon, even caviar-dipped maki.

Al stood next to the dumbwaiter in the corner of the kitchen, watching the crowd becoming more and more animated as the night wore on. He turned to the middle-aged man on the far side of the counter, returning to a conversation that had been interrupted earlier: "You know, the builders, they know that there's a lot of money coming in up here and they want a piece of it. Actually, the fact is they're charging twice what it should cost. It was cheaper for us to fly people up from Jersey and put them into a motel, including their travel time. . . . Just ask Mark about it, he knows all the numbers."

He paused, relishing a piece of eel-and-cucumber roll.

"But, you know, some of these town guys," he motioned around the room, oblivious to the fact that many of the contractors had already left, "they were just indispensable, so this is really a thank-you for *everybody*. . . . You have a Rodney who comes in, who's been plumbing for years, almost longer than some of us have been around. He's not used to handling three thousand dollar fixtures for the bathroom, and you have to say to him, 'Rodney, now listen to me. You have to be careful. These fixtures are very expensive and cannot be easily replaced. . . .'"

Mark and Al found themselves moving with their entourage into the living room, stopping to sample some of the double-fudge brownies and gourmet cookies that were being laid out for dessert. One of their new friends turned out—surprise, surprise—to be a high-end Realtor. He was more than a little tipsy and, realizing that he hadn't properly introduced himself, grabbed Al's hand at the same time he put his other arm around Mark's shoulder and excused himself for "crashing" the party.

"We would've found each other sooner or later," Mark remarked easily. "It's not hard to meet people in town. Actually, it's harder not to meet them, if you know what I mean."

The Realtor's nod was more emphatic than his ear-to-ear smile, and he continued to look at Mark, beaming, as he waited for him to go on.

"Al and I know two hundred people in town and, honestly, it's because we *want* to know them."

Al nodded as he turned to go freshen his drink.

"Remember I told you I was a civil service mediator for twenty years?" Mark continued. "Well, the deal was that *he*," he cocked his head toward the martini bar, "would keep bringing in the cash, and I'd make this dream of ours come true. So I gave up my job. For the house. That was the quid pro quo—my career for this house. It was something that he and I—"

"It was about *lifestyle*," interrupted Al, returning now with his martini. "This was our dream. The Cape, Ptown."

"That's why we're here—for no other reason. We'd been to Ogunquit, but we wanted to live in a town. We've already traveled pretty much all over the world except for Cuba, and we wanted to be in a place where we felt comfortable. It's like any other gay couple who has the bucks to move. . . . Why Provincetown? Because Provincetown is more comfortable than anywhere else."

"Yes, it doesn't matter who you are. Even a straight interracial couple—" Al interjected, not finishing the sentence.

"It's just *comfortable*, no two ways about it. It's open, we can be ourselves here. We certainly didn't move here because it's an artists' colony. Definitely not, and to be honest, we didn't even come for the beach, though it sure is pretty."

"We wanted Ptown," said Al.

"We had a time-share in the West End for years and had been coming back since ninety-one," Mark explained. "At other times of the year, we'd stay at the Boatslip and Harbor House. We watched most of the houses going up here on the ridge, you know, always saying we were going to live up here. Then in May of ninety-eight we started looking. We went to the Realtors' windows, looked at the ads, then we actually walked into Swan Realty. He faxed us some stuff after we left that weekend. . . . It was very interesting, pictures taken from the deck of our time-share ten years ago. This house was in the picture, you could actually see it in the background."

Mark was on a roll. He had seated himself on the granite ledge protruding from the base of the fireplace and had drawn quite a crowd. Many of his listeners were now sitting down themselves. Several lounged on one of the beautiful contemporary Tufenkian African rugs that were scattered throughout the room.

"We'd been coming fourteen years as a couple—since eighty-seven," he went on. "Al had been here before, the first time in seventy-nine with a woman. He said, 'What the hell am I doing here with a woman?' "

The group laughed.

"So we bought the house November 1, 1998. We signed the papers and moved in the same day. He went back to Jersey, I stayed here," said Mark, making a funny face at his partner. "It was like the most traumatic time of my life."

Mark was interrupted by the loud bravado of a middle-aged man dressed all in black, his buttons straining slightly over an extra twenty pounds. At the man's side swayed his companion, who appeared to be in his early twenties. The older man was Murray Klein, a longtime summer resident and the owner of a Greek Revival home in the East End, which was famous for its garden, a highlight on the competitive Secret Garden Tour hosted by the Provincetown Art Association in mid-July. Inclusion on the tour has become the most elusive status symbol of the new gay gentry.

Murray commanded the crowd to join him in a toast, as he raised his glass to the new homeowners.

"... and may you live here long and well, and keep the parties coming, and remember to keep me on your permanent guest list ... And, ah yes, thank you, thank you, thank you ..."

As his voice trailed off he took a large sip from his champagne glass and there was a round of applause. Murray now introduced his young friend. "Mark," he gestured, "Damon Pierce. Damon actually grew up here, can you believe it?" He grinned. "I've known him since he was a boy. He's only here for the weekend, because he's living in Boston—the hometown boy made good. He's studying architecture ... he's ... here for the weekend. ..."

Mark turned to Damon, genuinely interested in the boy's story. It was obvious that he was an anomaly in town, one of the few true "townie" kids who were going to make it out in the world off-Cape, and definitely one of the few openly gay ones. With a seriousness that belied his party manner, the young man acknowledged, "It's true. It's virtually impossible for a Ptown kid to graduate from high school here, go to college, then return and make a living in town."

He smiled coyly at his host, clarifying that this was not his situation, nor, if he had anything at all to say about it, would it ever be.

"It's impossible for the kids I went to school with to buy a home. There are no jobs. ..." Mark shook his head as Damon continued. "Besides, I think there was only a single kid born here last year. One."

"But that's staggering—*staggering*. Probably no other town in the country . . ."

". . . all summer," Al was suddenly saying to someone who'd asked how much time they planned on spending in town, and hearing this, Mark nodded agreement as his partner went on: "April through September, and every other week after that, right through. We want the house to be kept open. There are plants here, the house is alive. Eventually we want this to be our main residence. We're *here*."

As the conversation continued, the voices throughout the whole room seemed magically to rise as the volume of the music and the mood heightened. Mark brought their decorators out into the center of the room and called for a thunderous round of applause. The two men were well tanned. Both were smiling, totally at ease in the limelight.

After the toast, Mark found himself face-to-face with Todd Smith, a striking man in his thirties, slightly disheveled and unkempt, an up-and-coming artist, originally from Provincetown but showing primarily in New York and L.A. He had recently bought a home in town as well, a small, older cottage that he had *no* plans to renovate, he said—a boast or a declaration of faith. Smith was questioning the lack of contemporary art in the house. Mark listened politely, raising his eyes now and then to meet those of his other guests, but he excused himself when Smith referred to the Goya etching in the stairwell as "schlock."

That was too much. Mark hated to respond to what he felt were provocations, but even more he hated to be without adequate knowledge of something. They'd paid $2,500 for the Goya and maybe, as Smith seemed to be saying, they'd paid too much.

It just wasn't part of their world—art, that is. Until coming to Provincetown neither of them had even given art a thought. Mark had let the decorators use their knowledge or, perhaps more appropriately, their color sense to offer them selections to choose from—watercolors, lithos, oils, both new and old. But even their ship models, the steamer trunks in the bedroom, and the large antique frames that dwarfed many of their wall hangings, these were for design purposes, not for investment or aesthetics. The key always was "appropriateness"—the effect on the room or the area as a whole, not the spell of individual pieces.

Never one to ignore a challenge, Mark, and Al, too, for that matter, had become curious. Although they were the new rulers on the "hill," both admired their predecessor, David Davis, for his knowledge of culture and what was said to be his extensive collection. Davis had started the Schoolhouse Gallery, which showed some of the most cutting-edge stuff around.

Even before tonight Mark and Al had talked about it, turned over the possibility of hiring someone to give them a quick course next summer, but then they canned the idea. It seemed forced. Somehow . . . well, too precious.

Mark returned to the rest of the guests, most of whom had begun to leave. He placed his hand at the base of Al's neck as the two stood side by side for the next ten minutes, saying good night, shaking hands, finding rides for the few who were unable to drive themselves home. It was two-fifteen. The caterers had left over an hour ago, and the house was spotless except for a few glasses here and there. No one had been thrown into the pool. No one had gotten too drunk. They turned off the lights and retired to the bedroom, exhausted and glad to be alone.

It would only be a day or two before the thank-you notes and cards would begin to arrive, one more effusive than the next. The phone rang continuously through the week, with a long string of successive invitations, offers of sunset cruises, inquiries about their decorators. The house had made a major impression, an emblem of irrevocable change in the social history of Provincetown:

"Dearhearts, Mark and Al, It's nine-twenty pm on Saturday evening. The fireteams have gone. After having seen your gorgeous home we were tempted to return to our homes and torch our slums. Seriously, never have we been to such an exquisite and beautifully decorated home. The best part was the fact that you both were so very hospitable, so everything. Scrumptious buffet. What a treat to be invited. Merci beaucoup . . . We are sure Provincetown has seen nothing like it."

CHAPTER 2

ON THE EDGE

Existing in the liminal space where the eastern edge of America meets the Atlantic, Provincetown has remained throughout its history a haven for outsiders fleeing poverty and persecution.

The Puritans, warned by King James I that he would "make them conform, or . . . harry them out of the land," made their first North American landing in Provincetown Harbor. They found little game to hunt and few fields to till in these sandy lands, and after five weeks the *Mayflower* hauled anchor and sailed twenty miles west across Cape Cod Bay to land at Plymouth.

If they had stayed, Provincetown would have been a very different place. The Puritans, having found a haven for their own beliefs, were not of a mind to tolerate others. Colonists were forbidden to drink, smoke, play cards, or engage in "profane dancing." The disincentives were most effective: cropping ears, slitting noses, branding hands, putting sticks through tongues.

Still, sin survived, including, according to the records, buggery, bestiality, and incest. *The History of the Plimouth Plantation* relates the case of a teenage boy who was convicted of buggery with "a cow, two goats, five sheep, two calves, and a turkey." The boy was forced to watch as, one by one, the objects of his amorous dalliances were slaughtered and thrown in the pit. When the Puritans were done with the animals, they bestowed the same fate on the boy.

While the righteous of Plymouth were exacting cruel punishments on its errant citizenry, Provincetown, annexed by the Plymouth Colony in 1630, was becoming a haven for the lawless. The inhospitable terrain and distance from the mother colony made it a locus of transgression, where outlaws, deviants, and Indians could mingle freely in pursuit of those vices the Puritans proscribed.

Some attempts were made to make the town respectable. After 1670, the "Provincelands" were set aside as a fishing preserve for the Massachusetts Bay Colony, and fishing shacks began to appear on the area beaches. The town was incorporated in 1727, but its development was interrupted by the Revolution, which emptied the town of the more respectable residents and left it once more in the hands of the marginalized elements of society: smugglers; outlaw colonists; castaways; intrepid, profit-hungry fishermen; drinkers; and roving Indians.

The town had no government, no schools, and no families. The rectitudinous souls of nearby Truro were moved to petition the General Court in Plymouth to clarify the legal status of the Cape tip "in order that we may know how to deal with certain individuals there"; the rest of Cape Cod held to a similar view.

Alexis de Tocqueville, in *Democracy in America* (1835), spoke of the inherent tension—or perhaps hypocrisy—in the New England character, which cherished the principle of liberty but accepted all manner of social injustice and draconian punishments at the hands of their governing bodies. Provincetown, in its status as an outlaw society, stepped outside of this pious and contradictory state of affairs. A "sinner" was punished on the mainland; in Provincetown, a "sinner" walked free. The town has, over the centuries, continued to value liberty over law.

Twenty-five years after the American Revolution, Provincetown had grown to over two thousand citizens with the local economy revolving around fishing, just as it would for the next two hundred years. It was a makeshift affair, one observer noted: "Houses, saltworks and curiously built hovels, for uses unknown, are mixed up together. It would seem that God of the infidels, which they call chance, had a hand in this mysterious jumble." During the first U.S. census, which occurred in 1790, no one came to Provincetown, its populace apparently unworthy of being counted.

There was no road in the town, in large part because there was no road *to* the town. Provincetown was a virtual island. Everything was connected by a maze of sand footpaths, and, if you couldn't go by foot, you went by water.

Nevertheless, Plymouth was still attempting to keep the little community under control. The General Court served notice on the town to show why it was without a minister as "required by law" and donated money for the creation of a church, which was built in 1793. Public bars were banned in 1810, and the locals responded by distilling bootleg liquor and smuggling whiskey ashore from packets and fishing vessels. Private drinking clubs, called "tea rooms," flourished, ignored by the county sheriff, who, in what would become a Provincetown tradition, chose to look the other way.

In the first half of the nineteenth century, Provincetown changed from a one-horse town to a thriving community with fifty-five piers stretching along the town's two-and-a-half-mile waterfront and seventy-eight saltworks, producing almost fifty thousand bushels of salt annually for the burgeoning trade in salt fish, mainly cod and mackerel. The town's fleet consisted of fifty-six whaling ships and hundreds of Grand Bankers and Georges Bank fishing schooners. Sometimes, over seven hundred vessels would crowd the harbor, and packets ferried among Boston, New York, and Cape towns, carrying fish out and coming back with supplies.

Fortunes were being made as fleets of whaling vessels took the four-year voyages to the Arctic and Antarctic after whale oil, bone, and ambergris. The typical course for a Cape whaler was to head south to the Hatteras grounds, then on to the Azores and Madeira. From there it was just a short sail to the coastal waters of Africa and then, on advice from slaver ships returning to Rhode Island, tracking their prey clear to the "bottom of the chart." Contemporary records show that one twenty-five-month trip of the brigantine *Viola* produced two thousand barrels of sperm oil and seventy-five pounds of "first chop" ambergris—worth together $47,000. Another voyage, that of the *Bowhead*, even at the turn of the century when the whaling industry had started to falter, earned its skipper $115,000.

Newly rich captains and local businessmen with shares in the whalers built magisterial homes—three- and four-story Queen Anne houses of white clapboard up and down the town's "Front Street," many with the classic widow's walk. It was Provincetown's golden age.

By the 1880s, Provincetown residents enjoyed the highest per capita income in all of Massachusetts, but changes in the economy led to a slow, persistent decline. The huge catches of mackerel and cod had begun to dwindle, as had the demand for salted fish. Kerosene, discovered in 1859 and a better fuel for lamps, cut the demand for whale oil. By the late 1890s Provincetown's large fleet of schooners had shrunk to a mere fifty or sixty vessels. As their ranks grew thinner, the coopers and riggers, sail-lofts and ship-chandlers that stretched along the beach from one end of town to the other began to disappear. Even the wharves had begun to fall into disrepair, and many were finished off by the furious Portland gale of 1898.

Over the following thirty years, the Cape's once-great economy collapsed. Neighboring Truro, which for so long had outstripped Provincetown as a center of boatbuilding, became little more than a sleepy village, its once thriving boatyards abandoned. Wellfleet's whale fleet ceased to exist. The population on the Cape dropped from 36,000 to 27,000.

It wasn't until 1930 that Provincetown began to recover, its economy fueled by an influx of tourists. Having arrived at land's end, they could turn their back on the rest of the world, just as Henry David Thoreau had done almost a hundred years earlier. Arriving in 1851, for the first of his four journeys to Provincetown, Thoreau stood on one of the back beaches, looking out to sea, and summed up the attraction of Provincetown: "One may stand here and put all of America behind him."

CHAPTER 3

THE FOURTH OF JULY

The Fourth of July parade is a wildly eclectic community event, not so much a celebration of America's independence as the independence of Provincetown. American flags are hung alongside rainbow flags, middle-class families stand alongside shirtless muscle queens. It is a harmonious, almost surreal confluence of the gay and straight worlds.

The parade is led by the local contingent of the U.S. Coast Guard proudly marching with their rifles and the Stars and Stripes. Then comes the lone Provincetown fire truck, carrying the men of the volunteer fire department and a smiling baby, who sits with her father in the cab. Periodically, the truck's siren lets out a wail, and the crowd responds with enthusiastic whoops. Behind the fire truck comes the Ptown ambulance, with its simple sign: "Proud to be saving lives."

The next float tells you that you aren't in middle America anymore. There's a beaming geriatric drag queen dressed as a fairy standing atop this truck. She's wearing a great purple Afro wig and diaphanous wings. She uses her wand to bestow blessings on the crowd. Beneath her handlebar mustache she is beaming beatifically, and the crowd murmurs its appreciation.

Behind her, two lesbians carry a large banner that reads "The Bitches of Eastwood." There follows an endless array of queens, all the grand old dames of Ptown, some dressed as sailors with huge bouffant 1950s-style hairdos, others wearing only skimpy red-white-and-blue Speedos. They mince by, showing off their aged bronzed bodies. A man in camouflage carries a tall staff with a monstrous iguana perched on the top. The crowd is wildly enthusiastic about everyone who passes. A white convertible LeBaron eases by with Lil Howard, Ptown's "Senior Citizen of the Year." She gamely waves and everyone waves in return. The sun is hot, and she looks a little peaked.

The Stakeholders, a band composed of several musically oriented selectmen, ride by on the flatbed of a truck. Town manager Keith Bergman is on electric guitar. Mary-Jo Avellar, the longest-serving select-person, hams it up shamelessly as the group sings the Ptown standard "Stand by Your Man." The next truck is filled with the "Ptown/Truro Youth Hockey" kids.

This stitching together of recognizable small-town revelry with the adamantly gay captures the essence of Ptown life. The Youth Hockey kids Rollerblade behind the truck, while on another float there is a five-woman lesbian band called the Dyketones, singing the gay disco anthem "I Will Survive."

Waves of the so-called Gym Queens march by, buffed to perfection through a never-ending devotion to their bodies, their mirrors, Special K, and Ecstasy.

Gay men of every bent congregate on porches and balconies and stoops and drink and wave as the floats pass them by. Many of the straight couples, here for the holidays, stay close to each other. The gays call them "Klingons," because they cling to each other so desperately.

Still, the parade is a harmonious affair as straights, gays, lesbians, daddies, Gym Queens, bull-dykes, and all the rest of the polymorphous diverse mingle happily beneath the hot sun. It lasts several hours and, finally, as it makes its way down Commercial Street, the quarter-mile-long procession slows to a crawl. It has traversed almost the entire town now, running down Bradford Street, turning at the far East End, then meandering back to the center and then into the West End, where, in the heart of Gay Ptown, it tapers off near the Coast Guard station. For the duration of the parade, the town has been paralyzed. Extra police have been put on and paid overtime. Normal business has been halted.

But none of this matters. The Fourth of July is about freedom, and here, way out on the eastern edge of America, the parade is on some level a celebration of the freedom to be gay—and a celebration of the America that grants this freedom.

CHAPTER 4

PROVINCETOWN'S GEOGRAPHY: FACT AND METAPHOR

There is a certain suppleness to Provincetown's relation to the surface upon which it rests. Like its population, the town's terrain is in a state of perpetual metamorphosis. The waves and winds are relentless sculptors, moving the sand landward from the sea, forming dunes that echo the shoreline. If there are plants, such as the common beach grass *Ammophila breviligulata*, they will stabilize the dune. If not, the dune will traverse across the landscape until it is brought to a stop and anchored by vegetation.

These shifts have had an effect on the residents. Mary Heaton Vorse, the great labor writer and a resident of Provincetown for most of the twentieth century, noted that "The people in Provincetown do not regard houses as stationary objects. A man will buy a piece of dune land above the town and a cottage on the front shore, and presently up the hill toils the little house."

The land on which the town stands began its formation thirty thousand years ago—a mere millisecond of geologic time—when a huge sheet of ice began advancing on New England. After thousands of years of accumulating snow, the pressure of its own weight set the glacier in motion, and it ground down from Labrador, covering more than half of North America. As it advanced, it sliced off mountain peaks, smashed down hills, and created valleys. When it finally hit the softer margins of the coastal plain, it carved out bays and sounds and pushed relentlessly toward the sea. But this is where its advance ended. In the outer lands of Cape Cod it met strong currents of warm air and began to melt and recede. As it receded, it left behind millions of tons of rocks and rubble that it had carried from the mainland. These remnants formed ridges hundreds of feet high. The geologic formation is known as a moraine. The Cape's outer lands rest on such moraines.

Today, if one walks through the uplands of Truro, Provincetown's neighbor to the southeast, and digs a little, one can find the till—the gravelly material the glaciers transported to the Cape and deposited in moraines. Similarly, if you walk on Herring Cove and other outer beaches, the pebbles you walk on are the result of a collaboration of the glacier from thirty thousand years ago and the ocean, which over thousands of years worked diligently to break down the boulders and till into small pebbles, then into ever-smaller particles until they were sand.

But walking through Provincetown today, one is immediately struck by how verdant it all is. When the glacier retreated it left behind no vegetation, only huge ridges of stones. Birds brought the seeds in addition to those that the glacier had carried. Over the millennia that followed, as the ocean ground down these moraines, it left a halo of sand that followed the contours of the landmass. The ocean waves and currents created new formations, taking sand from the beaches to make the bars and shoals offshore. The bars became spits and then slowly transformed into peninsulas. The shoals became islands and the islands joined with one another to form long barrier beaches that ran parallel to the shore. These barriers created sheltered bays.

The hooked arm of Provincetown was formed when the glacier deposited its load and formed a moraine that the ocean waves pounded and smoothed out. Over millions of years the sand accumulated and finished off the supple landmass. But New England lore, and particularly that of the Cape, is filled with accounts of lost islands and peninsulas. Just as the ocean helped form these landmasses, it also obliterated them.

Nauset Island off Eastham, which many scholars think was visited by Leif Eriksson and which was mapped out by French explorer Samuel de Champlain, today lies under many feet of water. When Timothy Dwight, president of Yale, visited in 1810, he predicted that Provincetown would be swept away by the ocean. Modern scientists agree, saying that Cape Cod and the surrounding islands will be inundated in the next several thousand years—particularly as the ancient ice sheet in Greenland starts to melt, raising the sea hundreds of feet above its current level.

Because the Cape is almost completely surrounded by water, it tends to be cooler in the summer and warmer in the winter than the mainland. It lies near the juncture where two massive currents almost meet: the Labrador Current, which flows down from the north and brings the chilled Arctic water to local beaches, and the Gulf Stream, which comes up from the south and swings east around Nantucket to cross the Atlantic.

In the summer, the prevailing wind comes from the southwest. In winter it drives across the sea from the northeast. Winter storms are renowned for their ferocity and winds have been measured at over 110 miles an hour. Along with Cape Hatteras and Sable Island, the Cape's back shore, from Chatham to Provincetown's Race Point, is referred to as "the graveyard of the Atlantic."

Provincetown is built entirely on sand. It is so much a fact of life that, in 1838, when the federal government paid to have wooden sidewalks laid along Front Street, many townspeople resented the change and insisted on walking on sand. The shifting sands, which at one time threatened to utterly inundate the town, now are relatively tamed and the perimeter of the city is circled by large bulwarks to block the encroaching dunes. Still, the roads periodically clog up, and the trucks and tractors are sent out to clear them. When Thoreau visited Provincetown, he noted, "Sand is the great enemy here. There was a schoolhouse filled with sand up to the desks."

Some of the more dramatic dune activity is occurring in the Province Lands, the old Plymouth Colony fishing preserve that is now a part of the Cape Cod National Seashore. There the dunes frequently move over the Cape Highway, and year-round residents are well advised to purchase glass insurance for their autos, since windshields are routinely ruined by sandblasting.

Most of the forests of "oaks, pines, sassafras, juniper, birch and holly" described by the Pilgrims are now gone, used for houses, ships, docks, or burned up in fireplaces or furnaces. The boiling of seawater to extract salt at local saltworks also took massive amounts of firewood during the town's early days. As time passed, this ongoing deforestation resulted in greater freedom for migrating dunes. This posed a problem for those concerned with navigating the harbor, and in 1714, the first conservation act was passed, which restricted the felling of trees in the area, "to keep sand from being driven into the harbor." This law, according to most authoritative accounts, was blithely ignored by the residents of Provincetown, who in fact would often bring carts and wheelbarrows full of sand to dump on the shoreline so as to extend their property. More laws were passed in 1740 and 1786, and these, too, exacted little obedience.

As this deforestation continued, what little topsoil there was all blew away, leaving behind only sand. In 1874 a resourceful Provincetown man astounded other residents by creating the first artificial garden. Many of the ships that docked in the harbor used soil as ballast, so the man accumulated this international soil, carted it to his property, and began a garden.

Thoreau described the Cape as "a filmy sliver of land lying flat on the ocean . . . a mere reflection of a sand bar on the haze above." But Provincetown, despite its tenuous geographical position, is real. You have only to walk the narrow streets of town to see how many waves—physical and metaphorical—it has survived.

CHAPTER 5

WALKING TOUR

There are only two main thoroughfares running from east to west through Provincetown: Bradford Street, the two-way "service" road, for haste; and Commercial Street for leisure. More than forty-three perpendicular streets, lanes, and courts link the two, many lined with tall elms that provide shade for the area's many bed and breakfasts.

Commercial Street, traditionally known as Front Street, makes a forty-five-degree arc along the bay. It was originally no more than a sand path, and today it is still the same width as when it was laid out in 1835—twenty-two feet. This has caused more than a few bicycle accidents. On its two-mile trip through town, Commercial passes some of Provincetown's most elegant residences, Greek Revival, three-quarter Capes, classic saltboxes, mansard-roofed Victorians, houses with unusual details like the Figurehead House, built in 1850 with a traditional schooner's figurehead gracing the lintel over the door. There are even rebuilt fish sheds.

The houses in the East End are many and so closely sited, one to the other, as to earn Provincetown the distinction of being the most densely built environment on Cape Cod. Almost every residence in town is visible from the street, some with setbacks of less than four feet, some with none at all. Those on the waterfront, for example, were almost all laid out on a north-south axis, gable end to the street, partly so more structures could be fitted along Commercial Street, but also to present a slimmer silhouette to the fierce winter winds. "Here, we have no land," says a local historian. "Everything was compacted."

The East End has housed people as diverse as Admiral Donald B. MacMillan, the Arctic explorer who accompanied Admiral Peary to the North Pole in 1909; he lived at 473 Commercial Street. And the radical journalist and avowed Communist John Reed, who would eventually move to Russia to cover the Russian Revolution and write his classic book *Ten Days That Shook the World*. In 1916 Reed and his girlfriend, Louise Bryant, lived at 592 Commercial Street, along with painters Marsden Hartley and Charles Demuth. Eugene O'Neill camped out in the boat shed across the street.

A tourist traipsing by the American Legion building, a Civil War–era clapboard structure at 492 Commercial, is walking past close to fifty years of art history. Between 1957 and 1976 the building housed the Provincetown Workshop school, run by Leo Manso and Victor Candell. In 1977 the Long Point Gallery opened in its place, with a cooperative membership that included Manso, Budd Hopkins, Paul Resika, Judith Rothschild, Tony Vevers, Fritz Bultman, Robert Motherwell, Sideo Frombuluti, Nora Speyer, Carmen Cicero, Sidney Simon, and Varujan Boghosian. The building was sold in 1998 and rebuilt from top to bottom, with three separate gallery spaces; a high-tech mini-concert hall; scholarship studio space on the second floor; and a gourmet kitchen. It is now the Schoolhouse Center for Art and Design, the art showplace created by David Davis. Anyone wandering into one of the Friday-night openings would find them a far cry from the old Provincetown—champagne, even caviar. The gallery has become a major gay cruising spot, one of the hottest in town, and where Motherwells once hung there are now homoerotic photographs of young boys. One show, put on in early 2001, consisted of nineteenth-century daguerreotypes of tattooed seamen. Another featured camp pictures of Eva Perón.

Once Commercial Street leaves the East End, it enters the business district, which is filled with shops, restaurants, and galleries and seems to spread each summer with an ever-proliferating array of T-shirt shops and honky-tonk establishments. But the true town center is marked by two distinctive landmarks, the Provincetown Monument and the MacMillan Pier, the main wharf in town. The Monument, on High Pole

Hill, overlooks the harbor and is of Italianate design, its cornerstone laid by Teddy Roosevelt in 1907.

MacMillan Pier, almost immediately below the Monument, is home to the rapidly diminishing fishing fleet and the site of the still celebrated Blessing of the Fleet in late June. It is where the whale-watch boats tie up and the site of a new, expanding marina. For those who come to Provincetown by sea, the wharf is the main portal, with several Boston–Provincetown ferries dropping off tourists throughout the day.

Mixed in among the cluttered hot dog stands and clothing boutiques are several distinctive buildings: Town Hall with its imposing gable-ended roof; the Universalist Church, the oldest standing church in town, built in 1847 and famous for its trompe l'oeil interior; the new Crown & Anchor Hotel and the Whaler's Wharf Arcade, both recent reconstructions of historic buildings that were destroyed in a devastating fire in 1998.

In years past Provincetown was blessed with five supermarkets and three automobile agencies, but today there is one A&P that, reportedly, during the hectic summer months is one of the most profitable A&P's in all of America, and Land's End Marine, which sells paint, building supplies, barbecue grills, and beach chairs. If you want to buy a mattress or a business suit, visit a Barnes & Noble, or shop for a car, you have to drive to Orleans, twenty-seven miles away, or Hyannis, an additional thirty miles down the line.

When you leave the business district, you enter the West End, with its smaller homes, elaborate, lush gardens, and curved streets. Many of the town's oldest structures are located here, including the Seth Nickerson house, reportedly the oldest house in Provincetown, which was built in 1746 by a ship's carpenter from oak and timbers salvaged from shipwrecked vessels. A number of the West End houses were floated across the harbor on scows in the mid-nineteenth century from their original site on Long Point; to mark these buildings, the Historical Society had a local artist, Claude Jensen, design a blue-and-white enameled plaque showing a house afloat on the sea. In recent years, the West End has become an enclave for wealthy gays.

Provincetown is not immune to sprawl. There are pricey and fashionable houses on Somerset Heights, high above the flats as you enter town in the East End. The building goes on near the Moors in the far

West End, reaching the edge of the National Seashore. From Pilgrim Heights Road to Creek Hill Road and upward into Meadowview Heights the area is filled with new homes built in styles more commonly found in places like Malibu and the Hamptons. There seems to be no end to the current wave of building, and a number of environmentally concerned people have suggested that from this moment the town be thought of as "full."

CHAPTER 6

A BRIEF ART HISTORY

When people in Provincetown talk of change, they naturally fall back on the metaphor of waves, with the first wave being the Indians; the second, the outcast elements of mainstream Colonial society; and the next the Portuguese fishermen, who began arriving in the 1860s and eventually pushed out the Yankees.

But it was the wave that washed over Provincetown at the end of the nineteenth century that made the town a symbol of artistic liberty and sexual license.

The man first responsible for drawing the artists to the end of the Cape was Charles Webster Hawthorne. In 1899 Hawthorne opened his Cape Cod School of Art, offering students from around the country a chance to paint the Cape's soft, luminous light while staying in the inexpensive boardinghouses and renting studios for as little as fifty dollars per year.

Not every student who came found Provincetown a paradise. "It is none too easy to paint outdoors under the very best circumstances, but when the painting is done on the beach in the full summer sun, the sand reflecting every fierce heat ray into your eyes, when the famous Cape Cod mosquitos are biting at every exposed inch of anatomy and when hordes of little Portuguese children are playing tag in and out of the clustered easels and when an occasional gust blows picture, easel and all, flat on the sand, the whole thing becomes a nightmare," wrote a frustrated student in a collection put together by Hawthorne's widow.

By 1915 as many as ninety students had enrolled to learn Hawthorne's style of impressionist painting *en plein air.* Edwin Dickinson, Ross Moffett, George Yater, Henry Hensche, and Philip Malicoat were among those who spent summers painting in Provincetown. The principal style of the day was landscape painting, but modernism, which had announced itself at the controversial New York Armory Show of 1913, soon elbowed its way in.

Although a man named E. Ambrose Webster, who had become enamored of modernism in his student days in Paris, opened his Summer School of Painting in 1900, it wasn't until the Provincetown Art Association was formed in 1914 that the struggle began between the two groups. On one side were the traditionalists like Hawthorne, George Elmer Browne, and John Whorf; on the other, modernist crusaders such as Webster and Charles Demuth, whose style of "precisionism" produced a semi-abstract treatment of urban scenes. The struggle would last well into the 1950s, adding to the ferment that made Provincetown a vital summer community.

During what the artist Marsden Hartley called the "Great Summer of 1916," the town's cultural life reached a kind of critical mass. Because of the war, many who might have gone to Paris to paint headed for Provincetown. There were now six art schools, and joining the painters were a group of free-thinking, free-living bohemian writers and journalists who settled in for the summer in the East End of town: Susan Glaspell, who was later to win a Pulitzer Prize for her novel based on the life of Emily Dickinson; George Cram "Jig" Cook, philosopher turned farmer, turned writer, turned carpenter and prop-maker; journalist Hutchins Hapgood, who had trained under Lincoln Steffens and, like Jig Cook, had studied philosophy and believed that the theater should be an "ideal community," and Neith Boyce, Hapgood's wife, a short-story writer and playwright; and painter Marsden Hartley, and John Reed and Louise Bryant. Calling themselves the Provincetown Players, they were destined to become one of the most influential groups in the history of American theater.

With the help of one of its members, Mary Heaton Vorse, the group produced plays at an old fish shack at the end of Lewis Wharf the summer before. Then, in 1916, they discovered a struggling young playwright by the name of Eugene O'Neill, and in late July the Provincetown Players produced O'Neill's *Bound East for Cardiff* on their small, crudely built stage. O'Neill's premiere was a defining moment in the history of American theater, and it was also a turning point for O'Neill himself, who lived in Provincetown for the next nine years, solidifying a career that was to culminate with the Nobel Prize in 1936. (Unfortunately for those who crave real estate with a pedigree, the Peaked Hill Lifesaving Station, which had been bought by James O'Neill and given to his son, Eugene, as a wedding present, fell into the sea in 1931.)

By all contemporary accounts, never before in America had so many creative people been thrown together in one small place. The *Boston Sunday Globe* dubbed Provincetown the "Biggest Art Colony in the World," noting, "the thing that staggers visitors these days is the art students—mostly women—with their easels set up at nearly every house corner and street corner, on wharfs, in old boats, in lifts, in yards, along the beach, anywhere and everywhere you go—painters, painters, painters."

Acting as matriarch of this burgeoning art scene was Mabel Dodge, a banking heiress who traveled the town's narrow streets reclining on the red leather seats of her huge chauffeur-driven Pierce Arrow. Famous for her salon in Greenwich Village, Dodge, who numbered John Reed among her past lovers, was fiercely possessive of her position and entered into a rivalry with Mary Heaton Vorse for control of Provincetown's East End. For Vorse, the salon-happy Dodge was a rich poseur, "a women of shallow curiosities." For Dodge, Vorse's Lewis Wharf theater was nothing more than "a barn on the shore."

It was not long before novelists Sinclair Lewis and John Dos Passos stepped into the maelstrom of these warring coteries, as did the critic Edmund Wilson. The radical Emma Goldman, suffragist Margaret Sanger, and Max Eastman, the editor of *Masses*, the most important anarchistic English-language magazine of the era, also joined the scene. The energy—and argument—in the East End was barely containable. Women's rights, Freud, Buddhism, automatic writing, the neo-Grecian dance of Isadora Duncan, the injustice of monopolies and cartels, Gurdjieff, free love, all were the talk of the day.

And, of course, traditional painting versus modernism.

The fight between the two schools continued during the twenties, when the Provincetown Painting Classes of Ross Moffett and Heinrich Pfeiffer attracted such illustrious students as Jack Tworkov, the abstract expressionist. Attaching themselves to the other side were the sculptor Chaim Gross and Raphael and Moses Soyer, who arrived in Provincetown to study with Charles Hawthorne and managed to live on ten cents a day by sleeping on the dunes. By this time, Hawthorne and his allies Richard Miller and Frederick Waugh had taken over the Provincetown Art Association, and they made sure that few modernists were included in the exhibitions.

In 1926 the feud between modernists and conservatives hit a new high when conservatives managed to sneak a hoax "modernist" painting called *Hence the Pyramids* into the Summer Modernist Show, begrudgingly put on at the Art Association. It proved to the conservatives that anything could pass for modern art.

(The trick was tried again in the sixties. As the story is told, someone got a house painter, who was painting the interior walls of the Art Association, to set up a piece of Masonite and throw paint and paint rags at it, then submit it as an entry for the next juried show. When it was accepted, the traditionalists approached Hans Hofmann and triumphantly announced the hoax. Hofmann shrugged. "I don' care," he said in his heavy Bavarian accent. "Iz an int'resteeng peece of verk.")

Hence the Pyramids caused great embarrassment in modernist circles, but something good came of the hoax: The next year was the first full modernist exhibit at the Art Association. Not until 1937 was there a combined show, but even then, nonrepresentational works were confined to the small upstairs balcony area, while the huge, well-lit main gallery was reserved for the traditionalists.

The 1930s marked a changing of the guard. Hawthorne died in 1930, and although Henry Hensche held up the conservative side with his Cape School of Art, where he taught for more than fifty-five years, Hans Hofmann arrived and opened his Summer School of Art at Hawthorne's old studio on Miller Hill. Hofmann would divide his time between New York and Provincetown for the next thirty years.

Like the rest of the country, Provincetown was hit hard by the war. Both artists and fishermen left to fight overseas or work in defense factories. The membership of the Art Association dropped to its lowest levels since 1915, and they printed no catalogs between 1941 and 1946. But creative people were still drawn to Provincetown.

Tennessee Williams was in town during the summer of 1944, as was Marlon Brando and Brando's buddy the comedian Wally Cox. Williams, who was living with the painter Fritz Bultman and his wife, finishing *The Glass Menagerie*, had his own particular way of supporting the war. The Bultmans finally threw him out for bringing home too many young sailors. Jean Bultman recalled that "Tenn was part of a gay circle, but everybody knew."

Many of the gays the Bultmans knew were far less flamboyant than the men today. But Tennessee was "all over town," much as he had been ever since his first visit in 1940. His everyday vocabulary included "auntie," "butch," "cruise," "flaming belles," and the overly used "queen." His carryings-on, and what they say about the essential traditions of Provincetown, leap off the pages of his *Letters to Donald Windham, 1940–1965*:

July ?, 1944

Buddy-buddy-shipmate!

(That is a navy term of endearment which I have just picked up.) I have just returned from a most extraordinary all night party on Captain Jack's Wharf. . . . To begin somewhere, if not at the beginning, a couple of willowy, rather pretty Jewish-looking intellectual belles have opened a salon on the wharf, which for sheer chi-chi tops anything of the sort I have yet run into. One of them, to complete the definition, was a fellow student of Fritz' at the Bauhaus and assists Norman Bel Geddes at the Modern Museum . . . but tonight they had somehow come into possession of an immense creamy-fleshed blond sailor directly out of Melville . . . Well, everyone finally departed but the four of us. One of the belles was unbuttoning the sailor's pants and the other mine—we were all on one enormous inner-spring mattress on the floor. Then all at once things started to happen! The sailor extends his arm, I extend mine. In one dervish whirl both belles are thrown clean out of the charmed circle which from then on consists solely and frenziedly of Tennessee and the navy!

In that same year Jackson Pollock arrived with his wife, Lee Krasner, before moving on to Long Island, and Adolph Gottlieb visited for what would turn out to be the first of more than a dozen summers. Surrealists Roberto Matta, Arshile Gorky, and Max Ernst arrived, though Ernst was soon forced to leave because he was classified as an "enemy alien." Karl Knaths also settled in and soon found himself in the company of the great patron Peggy Guggenheim, who visited with her love interest, the French surrealist Jean Arp. William Baziotes, Robert Motherwell, and Helen Frankenthaler all made journeys from New York.

By the war's end there could be no question that Provincetown had become a center for international art.

CHAPTER 7

FORUM 49

"I consider it part of my artistic responsibility to help, support and encourage all that is young, vital, progressive and honest. This is the reason why I am a part of this Forum. . . .

—HANS HOFMANN, at Forum 49

Weldon Kees was a bit of a Renaissance man—a painter, poet, art critic, jazz musician, playwright, and filmmaker. He was also the prime mover in an art happening that took place in Provincetown in the summer of 1949.

With the end of the hot war, America had slipped into the cold war, and the political climate in the country was decidedly conservative. The Dies Committee had begun its investigation of the Hollywood Ten in California, and neither the cultural nor the political climate gave support to those who were "different." That summer, by producing a series of lectures that challenged conventional thinking, the Provincetown artists were taking a radical stand against the status quo. They were also assisting at the birth of abstract expressionism.

Kees had a distinguished roster of collaborators: artists Fritz Bultman, Adolph Gottlieb, Hans Hofmann, and Karl Knaths, and writer, poet, and editor Cecil Hemley, the founder of Noonday Press.

But it was Kees who was the major force, racing around town in the old car he'd bought from Mark Rothko for $175. (Rothko had called the battered old vehicle Tiresias, after the legendary seer whose ghost was consulted by another traveler, Odysseus.) When the conservative Provincetown Art Association refused to host the forums, Kees arranged to hold them in the old Ford Garage at 200 Commercial Street, which had recently been converted into a gallery. When seating two hundred people seemed an insoluble problem, the organizers, hearing that the local Methodist church was replacing its pews, bought up the old ones for nine dollars apiece.

On July 3, 1949, two hundred people paid sixty cents apiece to sit on Methodist pews in an old garage while Hofmann, Gottlieb, Serge Chermayeff, the head of the Chicago Institute of Design, and George Biddle, a painter who had been chairman of the U.S. War Artists Committee under Roosevelt, tried to answer the question "What Is an Artist?" Five hundred others were turned away.

The accompanying exhibit featured fifty artists, including four Provincetown pioneers in abstract art, Oliver Chaffee, E. Ambrose Webster, Agnes Weinrich, and Blanche Lazzell. Hofmann, the reigning master, showed two new canvases that drew raves, as did the paintings by Knaths, Byron Browne, Gottlieb, and Motherwell. Jackson Pollock's two, intricately spattered paintings were called "the most striking" by Elaine de Kooning. It was a gathering of a group of artists who were soon to be legends.

Jackson Pollock's painting #17 was also hanging in the gallery. It had just appeared in the famous *Life* magazine spread that provocatively asked, "Is He the Greatest Living American Painter?" There was a ballot box at the show where visitors could put their response to *Life*'s query. After a week, the ballots were counted. The modernists could not have taken much comfort from the fact that of the 542 people who voted, 39 said yes and 503 said no.

The second forum was to feature Dwight Macdonald, a major figure in the New York intellectual world and the editor of *Politics*, speaking on "The Dream World of the Soviet Bureaucracy." Kees encountered problems, as he wrote to Macdonald: "We've run into a certain amount of hysteria of a sort we hadn't counted on. Somebody got a look at our program, saw the word 'Soviet' in the title of your talk, and the next thing we knew the rumor was all over town that the Commies have taken over the building at 200 Commercial." The rumor didn't hurt. Once again, the lecture drew capacity crowds and people had to be turned away at the door.

Over the rest of the summer, Weldon Kees commented on the jazz music of the 1920s, accompanying his talk with recordings of Jelly Roll Morton, Louis Armstrong, and Bessie Smith. Francis Biddle, U.S. attorney general under Roosevelt, talked about "America's Responsibilities in the New World." There were also readings and discussions on James Joyce and T. S. Eliot, an unruly panel fiercely debating "French vs. U.S. Art Today," and a panel addressing the then fashionable Freudian analysis called "Finding Yourself Through Psychiatry." Although all the forums had an overflow attendance, the organizers were struck by the psychiatry panel's big turnout. But even then New York- and Boston-area shrinks commonly spent their August vacations in nearby Wellfleet.

Forum 49 was a low-budget affair, and there was no monetary remuneration for the speakers. Instead, each was given a bottle of scotch, which they no doubt shared at the parties that followed the lectures. The participants and audience would pour out of the old garage, talking and arguing, and then slowly make their way toward Weathering Heights, a ramshackle club perched on the edge of the dunes at the backside of town, along what is now known as Shank Painter Road. Provincetown was sweltering that July and August; the windows of the club were propped open, and the crowd overflowed outside, while inside Kees played jazz piano and the artists and their friends danced into the early morning.

In the aftermath of Forum 49—which ended on an appropriately open note: fifteen speakers from all disciplines participated in "Everybody's Forum"—Weldon Kees returned to New York, where he spent the winter. He recalled in a letter to a friend, "New York got to be too much of a struggle, at least for me, and one that availeth close to naught. Mostly got tired of the dirt and darkness. . . . Some of it had to do with the fact that we were living, if you can call it that . . . in a loft on the lower East Side, poor as hell, with a kerosene stove that only heated about a thirtieth of the room. We damn near froze."

At the forum debating French versus U.S. art, Robert Motherwell had exclaimed, "The conditions under which an artist exists in America are nearly unbearable," and Kees was in a bad way—broke, ill, and depressed. "I find myself getting more and more anti-social," he wrote. "It is an ordeal to get myself out of the house, and there are fewer and fewer people that I care about seeing."

Following a brief, underpaid stint as a critic at *The Nation*, Weldon Kees moved to San Francisco. He grew increasingly alienated from the New York scene, immersing himself in San Francisco's cultural life. According to poet Kenneth Rexroth, he was the first person to do a poetry reading at City Lights Bookshop, two years before Allen Ginsberg read "Howl" there. He did radio reporting and local journalism. He wrote pop sociology. And then he vanished.

"He was the most gifted and lively person of that whole epoch. . . . An individual of complete culture, and terribly witty," Fritz Bultman recalled. Weldon Kees disappeared in 1955, and his car was discovered in a parking lot near the Golden Gate Bridge. His body was never found.

CHAPTER 8

THE AUCTION

The woman was in her late forties, neither chic nor startling so much as Jewish zaftig, plainly dressed with short bobbed hair, and she marched purposely up the center aisle between the folding chairs that had been set up in the main gallery room of the Provincetown Art Association and Museum. She looked like a penguin. Her head was down and she didn't look at the several hundred people all around her who'd come to pick up a bargain at the annual end-of-season art auction. When she reached the podium, she turned and nervously cleared her throat, then began to read from a prepared statement that, earlier, she had been handing out to anyone who would take the single typed sheet at the door.

"My name is Jane Kogan," she began. "I've been living and working in Provincetown for over twenty years. Anyone involved in the art community here in the sixties knows that Walter Chrysler was famous for acquiring works of art and not paying for them. And it happened to me. He saw my work in a gallery and asked that I bring two paintings to his museum because he was interested in adding them to his collection. I was thrilled. Time went by but he never got around to paying me for them. The paintings went into storage and weren't readily available to me. Nor was Walter. I realized that I had no receipt. In the spring, I insisted on getting my paintings back or being paid. Chrysler offered to give me a reception and hang the paintings. And he did, after I repaired a hole in one canvas and a scratch in another.

"True to his word, there was a wine-and-cheese reception, and the paintings were hung in the museum. For one day. Not long after that, the Chrysler Museum left Provincetown and was moved to Norfolk, Virginia. To my knowledge my paintings were in storage for twenty years and never shown.

"My story is not unique, or even uncommon," she went on. "Many, many artists, some of them dead now, were ripped off by Walter Chrysler. Tonight, I'll be bidding twenty-five dollars to reacquire my own work. And I am asking you not to bid against me. If I sell them, hopefully to someone who will donate them to our own museum here, I will give the Art Association the same twenty percent of the sale price. The only difference is that finally some profit may go to the artist who painted the pictures, instead of to the Chrysler Museum that acquired them, shipped them out of town, and warehoused them for twenty years.

"Thank you for your consideration."

In the silence that ensued all you could hear was the creaking of the overhead fans turning slowly in the August heat, and now the auctioneer's assistants carried out a life-size oil portrait of Roger Skillings, the local novelist, short-story writer, and long-standing director of the writing program at the Fine Arts Work Center. Skillings had posed for Kogan in front of the Fo'c'sle bar in a T-shirt and jeans, barefoot, with a cigarette dangling from his mouth. His slouch seemed to say it all, a reminder of times gone by. The good old days. Camaraderie. A time when artists talked to each other and felt they were in it together.

The auctioneer asked, "What am I bid?"

"Twenty-five dollars," Kogan said firmly.

Silence from the large room.

The auctioneer called for more bids. More silence.

"Sold for twenty-five dollars," he declared, bringing his gavel down.

People in the audience turned to each other, grinning. Some hooted. Some wiped tears from their eyes, and after a moment everyone was up on their feet, still clapping as a few surged forward to shake Kogan's hand, to hug and kiss her as she stood there, looking stunned, her lips trembling.

The fat ghost of Walter Chrysler, millionaire collector, poseur, and thief, turned in his grave.

"I didn't believe it," she recalls years later. "I was astonished and moved because you just don't think people are that giving. This was a vindication, but it was more than just me. People were saying how they felt about Chrysler.

"The solidarity stemmed from the feeling that artists don't have a great place in society. Chrysler had the money, the cachet, the status, and could rip off the artists almost at will. The audience was mainly people who lived here. Not everyone was an artist, of course, but everybody there was interested in art, and they saw what had been happening.

"The only thing that recommended Chrysler was that he liked art and was interested in collecting it, but, frankly, a lot of what he had in his museum was the worst work of the best painters—like a tenth-grade El Greco that probably wasn't even an El Greco, or was like the worst day El Greco ever had."

Walter Chrysler, Jr., the quirky pederast heir to the Midwest auto fortune, had opened the eponymous Chrysler Art Museum of Province-town in 1958, in what had formerly been the Center Methodist Church, with a wildly heterogeneous, if uneven, collection; he also sponsored the first Provincetown Art Festival. In due course, Chrysler would show Robert Indiana and Roy Lichtenstein, just as he brought Andy Warhol to town, accompanied by the Velvet Underground.

The official explanation for the Chrysler Art Museum's 1971 departure to Norfolk, Virginia, was that the town of Provincetown refused to meet the mogul's demands for tax abatements. Kogan, like many locals, knows there were other reasons, too.

"I always heard that he wanted to be near the young sailors in Norfolk, which makes complete sense. I also think it's true that he was hitting on young kids in town—if not really young-young people then certainly people in their twenties, so I wouldn't be a bit surprised if he was told to leave 'or else.'"

Provincetown's street people, who often know more about what's going on than the aesthetic crowd, say that Police Chief Meads put a gun to Chrysler's head. Figuratively, of course.

It was already ten-twenty by the time the auctioneer got to the second of Kogan's two paintings, *Independence Day*, which was a large social satire. Again, the audience lèt her buy back her work for twenty-five dollars. No sooner had she done this then Alix Ritchie, a Ptown newcomer (and, later, a backer of *Ms.* magazine), stepped forward to buy it. "She offered me six hundred dollars and I was thrilled, because she was going to donate it to the Art Association, just like I'd asked. I also got to keep the other painting, which I gave to Roger," Kogan says.

"You know, the most amazing thing about the whole episode," says Kogan, running her hand through her close-cropped hair, "is how gullible I was. All artists are gullible, you know? We crave acceptance. We'll do anything to get our work seen. All Chrysler had to do was tell me he'd give me a reception and I let him take two paintings—I even brought them over to him myself. Money was never discussed. Then, when I finally confronted him a year later, even then I backed off, believing that there'd probably be a show and, at some point, money. I let myself get screwed. I was just so excited to be in a museum, you know? Total putty."

CHAPTER 9

CIRO & SAL'S

During the fifty years of its existence, Ciro & Sal's was the restaurant that put food in the bellies of the abstract expressionists.

Bronx-born Ciro Cozzi and his partner, Sal Del Deo, met in Provincetown the summer of 1947, and for a few summers both took drawing classes. Sal went into the army and Ciro briefly moved to Colorado to study fresco technique, but in 1951 both were back in Provincetown.

"An artist could afford to live here back then," says Ciro. "There were plenty of jobs and there was always fish. We'd go down to the wharf, a boat would come in and they'd say, 'Hey, kid! What d'ya need?' And we'd say, 'Whatever you got!' They'd throw us a big codfish. Or it could be a bucket of flounder. A bass, even. We used to *live* on fish."

Which might be all right for an artist, but Ciro, who had a wife and baby, needed a more reliable means of support. With the help of an uncle, he had bought a large ramshackle house at 4 Kiley Court, at the back end of the short clamshell-paved alley that ran off Commercial Street, a block and a half west of the Art Association. Trying to come up with a way to turn the unused space on the ground floor into a money-maker, he and his friend Sal decided to open a restaurant.

Ciro & Sal's started out small—a humble spot serving several varieties of sandwiches on the traditional Portuguese bread. It rapidly became so popular the overflow congregated outside on the street. It helped that the waitresses, mostly art students, were all knockouts. "I insisted," Ciro says, "that they wear shorts and T-shirts."

The crowd and the late hours led the neighbors to complain, and Ciro and Sal narrowly escaped having the town selectmen shut them down. They survived, a bona fide, licensed restaurant with a closing time of eleven-thirty, and the neighbors, who had only wanted a good night's sleep, gratefully donated silverware and dishes. The new restaurant, with its artist owners, was the hottest spot in town, but if the crowd was impressive, the food was not. When Ciro and Sal decided to upgrade the menu by adding a chicken dish, they bought the largest and most inexpensive birds the A&P had.

"I cut the damn things up to make my mother's recipe for chicken cacciatore," Ciro recalls. "I'm cooking it and cooking it all day. I'd take my fork and try to poke it into the goddamn meat. Finally I said, 'Jesus Christ, Sal, how long does this thing have to cook?'

"We didn't dare throw anything away, so, when the first customer ordered it, I put it on a dish, made it look pretty, and sent it out to the table. Sal and I looked through the window from the kitchen. He's eating. Chewing. He's not swallowing, just chewing. Finally, I went up to him and he'd actually broken out in a sweat. I said, 'How's that chicken?' He said, 'Oh, the flavor's great. But, boy, is it hard to chew.'

"The next day I called my mother. 'Ma, what happened? I cooked that damn thing all damn day.' Then I told her what I'd bought. She laughed. I'd gotten stewing chickens. 'Well, Jesus, that's for soup,' she said. 'You don't use that for chicken cacciatore.' That's when I had my first cooking lesson."

At the time, Provincetown cuisine, even at the established restaurants, ran toward hamburgers, fried clams, chowder, and cod drizzled with butter and paprika and then broiled to death. The best food available was at Cookie's Tap, a Portuguese hangout at the West End fronting Flyer's Boatyard, which offered kale soup and a squid stew so rich it was the color of chocolate.

Even so, Ciro and Sal made an effort. They expanded to include veal and pasta dishes, using local mussels and clams. They even started to make their own sauces, using bones left over from the half-sides of beef they butchered on the premises. By the late fifties, Ciro & Sal's had become the best-known restaurant in Provincetown.

Because Ciro was a painter himself, he became, over time, a mentor to the younger artists. "I was considered one of their elders. They used to bring their paintings to me, and we'd talk about what they were doing."

In those early years, painters without cash paid for their meals with a painting, much as early Provincetown artists had swapped canvases with the Portuguese for their lodgings. A lot of them wound up on the restaurant's walls.

Because the restaurant had no liquor license for its first eleven years, customers brought their own, usually bottles of Chianti, and this, too, contributed to the decor. When the straw-wrapped bottles were emptied, they were hung from the ceiling. The interior of the restaurant took on a charmed chaos: fishing artifacts, paintings by local artists, the innumerable Chianti bottles dangling so low that customers often walked into them in the half-darkness. When John Wayne showed up one night, he had to be seated at one of the side tables in "Outer Siberia," the area near the fireplace where the ceiling was higher than in the rest of the room; nonetheless, the six-foot-five movie star had trouble avoiding the Chianti bottles and was forced to eat hunched over.

The restaurant was always filled with the loud strains of Puccini, and both Sal and Ciro, but especially Sal, liked to sing along with the arias as they soared from the speakers that dangled on bits of picture wire amid the hanging bottles.

For a brief time in 1960, Ciro & Sal's had an even more unusual addition to the decor: the ashes of Harry Kemp, the poet of the dunes and the last surviving member of the group that had made up the Provincetown Players. For most of his years in Provincetown, Kemp had lived in an isolated shack on the dunes, shoveling out the sand every few weeks. Periodically, he would don his great cape and make a foray into town to pick up provisions and see his women, of which it was said he had many. During the fifties, Kemp had become so fascinated with the Portuguese fondness for nicknames—"Boozie," "Lamb," "Joe Baloney," "Spawn," "Jajoe," "Fidgey," "Tin Plate" ("He was strange, you know? Had a metal plate in his head from the war"), "Sally Big Nose," "Joe Hotdog," "Clarke Gable," "Mike Moon," and "Flyer Santos"—that he compiled a book of them, now a collector's item. Age finally forced the poet into town, where, in his cups, he could be heard having long, mumbled conversations in Elizabethan English with Francis Bacon and Shakespeare. Kemp spent his last days under piles of overcoats collected to keep him warm against the frigid sea air, surrounded by his collection of books, papers, and trash.

When he died, his friends remembered that he had always wanted to be cremated, half his ashes spread on the dunes, the rest in Greenwich Village. Shortly before his death, however, Kemp had converted to Catholicism. The Church, at that time, forbade cremation.

A friend, thinking to follow his wishes, put his body in the car and began the drive to the crematorium. She was intercepted by State Troopers and the poet of the dunes was installed in a funeral home to await a proper Catholic burial.

He did not rest in peace. The determined friend hijacked Kemp once more, deposited him at the crematorium, and then took him to his penultimate resting place, next to the cash register at Ciro & Sal's.

Ciro, on first noticing the box, asked, "What's that?"

The cashier replied, "That's Harry." Ciro nodded and went back to work.

The staff at Ciro's were as informal as the owner. A dishwasher might wander out into the dining room to serenade customers with his guitar, while the patrons slipped into the kitchen to drink with pals who were working the grill. Ciro later found out that the musical dishwasher was also an entrepreneur, subcontracting his dishwashing job out to others and taking a cut off the top. "There was this *parade* of dishwashers," Ciro recalls, "and I said, 'Wait a minute, this is your job. Who the hell are these people?' And he said, 'They're doing a good job. What are you complaining about?'"

Most of the staff were so eccentric as to be unemployable elsewhere. One of the dishwashers, known as Nina Gitana—"the Gypsy"— modeled for the painter Phil Malicoat and would drive Ciro nuts by wandering out into the dining room to do "drippings," picking up a flickering candle from one of the tables and using it to make hot wax designs on the tablecloth.

Julian Minsky, a sometime waiter and hanger-on, was an artist who did illustrations for the *New Yorker.* Another waiter was a Harvard grad student in literature who spent a month rewriting Andrew Marvell's "To His Coy Mistress" and T. S. Eliot's "Love Song of J. Alfred Prufrock," substituting references to the restaurant's veal scallopini. Once he was done, the rewritten verses were incorporated into the cover design of the next season's menu, which also featured musings on abstract expressionism and quotations from Hegel. The non-college-educated Ciro loved to talk about "my Harvard waiter."

Then there was Victor Joren, who appeared at the kitchen door looking for work one rainy night around 1959. Joren would go on to become the head antiquarian for the city of Boston, but that night, Ciro recalls, "Here he is in Ptown, dressed in a business suit, a handsome black man with an umbrella. He said, 'I'm looking for a job.' He was even wearing a tie, and I asked, 'What kind of work are you looking for?' He says, 'I'll take anything.' I said, 'Well, about the only thing we have that's available is cleaning up and helping in the kitchen, dishwashing and stuff like that.' I was embarrassed to offer that, but he looked at me and said, 'Fine, I'll take it.' He had a real low voice, very quiet, very elegant. And when he left that night, I looked at Sal and said, 'It's a weird one, isn't it?' He said, 'You hired him.'

"Victor was with me for fifteen years," Ciro continues. "One day I realized he was at Harvard, and I asked him what the hell he was doing there. And he said, 'Well, my major is mathematics, and it's a very good school.'

"Well, this goes on, and then I realized he'd switched majors and was now a *music* major. Then a couple of years later, he graduated and went to graduate school. But to *architecture* graduate school. I said, 'Wait a minute, you've never studied architecture before. First, you were a mathematician, then you became a musician, now you're going to do your graduate work in architecture?' And he said, 'Yes. What's so strange about that? I'm a member of a minority.' "

The staff all had tenure and the restaurant was home. The "family table" proved it—a long trestle affair that somebody had nailed together out of old two-by-twelves that seated a dozen or more at the back of the dining room near the kitchen door. The family table was reserved for staff and their comrades, who ate there before the doors opened for customers. Artists were welcome, and, Ciro remembers, in the early fifties, before he was famous, Andy Warhol would sit there, silent amid the raucous crowd. Franz Kline was another regular. Red Grooms, Richard Pepitone, and the photographer Paul Koch were also members of this special club.

People built their whole lives around the place—ate there, picked up girls, made gallery connections, even sold a painting occasionally. The bonding was communal, an us-versus-them thing that stemmed from everyone's sense that they were not, could never be, and never wanted to be part of America's white-bread mainstream.

More than anything, what fueled the popularity of the place was the art scene a stone's throw from the restaurant's door—the galleries, the museums, the artists themselves. Milton Avery's studio, where Avery did some of his best and largest canvases, was directly opposite Ciro's alley. Gottlieb lived three blocks up the street to the west. Fritz Bultman and his wife, Jean, were five minutes away, up on Miller Hill Road, almost directly behind the restaurant. The Art Association itself was less than a block away to the east, and a block beyond the "Art Ass," as it was known, was the Kootz Gallery, which during the mid-fifties had the hottest stable in town—David Smith, Ibram Lassaw, Jack Tworkov, and Marisol, in addition to Robert Motherwell and Hans Hofmann.

Friday nights, after the openings, the lines to get into the restaurant snaked all the way down the alley, out into Commercial Street. There was a chain across the door to keep the crowds out, and from time to time some out-of-towner stepped forward and claimed to be Ciro's cousin, or tried to bribe the maître d'.

In the summer of 1960, Ciro found himself at odds with his partner on several issues. There was a momentous and turbulent breakup and Sal left the restaurant to paint full-time. Ciro says he still thinks about it. "You know, in a restaurant, there are all those knives . . . it's a wonder that somebody didn't get hurt."

That same summer Provincetown's reputation as a haven for gays led the local business community to take action. Police Chief Francis H. "Cheney" Marshall advised town restaurateurs that all their waiters would have to register for "identity cards," because the town was going to initiate background checks, and anyone who showed up with arrests for "gay" offenses would be forced to leave Provincetown.

This was hardly what the Pilgrims had in mind when they penned the Mayflower Compact, but the town fathers were so fed up with

Provincetown's growing reputation as a haven for homosexuals that they didn't seem to care. The gays, they insisted, were destroying the town's tourist industry. Chief Marshall visited all the restaurants, announcing that all waiters were to be fingerprinted and photographed, their records circulated throughout the country, and if any of the men in question had been arrested for sodomy (a felony in most states back then) they would not be allowed to work in Provincetown.

One of Ciro's waiters—a soft-spoken man named Bobby Coal, who had toured with the Afro-Caribbean dance troop of Katherine Dunham—did have a record, so Ciro refused to comply. He wanted to make it a test case, but Coal asked Ciro to back off. Nevertheless, Ciro refused to fire Coal and for two years he kept him on in the kitchen, until the law was changed and Coal was allowed back on the floor. Reportedly, seventeen waiters lost their jobs that year, at a time when, nationally, homosexuals were second only to Communists as a target of law enforcement's search for "subversives."

Ciro wasn't alone in thinking that the Catholic Church, the most conservative force in Provincetown, had joined forces with certain entrenched business interests to push the crackdown on gays. Joe Taves, an accountant who grew up in Provincetown during the forties and fifties, says that St. Peter's Catholic Church was presided over by the fiercely pious Father Duarte. Taves describes Duarte as "righteous, saintly, but very antigay.

"He would corner people and say, 'Who are you renting to this summer? You shouldn't rent to them. I don't want you to rent to any homosexuals. You're a Catholic.' And the guy would look at him and say, 'But Father, they're paying me twice as much as I could get from anyone else, and they leave it in better shape than when they came, and they're no problem all summer long. . . .' And Duarte would look at them and say, 'You're Catholic. Homosexuals are sick.' "

The town called Father Duarte "the man on the hill," as in, "We'll do it if the man on the hill says it's okay."

A week after Chief Marshall's visit to Ciro & Sal's, he shut down an exhibition of monotypes by artist Tony Vevers at the Sun Gallery, declaring the nudes to be "publicly offensive" and "obscene."

Strategy sessions were held at the restaurant, where Vevers had once worked as a waiter. The cost of a lawyer was underwritten by Hudson

Walker, a multimillionaire timber baron, the benefactor of the Walker Art Center in Minneapolis and president of the Provincetown Art Association. His wife, Ione, a striking woman of six feet four inches who bore an uncanny resemblance to an ostrich, sat in the gallery every night until closing time. She knew that the jail wasn't set up to accommodate prisoners of both sexes at the same time; by adding a constant female presence, she made sure that no one got arrested. Hans Hofmann drafted a manifesto signed by nearly 150 artists and supporters, condemning the raid.

A compromise was finally reached, with the gallery hanging a half-curtain on the front window so children could not see inside.

Most of the artists who ate at Ciro's were dirt poor, except Robert Motherwell, who came from a prominent West Coast banking family. He'd been to Stanford and done a master's in philosophy at Harvard, studied at Columbia with the great art historian Meyer Schapiro, and then spent two years in Europe, hanging out with Arp and Léger. In later years, he married four times, drove a Bentley, had a house on the water, an apartment in New York City, and, later, an estate with a magnificent studio in Greenwich, Connecticut.

"Motherwell never had to stretch his own canvases, he paid someone to stretch them," Ciro recalls. Motherwell's wealth kept him alienated from other artists. "Bob tried very hard to be one of the boys," says Ciro. "But none of the other artists had any money. He was the only one. The others kind of resented it at first, but then I think they all realized he was a sincere painter and had something to offer.

"Motherwell, at the time, was a pretty good drinker. He could polish off a bottle of scotch between eight o'clock in the morning and noontime. But he never looked like he was loaded. He was one of the hardest-working painters in town. And he was also a very generous guy and never turned anyone down. Whatever he did, he did very quietly."

In 1955, Motherwell married the painter Helen Frankenthaler, who also came from a wealthy background. But Frankenthaler, whose work today hangs in the Whitney, MOMA, and other major museums, was never accepted by the local artists. "A lot of them didn't think much of her work," Ciro recalls. "I don't know why. I guess they held her background against her."

Toward the end of his career, Franz Kline also had a lot of money, which he used to buy flashy cars. "He had a beautiful Ford Thunderbird, but he was a menace on the highway. Thank God, he didn't have enough money to buy a car when he was in his prime," says Ciro. "He was broke for most of his life, maybe he made it the last ten years, and I remember him saying, 'Jesus, now that I've got money, I can't eat, I can't drink, I can't do a goddamn thing.'

"Some guys knew how to promote themselves," says Ciro, "like Ed Giobbi. Robert Rauschenberg was a promoter. Gottlieb, too. They made themselves available. They talked about their work. Larry Rivers was a big promoter. Most of the guys I know never thought too highly of him because he was always on a soapbox. They said, 'Jesus Christ, this guy is always talking about how great he is.' Sometimes people would just look at him and say, 'Shut the fuck up.' "

During the halcyon days of the fifties and sixties, there was only one place to get supplies—the Studio Shop, a tiny little hole-in-the-wall next door to Milton Avery's house. The owner was an odd, masculine-looking woman named Laura Easley. In 1953, when Easley told Ciro she needed an employee, he recommended his dishwasher, the artist Jim Forsberg, and when Easley finally died, she left the Studio Shop to him. Thanks to Forsberg's thriftiness, the shop had a look all its own, with shelves made out of old, warped stretchers and woodwork in a variety of colors as the painter-owner used up unsold tubes of paint. There was an amazing inventory for such a small store, and Forsberg would extend credit to artists who couldn't pay. Everybody went to the Studio Shop. "Hans Hofmann would never buy a tube at a time," Ciro recalls. "He'd buy a whole carton. Motherwell was a big spender, too."

The little art store was a marvel. "I used to get pissed off at painters who would come into town and then complain they could get supplies cheaper in New York. Jim would really get turned off by that, and he'd say, 'Well, goddammit, go to New York. I have to import this stuff. I'm not a big buyer, I've got a small place.' Motherwell used to get furious when he heard people complain. 'My God,' he'd say, 'you've got a gallery and a shop that provides everything you need and you complain?' "

When the store closed at the end of the eighties, and the space was converted into a small condo unit, many people thought it signified the end of Ptown as a vibrant painting community.

"Now," Ciro says, shaking his head, "if you want to buy paints, you go to the goddamn lumberyard. They're expensive and they don't have the selection. It's not run by artists. It's run by the guy running the lumberyard, who realized there was no one selling paints in Provincetown."

CHAPTER 10

CARNIVAL

August 30, 2000: A man in a hat walks by. He is a big man, deeply tanned, and all he's wearing is a small swimsuit. More startling is his hat; it is almost three feet high, an erect, rainbow-colored penis. The testicles are each just slightly smaller than the man's head, and the pubic hairs are tendrils of curled, iridescent plastic. The man is beaming. Families line Commercial Street, and they're pointing. Everyone is happy to see this man, and he's happy, too.

As he nears a large clump of people, a vivacious young woman darts out of the crowd and puts her arm around his shoulder. She smiles beatifically as her friend takes a photo. Photo finished, the man lowers his head and charges the crowd, like a bull. The crowd shrieks with delight, as the rainbow penis advances on them. At the last minute, just as he is about to impale an obese New Jersey housewife, the man with the hat swerves and runs skipping down the street.

The crowd roars and begins to clap and call him back. Welcome to Gay Carnival in Ptown.

It's getting near fall, and after several weeks of overcast skies and rain, the parade has been blessed with sun and a light breeze. The town is out in force, and hordes of tourists have come for the festivities. The mood is gay, both in the old and new sense of the word. One is immediately struck by the wide age range of the crowd. At the East End, the older folks hang out side by side with young families. The center of town is inundated with the pudgy, straight tourist set, a white, middle-class bunch for the most part, who've come to see Ptown's version of the Doublemint twins, two men with perfect tans and identical gym bodies holding hands as they walk down the street in their steel-toed boots and sarongs. The tourists will talk about the parade for weeks to come. As one continues toward the West End, the street is chockablock with young gay cyborgs. It might appear to an open-minded stranger as some sort of Utopian vision, gay, straight, lesbian, transgendered, bourgeois, working class—everyone mingling happily together. Of course, to Jesse Helms, it would be a nightmare, Dante's Hell. But sadly, Jesse Helms is not here. (If he were, the crowd would probably be so genial as to put him in a tutu and a tiara and plunk him atop a float.)

For the straight tourists, Carnival is a grand spectating event. They watch slack-jawed as the two Fabulous Hat Sisters mince by. The combined weight of the Hat Sisters is at least five hundred pounds, and they walk with a masterful strut, their hats monstrous creations, replications of flowering tropical bushes. A middle-aged lesbian walks by with her Chinese daughter, who is carrying a duck. A pair of men pass dressed as a hot dog and bun. They try to stick very close together and succeed admirably. A man dressed as a Cracker Jack box walks by; on the front of the box he has lettered "Eat Me."

This is what goes on in plain sight, during daylight hours, in a small town in the U.S.A.

A black Mercedes convertible drives by blasting Israeli pop. The two men in the front are wearing yamulkes, and a third, also in a yamulke, is manically waving an Israeli flag. Three magnificent queens in ornate tiaras and little else walk by with tightly linked arms; close on their heels is a black dump truck with a dancing gorilla in the back. The crowd isn't sure what this means but everyone claps anyway. A truck drives by, music blasting, with several hard-looking men in the back. They are in leather chaps with nothing on underneath, and one has a riding crop he uses to listlessly whip the bare buttocks of his compatriots. This is the Purgatory float. Purgatory is one of the venerable leather bars in Ptown.

A massive upright sow walks by and several little piglets fight over her extremely prominent nipples, when they are not jumping through a hoop held by a very buxom dominatrix. Following them is the Euro float, with a whole troupe of talented Mexican cabaret dancers. The crowd goes mad with desire.

In the crowd, men and women alike are draped in rainbow-colored beads and feather boas. Several older, more sophisticated women are wearing finely wrought Carnival masks, probably from Venice, and several of the older, paunchier gay men are in full drag and wearing bright red clown noses. All the bars are full and the drunken revelers spill out, wide-eyed, into the street. On the pier, a lone man plays a mournful bagpipe, and in front of Town Hall the huge Pearline is holding court. Pearline is like the Divine of yesteryear and gives a wildly successful cabaret show at an establishment called Steve's Alibi. As drag queens go, she is voluptuous without being extreme, and there is a certain daintiness to her carriage that can make one forget that, underneath, she is a three-hundred-pound behemoth in a skintight leopard-skin jumpsuit.

A man has painted himself black with a tarlike substance. It is difficult to ascertain if he is wearing anything at all, but it doesn't matter, since the crowd has shifted its attention to a Jeep carrying a rainbow-colored bear.

"It's Pride Bear!" they cry out.

Mothers maneuver their strollers to get a better view. Heterosexual men manage to clutch their girlfriends and crane their necks. An easily excited young queen melts away in a dead faint.

The parade meanders through the throng, music blasting from every float. Men are kissing on the streets. Obese queens weave through the crowd. In today's Ptown, there are very few queens who are not dipped in a postmodern irony before leaving their houses. In the year 2000, it's all about camp, with its garish colors, outrageous ensembles, and battalions of hairy-chested men in tight dresses. The Carnival used to be even more outrageous, until finally the town elders declared that they'd had enough, that the bacchanalia had to be toned down. According to locals, this year's Carnival was relatively demure, certainly more restrained than in 1989, when one float had a gaggle of men carrying signs, one of which read "Legalize Butt-fucking/Clit-licking."

That was also the year the town had its first Gay and Lesbian Family Week, which signaled another major flux. Lesbians had always been a presence in town, but now they'd "discovered" Provincetown. There were the feminists, and a younger group that had no apparent interest in either the arts or women's rights, but there was also a group that appeared over the Memorial Day weekend known locally as the Budweiser Dykes. These women, tough blue-collar lesbians from the working-class suburbs of Boston, Hartford, and Providence, lodged eight to ten in studio apartments and packed the Vixen and the Pied Piper, the town's leading women's bars. And there were Dykes on Bikes, riding Harleys. But the most aggressive group was made up of women who had not yet come out. They were in town expressly to "find themselves." Many of these were middle-class secretaries and second-level salespeople who hid their sexual preference in their daily life. In Provincetown, they insisted on proclaiming themselves, and this often took the form of refusing to let go of each other. As they walked up Commercial Street locked together, others were forced off the sidewalk.

The interaction between straights and the gay community is interesting. Some straight men are intimidated at how muscular all the gays are, but many of the young, straight townie crowd have begun to emulate the gay men in this striving for the body beautiful. Visit Mussel Beach, the gym of choice, and you're likely to find the man who delivers your heating oil at the Smith Machine pressing four hundred.

By nightfall the clubs of Ptown are packed. The shirtless, sweating men with the prominent deltoids jostle each other for space in the Crown & Anchor. A block away, the A-house is jammed. Every one of the four or five restaurants clustered next door are alive with voices competing with the beat of the Ramones coming off the dance floor, filling the alley.

On any given night during the high season, between one and four A.M., there will be one or two hundred men at the Dick Dock, the primary cruising spot in Ptown. Currently it is located on the beach in front of the Boatslip Motel, but it moves around. Two years ago it was farther down, at Flyer Santos's boatyard. Santos, an old-line Portuguese who did not appreciate his nightly visitors, installed high-powered night-lights and hired a guard with a dog to patrol the premises.

During the summer of 1999, a summer "rent-a-cop" shone his flashlight over the edge of the Boatslip onto the beach below, which was full of men servicing one another. When someone yelled at him to turn his damn light off, the portly cop, intent on making a bust, jumped off the balcony. He underestimated how high it was and hurt his ankle badly. While the cop cursed, over a hundred gay men in various states of undress laughed at him. The next night he was back, making a bunch of arrests, and the night after that, as well. He was transferred shortly thereafter.

As one knowledgeable observer of gay Ptown recently put it, "In Provincetown the cops know which side their bread is buttered on." The chief of police reports twice daily to the town manager, who, many say, is an advocate of upscale business development. Upscale business development, like the development of upscale private homes in Provincetown, tends to be a synecdoche for "gay."

If the cops do patrol the Dick Dock area, they take their time, make a lot of noise, flash their flashlights, and give everyone time to scamper away. The only people likely to get arrested are those so engrossed in what they're doing they don't notice.

Savvy men go to the Dick Dock before one A.M., because until that time the cops are busy patrolling Commercial Street. Until two A.M., they are patrolling Spiritus, the pizza parlor on Commercial and Court streets where gays congregate en masse when the bars let out. After two A.M. they might go by the Dick Dock.

Both in gay magazines and on the Internet, Provincetown is labeled "testosterone city," "Heaven on earth," and "the ultimate gym." The men who come to Ptown for sex—and that's most of them—have their own vocabulary:

RICE QUEEN: anyone attracted only to Asians
STICKY RICE: Asians who like only Asians
CHOCOLATE QUEEN: those who only like blacks
POTATO QUEEN: those who only like whites
DADDIES, or LEATHERMEN: those into hard sex, S&M, and bondage
BEARS: those preferring hairy partners
GYM QUEENS, or BUFF BOYS: bodybuilders, many of whom are
        into steroids (subdivided into those who are "big" and those
        who are after a more lithe, thus feminine, physique)

It is customary at these cruising spots to exchange names *after* the sexual encounter, not before. It is also taboo to make any noise at all. It is not uncommon to see twenty men entangled with one another, no one making a sound.

Occasionally, local straight men visit the Dick Dock to receive a competent blow job, but if they see the person who serviced them the next day on the street, they do not acknowledge him.

Since AIDS, most anonymous sex is restricted to fellatio and hand-jobs. "Barebacking," which is to say anal sex without a condom, and often between two HIV-positive partners, is not unheard of, but it is not common.

The dunes at Herring Cove Beach are the other main cruising spot. There, one need only set up a towel and wait. Or walk what the Park Service calls "Social Trails," which weave across the dunes and up around various knolls. These cruising trails have been in existence for decades, and there is no maintenance needed. They enjoy so much foot traffic, they never get overgrown. Lately, however, the Park Service has been closing off more and more areas so the fragile dunes may recover. Getting caught with one's pants down in the dunes is a misdemeanor, but people are rarely busted.

In addition to the Dick Dock and the dunes, during the fall, when the weeds have grown tall enough to provide protection, gays congre-gate in an area called The Love Canal, along the banks of a small tidal stream that wends through a marshy area near Herring Cove. From a good vantage point, one can see fifty to a hundred figures cavorting in the reeds and on the small beaches that form at bends in the stream.

Provincetown also has its "Circuit Party," one of thirty that are held all over the country every year in such unlikely places as Pensacola, Florida, and Columbus, Ohio. There is a group of men who build their lives around these parties, traveling from one to the next. Most are wealthy; others "work" the circuit as talent-for-hire. These events rake in huge amounts of money and feature DJs who have become interna-tionally famous superstars, people like Victor Calderone and David Knapp. Chris Cox, for example, was reportedly paid $100,000 to do the Millennium New Year's Eve Party in Australia and was then flown by private jet to L.A., where he was paid double his usual fee to do a New Year's Eve blast there.

Nowadays a number of these events are organized by the thirtyish Provincetown-based David Flowers, whose name meant nothing until three years ago. Now Flowers is famous throughout the gay community, profiled in the gay press as another Steve Rubell. Annually, his weeklong Fourth of July Provincetown event, called Summer Camp, brings upwards of $1 million into town.

At the July Fourth Circuit Party taking place at the Crown & Anchor, tickets went for $75 to $200, and nearly two thousand were sold, some seven hundred more than was publicly acknowledged in deference to local fire codes. The program ran the entire weekend, open-air afternoon tea dances, cabaret shows, boat cruises, and blow-out parties. According to reliable sources, only a couple of cases of beer were sold at the Back Room bar the first night, whereas they sold out of their 1,500 water bottles. Ecstasy, today's gay drug of choice, makes you dehydrated.

After the Crown & Anchor closed for the evening on the Fourth, the party moved to the Portuguese Princess whale-watch boat, which for $10,000 had been hired to sail around, out beyond Long Point, until dawn. Several hundred men were aboard. Drugs were rampant. Surprisingly, no one was lost overboard.

The best time to go to the town's favorite gym, MuscleBeach, is in the early morning. A sign outside the men's showers urges users to conserve water: "Longer Shower Will Not Get You More Dates." One of the gym's managers, a man in his late forties, explains that he has stopped going to Circuit Parties. "Most of the guys are assholes—airline steward types. They get deep into credit card debt—clothes, hotels, the drugs. There'll also be sponsors at these things—older guys who bring in five or ten younger guys."

This particular individual has, in the past, attended any number of Circuit Parties all over the country and knows whereof he speaks. There is the "Red Party" in Columbus, Ohio; the "White Party" in Palm Springs; New York's "Black Party" in late March; "Hope Weekend" in Boston; the "Pines Party" on Fire Island; and the "Black-and-Blue Party" in Montreal, which hosts sixty to seventy thousand and is the biggest of them all.

Starting about two years ago, the Crown & Anchor began holding occasional "Foam Parties," where a huge, enclosed area is filled with foam up to chest-level. Men go into the area in underwear or swimsuits, and there is much groping and "playing" but little fellatio, because the foam, reportedly, does not taste good.

Coke is out. Ecstasy is very in. GHB is in, Special K, too. Poppers remain popular. Viagra is also in demand and sells for twenty to thirty dollars a pill. Again, because they know "which side their bread is buttered on," the local police do little to arrest the dealers of gay recreational drugs.

Police also refused to disperse an East End afternoon garden party that had overflowed onto Commercial Street during the July Fourth weekend, 2000, although it was completely blocking traffic. Neighbors, irate over the noise, estimated there were five hundred bare-chested men present.

Although there are some monogamous couples among Ptown gays, they are fairly rare and tend to be restricted to older men. Some year-rounders practice what could be called "seasonal monogamy," forming a winter attachment and then, come summer, breaking up so that both can enjoy the "fresh meat."

There are two fully equipped dungeons in town, one belonging to a pillar of the gay community, who owns two downtown businesses. It is by invitation only.

CHAPTER 11

IF NOT US, WHO?

The gay community's struggle to carve out a place in Provincetown has not been without conflict. When the national organization Act-Up carried the inflammatory "Legalize Butt-fucking/Clit-licking" sign in the annual Gay Pride Parade in 1989, many locals felt the aggressiveness of the out-of-towners was unwarranted. The Provincetown Business Guild, dedicated to filling gay and lesbian guest houses, was loudly condemnatory. Police Chief Meads insisted he had been misled when Act-Up guaranteed that their contingent would not be confrontational—and afterward, the leaders of Act-Up were anything but contrite when they claimed that no one was paying attention to the fact that two men had been gay-bashed outside Town Hall only the night before. To focus on a single sign, they insisted, was proof of the town's homophobia.

Stephen Crouch, an Act-Up member who participated in the parade, called it "unbelievable" that the gays had no local power base. "Half the selectmen should be gay, the chief of police should be gay, the town manager should be gay—the government hierarchy here is totally straight," he claims.

The 1989 parade catalyzed a major political upheaval. Carnival, regarded as the high point of the gay tourist season, had been scheduled to kick off a week later; it was canceled because of anonymous threats. But Act-Up wasn't through. Later that month, in league with Provincetown People with AIDS (PWA), the group held a "Die-in" at the Outer

Cape Health Services clinic to protest the inaccessibility of aerolized pentamidine. About forty people walked into the clinic's waiting room, and, at an agreed upon moment, they all fell to the floor, a stylized mass death. The police were called and the demonstrators taken away, but a *Boston Globe* reporter was there to capture the story, which made the national wire services. John Perry Ryan, one of the organizers, recalls being ostracized afterward: "In such a small community it's hard to take on some of the people in power and not make enemies. To them, my response is 'Tough.' "

Prior to the protests, AIDS was perceived as a death sentence. Treatment had focused on taking care of the victims, in effect preparing them for death. But Act-Up and PWA wanted access to experimental medicines, as well as streamlined FDA approval for these drugs. They wanted information on how to fight the disease, not give in to it. They felt that the medical and scientific establishments were dragging their feet, and instead of dying with AIDS, they shifted the focus to *living* with AIDS. Their mantra, modeled on the oft-repeated slogan arising out of the Nazi holocaust, spoke eloquently:

> *If not here, where?*
> *If not now, when?*
> *If not us, who?*

Ptown had always been an apolitical place, a town of artists and writers, not academics and activists. The AIDS crisis was changing that.

Even before the Act-Up parade incident, there had been the so-called Spiritus riots, which took place late in the evening on August 15 and 16, 1986.

Spiritus Pizza is one of the last stops for food as one strolls down Commercial Street toward the West End. Just blocks from the Boatslip Motel, it had started as a hippie landmark in the early seventies. In operation since 1969, it was owned by John "Jingles" Yingling and Paul Schneider, two former hippies and college buddies, who had dragged an old pizza oven up from New Jersey to make their living in Provincetown.

By the end of the seventies, the crowd at Spiritus had changed. It was open until two A.M., serving a simple menu of pizza, coffee, and ice cream. It so ruled the after-hours scene that, when the bars closed at one A.M., the sidewalk and patio area in front would fill with upwards of two thousand men, some in form-fitting white tank tops that turned a shade of lavender under certain lights; some wearing black leather motorcycle jackets, chains, and shiny caps; some in Abercrombie casual, as though the wearers weren't in Ptown but at a Newport, Rhode Island, yacht club. Many were simply bare-chested. The crowd was so dense that Commercial Street, the town's main thoroughfare, was all but impassable.

Any number of straights in town had vented their spleen on this nightly congregation at Spiritus. Delores DeSousa, a member of the school board and a town selectwoman, was perhaps the most outspoken. Two years earlier she had urged her fellow selectmen to consider closing all eating and drinking establishments at the hour of midnight. For DeSousa and others who would later advocate mass arrests, the Spiritus crowds were not only indifferent to the needs of working people in the neighborhood, they also blocked the fire station just across the street; it could take ten or fifteen minutes for an emergency vehicle to get through, she argued, and the mob was known to shout insults and even throw pieces of pizza.

Others had suggested installing sprinklers to discourage people from gathering, or creating an after-hours zone on the outskirts of town, a reminder of Provincetown's notorious past, when pirates and mooncussers inhabited the infamous Helltown, a community of liquor and whores on the outer beach south of Race Point. DeSousa's final ominous words on the matter were "It's a powder keg, and it wouldn't take much to have a riot, and then what would you do?"

For years Yingling and Schneider had made attempts to work with town officials on what was now becoming the "Spiritus problem," but both were adamant that the crowds were not the fault of the business itself. In 1984, when the issue was first raised at selectmen's meetings, Schneider defended Spiritus's role in Provincetown's nightlife. He estimated he sold several thousand cups of coffee and a thousand slices of pizza nightly to the gathering throng, but that the food had "a sobering effect on them. If they were not here, they would be somewhere else," he told the local press. "And I can guarantee the problem will not diminish as the months go by."

Police Chief James Meads agreed with him, admitting he didn't know how to move the crowds without "a confrontation."

Thus, in 1986, in the weeks just prior to Carnival, there had been several meetings between the selectmen and the two business owners. Carnival, one of the last big parties of summer, was known primarily as an event to promote gay tourism, and with attendance that year expected to be higher than usual, it was decided that the police would deploy three times the usual number of officers—six, not two, and at Spiritus's expense—to keep Commercial Street clear "for reasons of public safety."

Unfortunately somebody forgot to tell the weekend bar crowd about this new protocol. As Selectman Munro Moore was to state later, "All of a sudden, the police were just *there.*"

It is debatable whether spreading word of the beefed-up police presence would have made any difference. Bar rush is a time that can accurately be described as bedlam and, more, the bewitching hour. For summering tourists, many of them used to closing hours as late as four A.M. in Manhattan, the night was young and Spiritus was the place to go to get hooked up for the night, if you hadn't already got lucky. When, on August 15, the police showed up in force and told the crowd, later estimated at one thousand, to disperse, not everybody moved; those who continued to linger were threatened with arrest. Soon people began chanting "Walk in the street!" and "Kill the pigs!" A handful of men standing on the sidelines began to march east on Commercial Street toward the town pier, to the cheers of the crowd. As the marchers grew in number, they called for others to join them, growing louder and more strident.

It was a scene worthy of Berkeley, only it wasn't Berkeley, it was Provincetown, and six people were arrested: three for rude and disorderly conduct; two for resisting arrest; and a sixth for "obstructing free passage." Early the next morning, Saturday, Chief Meads called an emergency meeting with the selectmen to review possible trouble later that night. The meeting, starting at two P.M., drew a small group of demonstrators objecting to Meads's insistence on a closed meeting. Meads held firm and, with the room cleared, the selectmen made plans for that evening, which they decided should include the State Police, police dogs, and a large bus-size paddy wagon in case they had to make mass arrests.

By late afternoon Saturday the rumors were flying up and down Commercial Street that there was going to be a demonstration at Spiritus. No one knew who the organizers were or what form the protest would take. But it didn't matter. When the selectmen released a statement requesting the patrons of Spiritus to keep the streets clear, people only cranked themselves into high gear.

The second night of the Spiritus riots was less tumultuous than the first, since only three arrests were made. But there was a big difference. People were more organized, there was a new and different political solidarity to it: Gathered five-deep from Carver Street to Winthrop Street, with the largest concentration in front of the pizzeria itself, many in the crowd showed up with signs and chanted slogans like "Homophobia has got to go!" and "We are one!" When the town's six police cruisers had roared the wrong way down Court Street and then swung into the parking lot at the nearby Seaview Restaurant to create a staging area for the State Police vans, the crowd responded with mock applause and hissing; some people threw slices of pizza, as if to express their determination to follow in the footsteps of the famous Stonewall Uprising, the modern turning point in the gay liberation movement that took place in the streets of Greenwich Village in 1969.

This was not the first time—nor the last—that the after-hours mob sent tremors through Provincetown's traditional Portuguese community. In the early seventies, police made sweeps to force loiterers to move away from the benches outside of Town Hall, the so-called Meat Rack that was the gays' principal late-night cruising area. A year later, Chief Meads staged an interdictive strike by storming Piggy's and arresting people for same-sex dancing. The raid was of questionable legality, of course, but that didn't matter. "He went around and every time he found a male couple dancing together he told them they couldn't do it anymore," recalls the club's DJ, thinking back fondly on the good old days, "and if anybody gave him shit, he'd just arrest them."

One *Advocate* reporter, who'd been tipped off to the raid ahead of time, explained that what it boiled down to was that Meads "just saw it coming. He saw the deluge, you know, that the dam was bursting and he thought, 'Somehow I'm going to stop it right now, and it begins here at Piggy's.' The women who were dancing with each other that night were left alone," he pointed out, "because so far as the cops were concerned that was like high school—that's what women do when they don't have dates. With the men it was something else entirely."

Meads was indeed making his stand, and he was no different from many other locals who were having trouble with "the direction" the town was going in. But only a fool or romantic could claim that the Portuguese hadn't been troubled in the past, going back thirty or forty years and more. Gays in Provincetown was nothing new. "The fairies," as the locals traditionally called them, had first started coming to town in discernible numbers as far back as the early twenties, drawn by the Wharf Theater, the successor to the Provincetown Players at the far West End, and its leading lady, Bette Davis, who even then was something of a gay icon. There were any number of gay artists around, too, two of the more notable of whom were Ethel Mars and Maud Squire, leading proponents of the White Line wood-cut method that had been invented in Provincetown.

During the forties, locals began renting to gays as a way of raising much-needed cash. Then, as now, the year-round Provincetown community was poor. For many Portuguese the lure of money was decisive, just as money would later move many a local to sell out altogether in the nineties.

"We didn't know what a gay person was, these were just people off the street. But once they got here, God, they flocked in," recalls Robert Meads, the brother of the town's police chief, whose mother and two aunts all rented to the new visitors. "Why were they accepted? It had nothing to do with Portuguese 'big-heartedness.' The Portuguese are as selfish and mean as any culture. The money did it. Provincetown was a damn piss-poor town. Besides, you'd rent to so-called beatniks and get stuck. The gays never beat you out of money, so even though you'd prefer to rent to your own kind, you rented to them."

Adds another local, less delicately: "Shit, it was all them artists. Gimme an artist, I'll show you someone who loves to suck cock."

Truth was, there had always been a mixed response on the part of the community. Aside from the fact that the gays had a reputation for keeping their apartments clean and paying their rent, they were also entertaining. The Portuguese women thrilled to the visitors' tales of New York and the big world beyond; for many they were also an antidote to their husbands' peccadilloes, or simply brought a little luster into marriages where the husband tended to be brusquely macho Mediterranean. They flattered the women's cooking, praised their hairdos even if the hairdos were pedestrian by big city standards, brought them gifts and . . . well, treated them like *women*.Consequently, in July and August many local females could be found at gay clubs such as Wuthering Heights and the Madeira Room, stone-crazy boozed, arm-in-arm with their tenants and their tenants' boyfriends. Sitting there surrounded by "queens," they happily took in the innuendo-laced drag shows and howled along with everyone else.

In 1947 one of the first openly gay guest houses, Five Winslow Street, had already hung out its shingle and was advertising a "mixed" clientele. Weathering Heights was doing a loud, capacity business night after night, thanks to the female impersonator "Bella Baiona," aka Phil Bayone, who'd wear a huge picture hat while being lowered from the ceiling on a swing, and more often than not insult her audience. One of the regulars was Clayton Snow, a local who'd "come out" in high school and started wearing a dress. He had earned himself the nickname "Claytina" and started mixing with the summer artists, including Brando.

By the mid-1950s, gay men were an established presence in Provincetown, and the mood among the locals, like so much else in America during that oppressive time, had begun to sour. Town selectmen sent out a famous letter that advised members of the community not to hire gays: "The boys are coming," the missive read, and so timely was the letter deemed to be that, despite its obvious and nowadays libelous bigotry, it was reproduced in the *Advocate*, the better to arm the community for the upcoming summer.

The man who was police chief back then, Francis H. "Cheney" Marshall, did his part by sending officers on horseback to raid the gays' favorite beach spot, a section of Herring Cove Beach then known as "Gaytona."

To make matters worse, throughout the fifties local teenagers, sensing their elders' approval, indulged in an orgy of "fag bashing." The town had a checkered history in this area, but the kids, who were tired of being taunted with "faggot" and "queer" every time Provincetown High went up-Cape for away games, began to set upon gay men. In one particularly vicious incident, four teenagers pummeled a man and left him unconscious near Adam's Drugstore, next door to Town Hall.

Another incident in the early sixties, one that went unreported in the *Advocate* but was whispered about over many a dinner table, involved a middle-age man who was beaten up and later found dead of a heart attack on the beach west of MacMillan Wharf. Other instances of what would later be called hate crimes included assaults with weapons ranging from broom sticks to BB guns.

By the sixties, it is safe to say, Provincetown was fissuring into straight and gay camps and the taunting of gays, not to say physical attacks against them, continued, even though the town government later embraced a host of sensitivity-training workshops. A couple of days after the Spiritus riots, an off-duty cop was heard yelling antigay remarks across Commercial Street. Meads summarily fired him, but the chief was well aware of how worked up locals could get over gays. Part of the resentment was class-based, the perception that the gay visitors were rich and arrogant. But another source of the year-rounders' resentment was that for years their kids, in addition to be being taunted by contemporaries at athletic meets in Orleans, Chatham, Dennisport, and other up-Cape towns, had often been ogled, and even propositioned, by the out-of-town, sometimes swishy visitors. Practically every kid in town could recall an incident that involved him or a friend. There was an exaggerated quality to the way many locals talked about it, but the scenario was essentially the same time and time again. Provincetown was a small town, and many of its citizens had only a high school education. They didn't know how to deal with the situation, and it made them dangerously angry:

"I'd be going to work down to the pier at four or five in the morning, you know," recalls one fisherman, describing the typical encounter, "and they'd follow you. They'd be walking right behind you, making remarks. Sometimes I'd just stop. I'd want to see if they'd stop, too, and I remember always telling myself that I was gonna smash 'em if they said anything to my face. . . . We all talked about it. Fuckin' faggots. You just don't know if you weren't there."

The biggest change of all was signaled by the formation of the Provincetown Business Guild in 1978. The Guild, or PBG, was not just the de facto Chamber of Commerce for the ever-expanding number of gay businesses in town but a political lobbying group dedicated to organizing the gay vote. Computerized mailing lists and ads in national gay publications were the instruments, but the strategy was to maximize the gay business dollar, to increase the number of gay restaurants, rooming houses, and retail shops until they outnumbered straight businesses. The goal was to control the town's tax base. If gay businesses could gain control, then gays would own Town Hall. "This was how gay people set out to get into Town Hall," says Sal Del Deo, restaurateur and painter, "and they have, absolutely. The Guild was their rallying point."

So strong was the PBG that many straight businesses signed up with the group, eager to grab their share of gay customers. With Paul Christo at the helm, representatives of the PBG would take their problems directly to the town manager. The traditional Chamber of Commerce was left stunned. What bothered the Chamber and their longtime president, Bob Harrison, who happened to be a gay man—albeit an "old style" gay man—who had lived in town quietly with his partner for several decades, was that Provincetown was being promoted strictly as a gay ghetto instead of a place for all people.

"You can't pick an *exact* date, but there's no question that sometime in the eighties was when they got political control," says George Bryant, who served as town selectman from 1976 to 1985. "John Perry Ryan used to come to the Board of Selectmen almost every Monday during the summers and bring some guy he said had been hurt in a gay bashing episode. This was meant to intimidate the selectmen and other town officials, to try to make them feel as though the gays were a besieged minority, when they were actually becoming a majority. They were trying to set the stage for the complete gay takeover, and the thing is, when town officials are besieged with this sort of stuff, the good people leave and the bad people stay. It's just too difficult to deal with."

One week after the Spiritus riots of 1986, the selectmen called a public meeting. About 250 angry people filled the wood-paneled Judge Welsh Conference Room in Town Hall and lambasted the town officials, demanding that all charges against "rioters" be dropped and calling for an end to what they termed "selective law enforcement." Chief Meads, the selectmen, the media, and even the town manager, who'd been away the previous weekend, were all to blame, they said. Selectman Paul Christo got the loudest ovation when he said that for anyone to believe that the Spiritus situation wasn't a gay issue was "to be naive." "Provincetown is a gay haven, where people come to be free and recapture a feeling of being alive," he yelled, adding, *"And we're here to stay!"* When the applause died down Selectman Munro Moore, widely regarded as the town's leading progressive despite his proclivity for plaid belts and silly green yachting pants, rose to say that he was appalled that the selectmen and the police had been labeled antigay. The crowd only booed him. Delores DeSousa got up next, saying that she shared Moore's outrage. Now the audience guffawed, as though to point out that this was the very woman who only the week before had suggested that police load the demonstrators into school buses and "take 'em all back to Greenwich Village where they belong."

But it was Pat Shultz, a longtime resident who'd risen to become the town's most successful Realtor, who voiced a sentiment that touched all parties at the meeting.

"Being gay does not make you right, it makes you human. This is our home," Shultz said. "We have a total commitment here, not just a weeklong commitment. Just because tourists come to Provincetown and spend money here, they don't have the right to create a situation that would make residents want to leave town."

Most of the crowd knew that Shultz herself was gay, but the Realtor's comments, like those of the WASPy Moore, elicited more hisses and boos.

Little came of the meeting, and so it was no surprise that as the power of gays grew exponentially through the eighties, Spiritus erupted again during the summer of ninety. This time it was "the Golden Plunger Riot," because the disturbance took place on the eve of the Annual Golden Plunger Awards—an event modeled after the Academy Awards, where fans, drag queens, and the whole gamut of performers making up the town's entertainment world gather together at summer's end to celebrate the "Best of the Best"—the "Best Entertainer," "Hottest 'Tron" (as in "Waitron"), "Babe of the Year," and "King and Queen of Provincetown." Then, as now, it was a tongue-in-cheek affair, full of flamboyant wit, shrieks, sequins, and high camp, with actual toilet plungers spray-painted gold given out as awards. Late the evening in question, a passing motorist yelled antigay insults in front of Spiritus and one of the award winners chased the car down the street, wielding his plunger above his head. An angry crowd followed suit, and the car was forced to the curb. Lenore, the drag queen who'd led the charge, smashed the vehicle's windshield with her high heel, the police arrived, and there were more arrests.

Despite the predictable outcries of harassment and sex discrimination, the evening was ultimately a joke. The Golden Plunger Award? An attack on a drunk local by a queen with her high-heel shoe? A so-called riot revolving around thrown pizzas and ice-cream cones?

But for all the humor, the Spiritus events were, in the words of one Cape newspaper, "a litmus test of where you stand." The marchers had unearthed resentments that had been simmering for years. But the conflicts couldn't be reduced to gay-straight. Whatever the psychic complexities of the situation, the underpinnings of what was happening were ultimately economic. The major, in fact singular, after-effect of the eighties real estate boom was that a lot of townspeople, including many second- and third-generation Portuguese, had started to sell their property and were moving to Truro, leaving behind a situation that was in fact patently unique: a town where gays were well on their way to becoming the numerical majority. Pat Shultz's complaint after the Spiritus brouhaha had been directed at gay *visitors*, people who came for a week or two during high season; now it could just as easily be applied to the "new" gays who were buying property so they could spend their summers, or just a month or even several weeks of the summer, in town, then move on to their other homes in San Francisco, South Beach, Malibu, or Palm Springs.

Many of these people had considerable money. What their peripatetic living habits signaled was that in Provincetown there was now little possibility of a functioning year-round community.

Jay Critchley, a gay artist and activist, spoke to the gay community: "What we need to do is to stop thinking of ourselves as victims and begin to honor the minority rights of the straight people, the Portuguese people, the children who live in this community. We need to be very conscious about including other voices in all the decisions that affect our community. Surely gays should understand that better than most."

Unfortunately, only a small number of the newcomers seemed to be listening, and for many traditional counterculture romantics, the party, as they say, had ended. The whole complex of anarchic, nonmainstream values and personalities that had been the town's lifeblood since the turn of the century—all were diminished, and for some displaced completely by visitors driving Rovers and BMWs.

"The democratic dream that there's going to be a fisherman dancing next to you with big boots and then there's another guy at the Fine Arts Work Center who won the Yale Younger Poets thing, you know, that dream that there's going to be this extraordinary community of straights and gays, of people deeply *involved*, going at it side by side . . . that was *gone*," says Lou Postel, the straight editor of *Provincetown Poets*. "There was a sadness because we didn't know what to do. We'd lost who we were, so a lot of people just went back to Boston and Manhattan. Others who had private money stuck around, waiting for the worst."

CHAPTER 12

TONY JACKETT:
THE SMUGGLING STORY

Third-generation fisherman-turned–pot smuggler, now Provincetown's shellfish warden at a salary of $27,000 a year, Tony Jackett has just turned fifty-two, although from his looks you would never know it. He is the father of four children and has been married for the past twenty-nine years to Susan, a blond with high cheekbones and alabaster skin, another local with Portuguese roots who has long been regarded as the most beautiful girl to come out of Ptown High.

Jackett himself is dark-skinned, with jet-black hair—"dark and marvelously good-looking," to borrow the John Dos Passos description of the Provincetown Portuguese, whom he found such a contrast to the local Yankees with their "hard-looking hatchet faces." Jackett has a well-proportioned, lean face, perfect white teeth, and large lambent eyes. When he goes a day or two without shaving, as he often does, he's an Errol Flynn look-alike. His father, uncles, cousins, and grandfather have all been among Provincetown's most celebrated fishermen—"highliners," as they're called, the best of the best. Tony, in the face of today's fishing crisis, is having to decide whether he can resurrect his aging boat and carry on the family tradition. In the meantime, he checks out the shellfish.

It's a perfect dawn in midsummer, with thin tufts of clouds spread

out across the horizon, and a gentle breeze causing the slightest of ripples to course across the stillness of the bay. The streets are quiet.
Everyone is still in bed recovering from last night's carousing. But Tony
Jackett is up, driving down Commercial Street through the East End of
town. He pulls over briefly to check on the moorings of a float, finds it
solidly anchored, and looks out across the wet sand shimmering in the
morning sun. Off in the distance he spots an older man—the man is with
a little girl, and he's digging into the sand with his heel. Tony recognizes
the motion. The man, who has a bucket next to him, is harvesting quahogs in a restricted area. For the past month or so Tony's been cultivat-
ing several quahog beds here. The beds are still in a fragile state. It is these
shellfish, when mature, that will seed the beds for generations to come.

Since the turn of the century, humans have been harvesting quahogs
in this area. Read about Cape Cod and you'll read about how clam digging is a Cape tradition, a ritualistic part of summer. In the fifties and sixties, seaplanes used to fly in from Boston, fill their cargo holds with
shellfish, and fly back. Even Mick Jagger of the Rolling Stones, whenever
in Boston for a concert, would special-order local shellfish. By the early
seventies, there was nothing left.

Tony goes back to his car, gets his shellfish warden badge, and
walks out toward the man.

"Good morning, sir."

The man looks up, surprised. Tony is barefoot, wearing shorts, and
only the small, open clam on the left side of his tank top, and the let-
tering underneath, "Shellfish Warden," indicate that this is an official
encounter.

Tony reaches in his pocket and pulls out his badge. "You know that
this is a restricted area for shellfish harvesting?" he asks rhetorically. He
walks over to the man's bucket, which is overflowing with young, pink
cherrystones.

"Where are you from?" Tony asks.

"Rhode Island," the man says, and he looks uncomfortable as he adds,
"I'm actually on the town shellfish commission out there. We're going to
dump these out. I just wanted to take my granddaughter out clamming.
It'll give the seagulls something to eat. . . ."

Tony looks at him. "Actually, sir, you know what you're going to do? You're going to rebury them. That's what I ask people to do when they've dug up clams in a restricted area." Tony is smiling.

The man looks nervously at the little girl standing next to him. She is about eight years old and is watching with interest. "Yes, well, I guess that's what we'll do. . . ."

Tony beams. "Thanks very much. It's a lovely morning, isn't it? So how long are you visiting Ptown for?"

"Just another couple of days. I've been coming here for fifty years. This last week's been great." The man is relieved that he's not going to be busted. "I'm actually a judge up in Rhode Island," he admits suddenly.

Tony grins, showing his big, infectious smile, and turns to leave. "Listen, make sure you bury the quahogs good and deep—and spread them out a little, too. Have a good stay in Provincetown."

Tony makes his way back toward his Jeep. Before he steps off the beach, he looks back. The judge is on his hands and knees in the flats, reburying the quahogs. The granddaughter waves.

Ptown is eerily silent. Confetti and the odd balloon are the only remnants of last night's festivities, the once-a-year gay parade known as Carnival. The Jeep rolls by Town Hall with its ornamental Queen Anne gables and copper-clad clock tower, and then the Coast Guard station. Tony parks near the Pilgrim Memorial Circle, where the breakwater shoots straight out to Long Point.

Just as he's about to get out of the car, he sees a big street-sweeping machine coming his way. He restarts the engine, pulls out again, and parks on the other side of the narrow road. The street sweeper rumbles by and Tony nods to the driver, who stops the machine and hops out. He's in jeans and a T-shirt, another handsome sinewy Portuguese.

"Hey, Tony! You didn't have t'move the car. I coulda gone around!"

They shake hands and exchange news, fishing mostly. Five bass caught off Wood End, a six-hundred-pound tuna off the back shore. Then Tony notices the man's shirt. On the front there's the Provincetown seal. On the back in big block letters it says "DPW."

"New shirts?"

"Yeah, the town's been givin' 'em out."

"DPW—Department of Public Works. Nice. They didn't have those when I worked for 'em."

The man grins. "That's not what DPW stands for, Tony. You know what it really stands for?"

"What?" Tony grins back at him.

"Dumb Portugee Worker!"

The Portuguese of Provincetown have always had an us-and-them mentality. People often forget that the majority of locals are an African people, a mixture of Sudanese Negro, Arab, and mainland Portuguese. For many, the law represents "white." Most came to this country in a state close to indentured servitude, something few of them care to discuss today. Typically, during the years after the Civil War, Yankee whaling captains would leave New Bedford, Nantucket, or the Outer Cape ports with a skeleton crew and sail straight for the Cape Verde and Canary Islands, though sometimes they'd go to the Azores to pick up additional hands for the ugly work of stripping and boiling of whale blubber when the vessel reached the killing grounds of the Pacific. These dark-skinned crewmen would be paid next to nothing, usually ⅟₇₅₀ of a share. Skippers, by comparison, got two or three shares—numerically three to four thousand times as much as the Portuguese crewmen. And the islanders rarely got even their 750th share, since they had to pay for clothes gotten out of the ship's swap chest, for the grog they drank, and for any infraction of the Master's rules. By the time a man got ashore at the end of a two- or three-year voyage he might have five dollars in his pocket, which would be quickly spent in the local bars. Some of the seamen chose to make Provincetown their base, but many more simply found themselves stranded, unable to return home. There is still a feeling among the Portuguese population that the New Englander looks down on them, viewing them as objects to be used.

At Provincetown High, Jackett was something of a golden boy—a respectable B-student, king of his junior prom, a tireless Little Leaguer as well as co-captain and high scorer of the school's basketball team, the Fishermen. Unlike his older, "cooler" half-brother David, Tony never got into trouble. On the contrary, he was known to most of the town as a good boy, the exemplary Jackett kid who worked at the Dairy Queen during the summer months, where he went out of his way to chat with the old folks as much as with the bubbly teen queens, many of whom would queue up at the fast food window expressly to ogle him. Even then he was handsome and, doubtless because he knew it, there was an ease to the way he carried himself, a certain stylized flair.

Although he made sure that no one saw him, at home, alone in his basement bedroom, he sometimes practiced poses, pretending to be Roy Orbison, the great rocker, studying himself in the mirror lip-synching "Pretty Woman." His heroes were Brando, Dean, and Steve McQueen. Later, he came to envision himself as Warren Beatty in *McCabe and Mrs. Miller*, his favorite movie.

Tony was a Boy Scout and a choirboy at St. Peter's, the Catholic church that had been built in the late nineteenth century, when the Portuguese population had grown so large it made up a third of the town. After graduation, he went off to business college in Boston. This descendant of a long line of fishermen thought he might become a court stenographer. At one point, in deference to his mother's pursuit of the American Dream, he even considered law school. Then he met Susan— "like *bang*," as he recalled. "I didn't care that I'd never liked fishing; it was 'I'll go fishing,' since it was the quickest way to raise money so we could get married and buy a house."

They met while Tony was back at the Dairy Queen, the summer after his second year at school. Susan was living near the Jackett's house in a cramped, two-bedroom apartment in Young's Court, a cul de sac between Bradford and Commercial streets, not far from the town pier. She was at the end of a marriage, waiting for her divorce to come through.

Susan had two children, Lakota Sioux Indians she'd adopted. And she was four years older than Tony. Susan's mother, a mainland Portuguese of the old school, did not approve when Tony moved in with Susan. Susan's father, an Iowa-born, ex–coast guardsman, who had worked for years in the plumbing department at the town's main hardware store, didn't much like the arrangement either.

But the person who was most upset was Tony's mother. Tony was her favorite, her "love child," and she regarded Susan as the woman who'd taken advantage of her son's innocence. When Tony and Susan married that fall, she was, nonetheless, at the wedding. But it was awkward. Tony's father, Anthony, had left her only the month before.

•   •   •

The Jacketts were a fishing family. Tony's grandfather, a swordfish har-
pooner from north of Lisbon whose name was originally Jacquetta, had
not come ashore until he was well past seventy, and only then because
he was disgusted with his crew, who refused to go out in bad weather.
His father's brothers-in-law, Louis and Freddy Salvador, were the biggest
"highliners" in town, and their boat, the *Shirley and Rowland*, had set
the standard for the fleet ever since the glory days of the early fifties.
Tony's father, Anthony, whose boat, the *Plymouth Belle*, wasn't far
behind, was delighted that Tony was marrying and joining the crew,
which already consisted of Tony's brothers, David and Tommy, and his
uncle, Oscar Snow. It would have been hard for Tony to escape the life:
In addition to his uncles, his father's best friends were Frank Parsons,
Henry Passion, and Manuel Henrique, who owned boats that were
successful as well.

"I grew up being very proud, coming from that heritage," Tony
recalls. "My dad's boat had the best lines, she was *everyone's* favorite, and
every year at the Blessing of the Fleet I felt privileged. I was six when
my dad got her, but to me he'd *always* had the *Plymouth Belle*, even
though he'd been fishing with my uncle Louis a half dozen years before
then."

In a town the size of Provincetown, such a pedigree is equal to
being a Trump in today's Manhattan or the racer son of Mario Andretti.
Whenever people looked at Tony Jackett, they thought of his father,
Anthony.

Like the vast majority of local fishermen, Anthony had little formal
education. After quitting school at sixteen, he'd gone to work for the
local ice company, and it wasn't until he returned from World War II, a
veteran of Omaha Beach on D-Day, that he went fishing.

Provincetown was riding the wave of the nation's postwar prosperity, and the Portuguese were the biggest beneficiaries. Men who'd
worked as deckhands had returned with wartime savings that allowed
many to buy vessels of their own. Fish stocks, extending from the
nearby Stellwagen Banks all the way out to the Georges Banks, were at
an all-time high after the hiatus in fishing during the war years. The revitalized industry had taken on new importance to those who had businesses ashore—the bankers and insurance brokers, the fuel companies
and boatyards. All looked upon fishing as the keystone of the local econ-

omy, at one with the town's future. They also looked on Anthony Jack-ett as a sure bet. For seven years he'd toiled as a crewman aboard sev-eral local boats. Then, as a hired skipper, he'd turned the *Plymouth Belle* into one of the most profitable draggers in the fleet. In 1957 Marcey's Oil Company and Anthony's brother-in-law Louis Salvador loaned him enough money to buy the *Plymouth Belle* from its absentee owner in Fall River. Anthony Jackett was in a position to earn money like he'd never earned before.

By the time he bought the *Plymouth Belle*, Anthony had married, fathered two sons and a daughter, and also taken on the responsibility of helping to raise his wife's son by her earlier marriage.

When Tony joined his father's operation in 1971 after marrying Susan, he knew little about harvesting fish from the ocean floor, though he'd worked aboard the *Plymouth Belle* intermittently while in high school. He learned to mend nets, to navigate, to smell fish in the water, and, at last, to overcome his tendency to get seasick, one of the principal rea-sons he'd decided not to fish in the first place.

The smell of the fish and the toss of the boat makes seasickness not uncommon in novice fishermen. Anthony remembers that his son Tommy was determined to overcome it. "And he did, cuttin' fish and throwing up over the side at the same time. But Tony, when he first started he just left the boat to work at the Dairy Queen, because he didn't want nothin' t' do with it. Then he came back and got seasick all over 'gain like you wouldn't believe. It was worse 'an before, really. But then one night at dinner it was just, 'You know something, Dad, I didn't get sick today.' "

From 1971 through 1976, Tony worked aboard the *Plymouth Belle*, while his father, who was known as a demanding, difficult captain, tutored him relentlessly. Every morning he'd take the wheel as the *Ply-mouth Belle* pulled away from the pier, and whether they were going just outside the harbor or steaming south through Cape Cod Canal and then due east out to the Georges Banks 120 miles offshore, the routine was always the same: The old man would go below to sleep or play cards and after a few hours the son would call down, "We're here, Dad." Back in the pilothouse, Anthony would consult his charts and find that his son had brought them to exactly the right spot: Tony had mastered the Loran, the fisherman's satellite-guided navigation system. At home, down in the basement, Anthony had built a big chart table for Tony and his brother Tommy; now it was paying dividends.

Aside from his son's growing navigational skills, Anthony also boasted to his friends of how Tony was overcoming his terror of bad weather. The *Plymouth Belle* was sixty feet at the waterline, heavily built with high chines, which made her a superb sea boat, but this guaranteed nothing. One winter northeaster caught them fishing off Truro's Highland Light in open water with the wind blowing eighty miles an hour; when they ran for shelter, it took more than four hours, not the usual two, to get back to Race Point. Rounding "the Race" the seas were even higher, with twenty-five-foot waves coming over the pilothouse. "I remember that till today," Anthony recalls, still shuddering. "Him and Tommy were standing at the stern of the boat behind the wheelhouse and I should've had them inside with me. I know that now, but back then I thought different. I told 'em they had t' be on their own."

At night it could be even more frightening. Sometimes it was so black you couldn't see the white froth of the waves curling just below the gunwales, almost close enough to touch. All boats will take water over the stern when they're loaded after a good day's fishing, but in the dark there is always a greater probability of foundering in a following sea; it is necessary to ride the wave crests so the craft won't yaw sideways, to keep her straight-on to the seas; without the right rhythm you could sink very quickly. There is also the possibility of losing someone overboard. One night Tony stood awestruck as a crewman disappeared over the side, and his father kept calm enough to do a perfect triangle "on the compass," which brought them back to exactly the right spot where they found the man and, in pitch darkness, hauled him back aboard.

Tony became a fair fisherman, not the equal of his father, certainly, but good enough. More than that, he'd found a calling. "It got into my blood," he says. "It was something that was empowering. It helped define you as a man. I'd never wanted to fish when I was younger, I'd gone into it 'cause it was the only way of making money so Susan and I could get married, but now it had become my life."

• • •

The Portuguese are the world's greatest fishermen. They'll go out to the middle bank, tow a net along the edge of a rock pile. They don't know anything about geology or the glacier deposits, but they know the bottom—the rocks, the trenches—and they can avoid obstacles like you can't imagine.

Their skill is almost a sixth sense, and the challenge of living up to this tradition, of measuring up, had gotten under Tony's skin.

In 1976, after getting no response when he badgered his father about when he might reasonably expect to take over the *Plymouth Belle,* Tony bought his own vessel, a forty-five-foot steel-hulled ex-government pilot boat built in 1955. Although the *Josephine G* was smaller than the usual Eastern-rig dragger, she had potential as a wage earner. There were a number of similar "mosquito boats" in the harbor. They were day-boats meant to fish local waters rather than far offshore; their crews were small, two and three hands instead of the usual six found on larger boats. They might not make the hauls of the bigger vessels, but the smaller crew meant fewer to share the money and less expense on maintenance. Happily, the *Josephine G* was in good shape. During the first half dozen years he had her, Tony fished with a varying crew, his brother Tommy, cousins Adam Snow and Chris Landry, Buddy Johnson, Roger Diaz, Bobbie Giovinno, and Mike "the Coma" Doucette, the town drunk, who slept on the boat and looked after things. He also took on Chris Busa, the son of the late abstract painter Peter Busa. Chris, a tall, barrel-chested man now in his fifties, is the cofounder and editor in chief of *Province-town Arts,* the award-winning magazine that has documented the cultural life of Ptown for the past fifteen years. Back then, he went fishing to gather some "real life" experience. Tony didn't go out each and every day like his dad, but the boat produced.

"We had fun and didn't kill ourselves," said Giovinno. "I made enough to get by, Tony made enough to pay his notes. We could've gotten rich, but that's not how we wanted to play it."

Overall, life was good. Susan had already had three of their four children—Braunwyn in 1973, Beau three years later, and Luke in 1979. Kyle, their youngest, would be born in 1981. Kim and Shelby, her adopted Sioux children from her first marriage, also lived with them in the three-bedroom ranch house they'd bought in Truro. The house wasn't huge, but it met their needs. Susan had furnished it with unpretentious furniture, a lot of it secondhand stuff she'd picked up at yard sales, but they also had a large twenty-five-inch Zenith that Tony had gotten on credit at Sears in Hyannis. There was a dog, several playful cats, and everybody was happy. The fishing was good and the *Josephine* G continued to bring in enough money so that Susan didn't have to give up being a full-time mother and go to work, as she would later, cleaning rooms in a nearby local motel.

Tony, of course, still dreamed of taking over the *Plymouth Belle*.

Fishing is a cyclical business. One year the sea is a cornucopia; the next, the waters are barren. The early eighties were terrible years for the New England fishing industry, and when the fates intervened and Tony was offered a chance to earn a phenomenal amount of money, he decided to take a chance. A big chance.

His adventure turned into one of the most bungled dope runs in the history of Ptown.

CHAPTER 13

WARM NIGHTS

When you look back at its history, you can see a progression in Provincetown, things getting wilder and wilder, the outlaw element becoming the norm. Provincetown had never been a typical New England town, not even in the eighteenth and nineteenth centuries, and it was certainly not a Puritan one. But by the fifties and sixties, private vice had gone public.

"It was the most sexually active community I'd ever been involved in," Ciro recalls. The town's art schools drew many women, some who came as students, some as models, and, says Ciro, when he split from his first wife, Ero, "I was in hog heaven. I had a housekeeper who used to say, 'You know, you've got to be careful. I've been changing these sheets almost every day.'" Older women, usually married and often wealthy, came each summer in search of "Latin" lovers among the local Portuguese fishermen, many of whom were happy to oblige. Manny Zora, a fisherman friend of Ciro's, drew the New York ladies until he was in his mid-seventies and left town to retire in the Algarve.

Aside from the warm nights and the many nearby beaches, what made Provincetown so special was that rarely did anyone fuss over anyone else's partners—their income, manners, social status, or even gender. If art was everyone's raison d'être, sexual play was the town's number-one diversion.

During the late fifties and early sixties, the wildest, best-known

parties were at the Hawthorne barn atop Miller Hill Road that Norman Mailer rented over the summers of 1959 and 1960. This was the
writer's "existential" phase, when he was experimenting with orgy and
the so-called transcendental powers of marijuana. Mailer's guests often
found themselves making their way up and down the hillside through
clumps of writhing bodies.

One party erupted into a fight involving Mailer's wife, Adele, and
Harriet Sohmers Zwerling, an editor on the *Provincetown Review*. Both
women were big, drunk, and jealous, and at the center of their brawl
was the Obie Award–winning Cuban playwright Maria Irene Fornes.

"That party was such a pile of shit," Sohmers Zwerling recalls bit-
terly years later, "and what the fight was really about was Adele's being
a toy of Mr. Mailer, of having no will of her own and not too much sense
either. The two of them had been involved with Irene, and, when I got
involved with her, she dumped them. In the middle of the evening
Adele came over to me and said, 'If you're not a coward, you'll come
outside.' I said, 'Well, you know . . .' and before I could go any further
she smacked me in the face.

"So we went out on the hill, and the next thing you know, we're
rolling around and all the guys are watching, yelling, 'Go! Do it!' Norman was probably coming in his pants. I remember at one point I was
on top of her, holding her down, and she tried to bite my breast, so I
socked her and that was it. Her head went back, she went out. When
she came to, she was crying, I was crying, and Bill Ward [the editor of
the *Provincetown Review*], who I'd come to the party with, helped me
down the hill, staggering along. Norman was standing there in the
dark, screaming, 'Cancer hole! You're going to die! *Die! Die!*' "

That was one of Mailer's frequent descriptions for women at the
time—"cancer hole"—and several witnesses later claimed that when
they'd tried to break up the fight, he intervened, a Marquess of Queens-
berry figure citing the need for "honor." By the end of the next year he
had flipped completely and made headlines after stabbing his wife in
the chest with a penknife at a party he threw in New York. The wife
survived (though the marriage did not) but Mailer was arrested. At the
time, the writer's psychiatrist advised the admitting staff at Bellevue
Medical Center that Mailer was having "an acute paranoid breakdown."

In Provincetown, however, the day following the Sohmers Zwerling–Adele brawl there was a cocktail party at Fritz Bultman's house, next door to the Mailers' on Miller Hill Road. Mailer was there and he was nothing if not courtly. Sohmers Zwerling was also present, again accompanied by Bill Ward, and, like Adele, she was covered with bruises. The Bultmans politely ignored this, as did the other guests, all of whom had heard about the previous night's brawl. There were few people in town who hadn't.

"Absolutely nothing happened," says Sohmers Zwerling. "Norman was on his best behavior, entertaining people with all his usual bullshit stories, and Adele and I avoided each other."

Mailer's parties continued after he and his fourth wife bought a new place on the East End waterfront in 1964. The house, which was next to one previously owned by John Dos Passos, had a deck supported by two stanchions. Macho-man Mailer had strung a tightrope between them, and one guest decided to walk it. After two or three hesitant attempts, the man, urged on by a crowd of squealing women, worked up his nerve and went for it full-out. He landed on his skull, making an ugly thudding sound as he hit and left a pool of blood behind after someone took him inside to wait for the Rescue Squad. Another time, the actor Kevin McCarthy, who'd flown in from the West Coast to see his sister, novelist Mary McCarthy (then married to Edmund Wilson and living in Wellfleet), was boozed and dancing his brains out when he suddenly ducked outside. When next seen, he was prancing across the flats, a solitary figure in the pale early morning light, doing a recitation from *Richard III*—stark naked.

This was the period when Mailer was championing prisoners, and one of his guests was a young black in his mid-twenties who had just been released from jail for attempting to blow up the Statue of Liberty. It is not known whether Mailer's faith in him wavered after the young man "borrowed" the writer's new Corvette and crashed it at the New Beach rotary.

A high-ranking CIA officer, a guest at another party, which included George Plimpton, Grace Hartigan, Jimmy Breslin, detective writer Rod Thorp, and Mailer's buddy, boxing champ Jose Torres, remembers going to the bathroom, seeing the shower curtain move, and hearing a male voice proclaim, "I love you, I love you."

To which a female voice responded, "Shut up and fuck."

Leaving the bathroom, the CIA man was unable to resist lingering long enough to find out who had been behind the curtain. When the door opened, he saw one of the most respected names in New York publishing, followed unsteadily by one of Mailer's most devoted followers.

Alcohol didn't entirely blur the focus on art. At another gathering, the painter Sidney Gross began throwing furniture around because of an unresolved argument over Soutine.

Former Golden Gloves boxer, occasional short-story writer, and full-time Mailer acolyte Eddie Bonetti got so crazy on grass that he made a speech proclaiming that he was always faithful to his wife. He had never betrayed her, he informed the crowd, because "I only let my girlfriends go down on me." This fine reasoning didn't save Bonetti later, when he was committed to a mental institution. He said he knew things "weren't right" when he found a group of patients staring intently at a TV with nothing on the screen but static.

Mailer's parties may have been the ones people talked about most, but the booze was everywhere. For the artists, liquor was the lubricant of creativity, for vacationers it was a chance to cut loose. Only in Ptown, the nutty behavior was somehow *nuttier*. Lettie Cowden, a summer regular since the mid-fifties, often bared her chest at parties. Even when she disrobed in the Flagship or Rosy's, no one can recall anyone ever calling the cops. Another stripper was a young artist who worked as a waitress at Ciro's. She would sit alone at the end of the bar after work, quietly sipping her piña colada, completely bare-assed.

Liquor fueled the whole mélange of characters and hangers-on at the Old Colony, Foc'sle, Ace of Spades, Pilgrim Club, and the A-House, and if the fishermen were hard drinkers, the types who clustered around Mailer took it as a personal challenge to outdrink them. Bill Ward, Harriet Sohmers Zwerling's friend, just couldn't keep himself in line. Wherever Ward went, there'd be a fight. He never did mend his ways, even, according to stories that filtered back to the Cape, after he tried taking on a half-dozen Puerto Rican street kids in New York and was badly beaten. Another difficult drunk was Eldred Mowry—Harvard grad, carpenter, and Caribbean sailor extraordinaire, who later went to jail for looting Hans Hofmann's studio. Mowry could always be counted on to accept Mailer's challenge to a head-butting contest, a stunt they often did in the front-window booth of the Old Colony, while passersby on Commercial Street stopped to watch.

Boozy behavior wasn't limited to the artsy types. Ptown could be a rough place, and arguments in the bars were usually settled outside on the beach, or in the alley alongside the Old Colony tap.

What got most people's attention in August 1960, the same month Cheney Marshall was censuring art shows and trying to purge Ptown of gays, was when Mailer, staggering out of the Old Colony one afternoon, got himself clubbed by the cops and subsequently mounted a court defense that was hailed as a local civil liberties landmark. Richard Dickey, a local fisherman who later went to jail for pot smuggling, recalls:

"It started in the Foc'sle and went on to the Old Colony, and Mailer was bopping around, irritating people. Nobody in town liked him anyway, the townies, the waterfront people. I don't remember him being with his sycophants that day, Bonetti or Eldred, but he kept bothering us at our table, butting into our conversation, and so far as we were concerned it was just, 'Fuck off, leave us alone.' He was *a pain*, you know? He wanted to be one of the boys—like he used to wear a watch cap and bell-bottom jeans because he thought that was what authentic seamen wore, like it was cool.

"Now this particular day he was coming on real strong. I was with a guy I fished with out of New Bedford, and we wanted to get down to the West End, so we left. In those days you had to watch out when you left the bars, see, the cops would be there waiting, outside on the street. Anybody drinking got fucking arrested and thrown in the drunk tank, right? They'd call you over to the fucking car. They smell booze on you, you're in the backseat and on your way. You had to face Judge Welsh in the morning, and I mean it was *bad*. Even if you weren't acting up, they'd call you over to the car, and *bam*, you're in the backseat and on your way.

"All this was coming from Cheney Marshall, of course, who'd slapped me 'round some, too, and what happened that day was we were standing across the street from the Old Colony, straight and proud, you know, and Mailer comes out after us and goes to the taxi stand at the corner. But there aren't any taxis there. So he's hanging on the taxi sign, looking up and down the street. He's drunk—just as drunk as we are, and we're fucking loaded. He's dancing around there, and the next thing, the cruiser comes along. But you couldn't tell it was a cruiser 'cause it was getting dark. It had the bubble gum thing on top, too, like the old-fashioned police cars had, and I got to admit that you could confuse it with a taxi.

"So Mailer steps out into the middle of Commercial Street and goes, 'Taxi!' He might've been fucking around, I don't know, but I don't think so.

"They stop and tell him to get in. He says, 'No, no. I just want a taxi. I'm going home.' I don't remember who was driving, but Cobra, who was Cheney's right-hand man and a real bastard, he tells him, 'Get in.' Mailer says, 'No, I'm going home.' So Cobra gets out and orders him into the car. He opens the back door and pushes Mailer's head down, but Norman backs out, so he takes his club and bops him one on the back of the head, then shoves him inside, and they take off with him.

"Now I don't know if he spent the night in jail, but the next morning we heard there was going to be a big trial, that Norman's already got lawyers up from New York, so we went over to Town Hall, which was where Judge Welch used to hold court. When we came in the side door, the place was packed. You had to stand on your tiptoes, you couldn't see shit. But you could hear, and I remember the judge asking Norman a couple questions, and the next thing you know the lawyers are spouting laws and shit, and I thought, Jesus, he's won. He didn't win, actually, but that didn't matter. Because Judge Welsh took the opportunity to tell the cops never to pick up another man just for being drunk if he wasn't bothering anyone."

It was "a great victory" and for days afterward the word around town was that Mailer had "straightened out the police force." For the rest of the summer Mailer's behavior was worse than ever. "He was aggressive, you know? He liked to talk about Norman, and nobody else did," Dickie recalls.

Nat Halper, the director of the HCE Gallery (the name taken from Here Comes Everybody, from *Finnegans Wake*), was treated to the same egomania when Mailer tried to get him to show his wife Adele's paintings. The day in question, Mailer came into the gallery, bought a Jan Muller painting, then produced a canvas of Adele's, which Halper agreed to put in the last show of the season.

The painting was "All right. It really wasn't bad," Halper recalls later, and he hung it between a Motherwell and a Marsden Hartley. But this happened to be in the second, smaller room of the gallery, and at the opening, when Adele came in, she looked around and couldn't find her painting. When she finally spotted it in the little room, she turned and stalked out angrily.

About fifteen minutes later Norman arrived, alone, and took Halper aside. "I suppose I'm allowed to withdraw the picture?" he said. Halper nodded, to which Mailer replied, "I just don't understand it. I'm a guy with some sort of reputation, and it would be good for you to have my support. I've already bought one picture, I'm talking about buying another, and you won't play ball."

He didn't actually take the picture off the wall, Halper recalls, but it was at that point that the art dealer made the remark that became celebrated around town and made Mailer stop speaking to Halper for four or five years.

"Norman," he said, "little did I think that you would ever turn out to be an artist's wife."

Halper got Adele's painting back to her and hung an Avery in its place.

CHAPTER 14

THE BARS

Despite Police Chief Cheney Marshall's harassment during the early 1960s, Provincetown had always been a haven for homosexuals. Back in 1928, Eugene O'Neill wrote his son a letter warning him not to listen to the gossip of the Provincetown ladies, then felt compelled to add, "and he-ladies of which breed P'town is full." Even the Portuguese accepted the gays, although, says Joe Taves, the town made a distinction between year-rounders and day-trippers. "It was the summer gays who bothered you. I always refer to them as 'the New York gays.' They came up on the bus. They were cheap and would just hit on everybody. They'd stand on the bus the entire trip, drinking the whole way, then party like hell all weekend and leave at six o'clock Monday morning. And those guys were not appreciated, let me tell you. The gays in town didn't like them, and neither did the straights. The year-round people were a community. We stuck together. When I was a kid, I knew plenty of year-round gay guys—Phil Bayonne, Peter Hunt, a bunch of others. Never had a problem."

In the late forties and fifties it had been the Weathering Heights and the Ace of Spades that catered to gays, but those bars hadn't been exclusionary. Straight couples were also welcome.

Arnie Charnick, a muralist, recalls how, at Piggy's, the legendary disco located on the outskirts of town, straight men would dance with gays. "I myself had some of the best fun dancing with men," Charnick says. His favorite dance partner was the short, totally affable Howie Gruber, who was active in Ptown theater and one of the best commercial chefs in town. Gruber was among the legions of men who died of AIDS in the 1980s.

"I used to call myself a straight fag," Charnick explains. "You'd dance with everybody. There was never any prejudice or bias. I was no different from a lot of people, gay and straight alike. It worked in Ptown very well during those years, and it worked particularly well on the dance floor—you'd be dancing with a woman, and then you'd be dancing with a guy, just switching back and forth. It was uncomplicated. It was like a family. It's different now."

In the late sixties and early seventies, Vietnam War protestors across the country were chanting "Make Love, Not War," but Provincetown residents, more interested in sex than politics, had already made that choice. Provincetown had become the country's best-known vacation spot for lesbians and gay men, and the club scene was exploding. There was the Pied Piper, the Pilgrim House, the A-House, Gifford House, Town House, and the Crown & Anchor, all within several blocks of one another in the center of town, not far from MacMillan Wharf. Weathering Heights, Ptown's earliest drag-queen bar, was located farther out, near Route 6, but it was still going strong. The Moors, a rustic fishnet-and-buoys-type place in the far West End, was known for its frolicsomely social sing-alongs, featuring songs by Judy Garland and Ethel Merman every afternoon at teatime. The Boatslip, with its big beachfront deck just west of the town center, also offered late afternoon entertainment with its highly popular daily "Tea Dance."

Even the "straight" bars like Rosy's and Piggy's were serving larger and larger audiences every day. Mixed, gay, bi—it was a bazaar that promised to satisfy every taste.

The Crown & Anchor, doors down from the Universalist Church, was perhaps the most visible indication of what was happening. More than a club, the "entertainment complex" was owned by a squat, balding man in his mid-forties by the name of Staniford Sorrentino, who had come to the Cape in the early fifties as a penniless high school music teacher. A former opera singer with a degree from BU, Sorrentino had had several stints with the Boston Symphony and Boston Pops Orchestra, where he'd actually sung under the direction of Leopold Stokowski;

as a teacher, he gained enormous favor with his students at Provincetown High; and living modestly, in 1957 managed to buy a Beach Point motel to supplement his schoolteacher's income. Then everything changed: Sorrentino was tapped as a potential business partner by two Bostonians, Henry and Carmine Vara, who specialized in running gay bars. A streetwise columnist for the *Boston Globe* had called Henry Vara the "Babe Ruth of sleaze," pointing out that he was "to a neighborhood what a Mediterranean fruit fly is to a plum." The match between Sorrentino and the Vara brothers proved to be a dynamic one, however, when, in 1961, the three purchased the Sea Horse Inn, a traditional three-story hotel of forty rooms overlooking Provincetown's harbor. Renaming the place the Crown & Anchor, they quickly turned the former inn into a svelte waterside club consisting of three bars, a swimming pool, and a poolside disco known as the Back Room. One of the bars, the Ms. Room, hosted performers like Nina Simone and Eartha Kitt, who packed the place with a lesbian crowd that equaled the masses of bikinied men at poolside. There was a clam bar and two full-service restaurants, but in the evening, the Back Room was where it was at, with two bouncers at each door and a darkened seating area off in one corner where patrons were free to grope one another without being seen. Strobe lights, an insanely powerful sound system, and shirtless waiters were part of the draw. Some of the waiters had rings piercing their nipples, their bodies were flecked with iridescent glitter, and many wore metal-studded neck collars. A further draw, upstairs, in what had once been innocuous, ordinary seamen's quarters, were the row upon row of cubicles that Sorrentino had had built and rented by the hour.

Clearly, catering to gays was the way to go, and one of Sorrentino's main competitors who was quick to take note of this was Reggie Cabral, the proprietor of the nearby Atlantic House. The A-House, as locals called it, was a large, gabled Greek Revival mansion only two blocks west of the Crown, down a narrow alley off Commercial Street known as Masonic Place. Originally, it had been a stagecoach stop and inn where, it is said, Thoreau stayed while making his famous walking tour of the Cape in 1841. Yet Cabral was anything but a Yankee, and indeed, even more than Sorrentino, he was an odd combination of hubris and originality, a fisherman's son with little formal education who had, on his own, discovered art, which he'd come to love as much as the local artists themselves. He had been a coast guardsman and was a World War II vet, a member of the local VFW Post, King Hiram's Masonic Lodge, and the Friends of the Provincetown Council on Aging, but after buying the Atlantic House in 1949, he opened the doors of his club to such young and rising painters as Mark Rothko, Claes Oldenburg, Robert Rauschenberg, Larry Rivers, Franz Kline, and Red Grooms, with the result that he assembled the core of an important collection, one he supplemented with regular purchases of works by other Provincetown artists. Cabral did not limit his collection to those who bartered their paintings when they couldn't pay their bar bills.

There were *many* collectors in Provincetown during the fifties and sixties, of course, ranging from Walter P. Chrysler (whose resources were near limitless) to Hudson Walker to Ciro Cozzi. But Reggie was smart; he not only traded drinks for paintings and sculpture, he also collected theater and literary memorabilia, and by the time of his death in 1996 he'd amassed a considerable collection of original material by Eugene O'Neill, Edna St. Vincent Millay, Susan Glaspell, and other early Provincetown Players, as well as manuscripts and first editions of Tennessee Williams and Norman Mailer, both A-House customers.

"History," Cabral told the *Advocate* at one point, "is only as good as the material you have to work with. I was born here, and I know that everybody had a story about O'Neill and his friends, and that the myths and the stories were simply not true. Everybody told them, not because they cared but because they wanted to grab on to the glory."

Cabral could be gruff, impolite, and overbearing, and he was greedy and immoderate as well. Seeing the success of the Crown & Anchor, he decided the A-House had to "go gay," too. The A-House had always been "mixed," with a long history of headlining live entertainers like Zoot Simms, Mose Allison, Miles Davis, Gerry Mulligan, Ella Fitzgerald, and even Billie Holiday (Cabral hired the great "Lady Day" after New York City police confiscated her cabaret card following an arrest on narcotics charges), but now Cabral instructed his bartenders to set up a two-tiered price list and hike the price of drinks for women *fourfold*. A gin and tonic suddenly cost $12, not $3. If customers complained, he instructed his staff to tell them they were invited to take the club to court. None did, of course, and soon Reggie had himself an exclusively gay nightspot.

The changeover, which took place during the summer of 1976, had an immediate effect on the club's decor as well, which meant everything in a town as artsy as Provincetown. Previously, the walls of the large main dance room had been filled with paintings worthy of a small museum— several Klines, a Hofmann, a Karl Knaths, and a huge James Wingate Parr, and also works by Avery and Bultman, to name the more famous. There was also a tiny Larry Rivers oil, a portrait of Reggie and his wife that had hung at the end of the bar for a dozen years or more.

One effect of the change was that the art was replaced with kitsch. Not because Reggie feared that the wild gyrations of the club's dancers might endanger the art, or that the paintings might be compromised by the room's habitual clouds of thick, dense cigarette smoke. On the contrary, the reason was that Reggie had finally come out of the closet, declared himself to be gay like most of his staff, and his high-strung wife was going after anything of value she could lay her hands on.

Meara, mother of Cabral's three children, had been anything but pacific during the course of their twenty-year marriage; her response to the "new" Reggie was to rush into the club late one afternoon, screaming, "Where's that motherfucker husband of mine?" The bartender, a gentle soul who'd been alone in the empty dance room, cutting lemons and doing prep for later that evening, shook his head.

"Meara, honestly, I don't know," he said. "But he's not in the office."

"Don't you lie to me!"

"No. I'd tell you if I did."

Frustrated beyond words, she scanned the room wildly, then she grabbed the paring knife off the bar, ran to the side of the room and started slashing at the small Larry Rivers portrait. Again and again she hacked at it until her husband's face fell, hingelike, from the painting, attached only by several threads. She pulled the small piece of canvas free and threw it to the floor and started stamping on it.

"There!" she screamed as she walked out. "That'll teach him!"

Overnight, the main dance room was stripped. Everything came down off the walls, the paintings were crated and shipped out of town, supposedly to Reggie's estate on the Costa del Sol. Where the collection actually went remained a secret, however, as Cabral owned no property in Spain, nor anywhere else in Europe that anyone was aware of.

In addition to the now denuded main dance room, the A-House

had two other bars: the Small Bar, also known as the Little Bar, with its separate entrance next door to the main disco; and the Macho Bar. You gained entry to the Macho Bar by climbing a steep flight of stairs, guarded by one of Reggie's bodybuilder employees, while Reggie himself stood by, slapping young boys on the behind with a riding crop as they ascended. The Macho Bar was definitely on the cutting edge, even by Ptown standards. One of the more outrageous gay men, Terry Catalano, during his tenure as a bartender, used to wear only a pair of Calvin Klein underwear, cowboy boots, and a red handkerchief around his neck.

A year after the club had decided to exclude women, town selectman and finance committee head Paul Christo was arrested and charged with committing an "unnatural sex act." Undercover police had found Christo dressed in a Nazi SS officer's uniform, using a belt to vigorously beat a man who was tied head and foot, while a third individual was simultaneously performing fellatio on the thirty-three-year-old selectman to the huge enjoyment of a crowd of drunken, cheering onlookers.

All in all seven people were arrested, and although the bust made the front page of the *Advocate*, it was treated as a joke by many in town. Christo himself would soon be reelected for his second term as selectman, as well as chosen to chair both the Board of Selectmen and finance committee, two of the most prestigious, influential positions in Town Hall.

In its heyday, the Macho Bar had a narrow spiral staircase leading up to where the DJ now spins. From there, members of the audience could pee on their favorite gay porn star, who was waiting in a bathtub below. Needless to say, the audience would often get peed on, too, and at one point health department concerns kicked in, and they had to switch to using a hose to simulate peeing. This event was called "The Piss-Call."

Nowadays, the Macho Bar and other gay clubs prohibit the showing of the phallus, with a strictly enforced "keep the rockets in the pockets" rule and "Weenie Patrols" to make sure everyone is complying.

Cabral, for all his outlaw nuttiness, could be a great softie. He could always be counted on to donate money to the local AIDS hospice, Foley House, to the new senior center, or the Heritage Museum. With Ruth Hiebert, the daughter of the town's longtime physician, he gave unstintingly to the Fine Arts Work Center and to the Provincetown Art Association and Museum, as well as to artists down on their luck or just in need of free booze. He bought paintings by young people and paid for the funeral of painter James Wingate Parr, who was found dead in the sand dunes, presumably murdered by a trick, in 1969.

But the truth was that Reggie, patron of the arts, had for years not only been buying it and swapping for it, he'd also been stealing it.

This had started roughly in the mid-sixties, and any number of locals were aware of what was happening and accepted it just because it was Reggie, or because they themselves were accomplices. Reggie had always traveled with a small entourage, much like his daughter April, the current owner of the A-House, does to this day. But two locals in particular worked for him, guys who had definitely seen too much television. The senior of the two, Raul Matta, whose father ran the general store, drove around in Reggie's convertible with the top down in any kind of weather. He dressed in a black leather trench coat, sported a Vandyke beard, and lived with the biggest-breasted woman in town. Although there was a Katzenjammer Kids quality to the art theft operation, Raul and his sidekick still managed to snag a fair amount, not only by breaking into empty houses during off-season but by venturing off-Cape to steal from low-security university art museums.

Their failures were more interesting than their successes. On one occasion they snagged a Gainsborough. They'd already successfully heisted a Moore and a Jasper Johns, but the eighteenth-century English masterpiece proved too hot to fence; when they couldn't find someone to take the painting to Europe they destroyed it, reportedly by slicing the masterpiece into shreds. On another occasion they stole a historically important Hieronymus Bosch, *Landscape with Conflagration*, from the Walter Chrysler Museum. This theft made the front page of the *New York Times*, and once again they found themselves in over their heads. When Police Chief Jimmy Meads leaned on them—and Meads leaned on them very, very hard—the two returned the sixteenth-century masterpiece by breaking *back* into the Chrysler Museum, where the next morning sleepy guards found the painting once again back on its peg.

Ciro Cozzi recalls Reggie's man knocking on his door one afternoon to offer him a Constable.

"Ciro, I got something I think you might like," said the thief, producing the small gem of a landscape, still in its institutional frame, acquisition numbers and all, along with a newspaper clipping that chronicled how the work had been stolen from a regional Massachusetts museum. The asking price was $5,000. "A steal," the man put in quickly, explaining that the news article was proof positive of the painting's authenticity and provenance.

More often than not, these stolen works went into the maestro's own collection. But Reggie maintained he knew nothing about the art thefts, even when his Number One got hauled in after the Bosch heist, just as he pretended innocence when, in 1977, town selectmen voted to revoke his club's liquor license, the first such revocation in anyone's memory. The A-House, Reggie announced, would remain open as "a juice bar" and still offer music for dancing. At the selectmen's meeting packed with his supporters, he stabbed the air with his upraised index finger and spoke of homophobia and the denial of civil liberties.

"The whole thing is unjust," he said. "We've worked hard to provide a comfortable atmosphere for customers, to enable you to continue your right of . . . life, liberty, and the pursuit of happiness."

It was little short of a comedy, this small Napoleonic figure defending public blow jobs on the grounds of "freedom of choice." But it was Ptown. It was also Reggie. In later years he was quite proud that he was buying Robert Mapplethorpe photographs long before anyone had heard of Mapplethorpe, or indeed before Mapplethorpe began taking the controversial photographs that made him notorious.

At the time of Cabral's passing, a friend and admirer told the press, "If Provincetown nowadays is becoming more of a Yuppie playground and less of an arts community, Reggie's death is especially saddening because it's emblematic of what is happening in town. He was one of the great figures and they have all been dying out."

Another Reggie fan, the artist Paul Bowen, spoke of Cabral as the consummate Provincetown collector. "His taste was very much his own, he never stopped looking at new artists, and so many of us benefited from that."

Down the street at the Crown & Anchor, the Ms. Room, the lesbian bar, overlooked Commercial Street and provided the best theater in town.

On a given day you could see a midget and his tall partner posing as Christ and God-knows-what, dragging a huge cross up Commercial Street. There were the drag queens: one of them, habitually dressed only in red, black, and white, was reputed to be a real-life sheriff from Rhode Island. Another was an upper-class horse breeder from Kentucky. There was "Charlotte," a cross-dresser in his seventies who adored high heels; Charlotte's biggest kick was to take a deep breath and walk down Commercial Street like Miss America on the ramp, fishnet stockings, miniskirt, lots of makeup, big pearl earrings, and all. "I did it," he'd announce, coming back to the club's main lounge. "I went all the way up to the Foc'sle today!" Or, "Hi, my name's Charlotte. I'm the oldest living drag queen. . . . I've got the best legs in America."

Once a year the Crown & Anchor would host a gala drag contest. Queens would fly in from all over the United States to compete, with many of them spending thousands of dollars on their gowns, their shoes, their hair, and their surgeries. It was a very competitive bunch; those who lost were convinced they'd been cheated. Once the winner was announced, the fights would start and the second part of the show played itself out in the Crown & Anchor parking lot, where wigs were ripped off and punches thrown. The melees were often so spectacular that crowds gathered on Commercial Street to watch.

A wild cast of characters swirled around the Crown. A singer known as "Mr. Peanuts" got so high on heroin one afternoon that he locked himself in a phone booth and refused to come out and perform. He insisted he'd gone blind. A huge crowd gathered, and he only emerged after his fellow band members pleaded with him, pointing out that if he didn't sing, they'd lose the gig and they needed the money.

"There was this screaming queen," Carolyn Tacke, one of the Crown & Anchor's favorite waitresses, recalls. "I don't even know if he was gay or not. He was a very tall man, very garish in his makeup and his dress, and he used to go up to the Presidential Suite upstairs and stand out on the balcony overlooking Commercial Street, where he'd sing a single note as loud as he could and for as long as he could. Anything to get the people to look at him."

When the painter Arnie Charnick was hired to create a mural on the walls of the Back Room, he naturally decided it should have a sexual theme. He settled upon the idea of a jungle motif. For five weeks he painted and painted, starting with a massive eight-foot circumcised cock in the bathroom. The cock was ejaculating, and the ejaculate coursed across the bathroom wall, out the door, and circumnavigated its way around the whole room. By the time it reached the main dance area, the stream of cum had assumed riverlike proportions. To people who had not been in the men's bathroom it would appear like a river coursing through a jungle vibrant with wild animals; to those who had, it was a huge wonderful joke.

"Everything was sexual," Charnick recalls. "There were panthers hanging in the tree, they were like black guys, and one of the panther's tails came around and looked like it was a big hanging cock. Everything was male-oriented, sexy as hell, and there were things leaping. There were plants committing buggery, and across the ceiling there were stars like it was a jungle. It was mad. People loved it; it was great."

Staniford Sorrentino, the decadent, roly-poly Nero who presided over the club, "loved the scene," recalls Carolyn Tacke. "He'd sit back and giggle, 'Oh! This is too much!' while he watched the queens screaming at each other. The fights could get very vicious, and each time Stan would say, 'They're fighting again! What should I do?' But he loved it because it was so wild. He loved the drama, the opera of it. . . ." Carolyn says she cannot recall a time when Sorrentino wasn't either on cocaine or high on uppers. But instead of getting skinnier and skinnier, the usual result of the drugs, Staniford Sorrentino just got fatter and fatter. And the fatter he got, the better the Crown & Anchor did.

Stan Sorrentino and Reggie Cabral had always been competitive. If the Crown & Anchor had an outdoor patio, then the A-House would have one, too. If the A-House, which was just up the block, installed an S&M bar, the Macho Bar, then the Crown would have one, too—The Vault. During the 1970s and early eighties, these were "back rooms," places men could go for anonymous sex—analogous to the sex clubs and the famous "baths" in New York and San Francisco. So when the A-House began shifting its focus to an exclusively gay crowd, Stan Sorrentino decided to follow suit. Previously, the Crown & Anchor had catered to a wonderfully heterogeneous, drug-addled, high-energy mix of gays and straights. Dancing seemed to inspire many of the young women to strip off their clothes; then they would climb up on the pedestals that stood along the back of the dance floor and dance topless.

Out on the beach-side patio, any number of women, straight and lesbian both, would strip before jumping into the pool. One handsome
blonde, whose family went back three generations in neighboring Truro,
remembers that her friends found it hilarious when she was finally
banned from the club because she refused to keep her clothes on.

"I mean it was such a joke," she recalls years later. "They were making this grand gesture in the name of propriety, when every night there
were guys under the tables giving blow jobs."

But now, looking over at the A-House, Stan decided it was time for
him to make a move. So he did what any right-thinking, rational club
owner would do: He built a large wall down the middle of the Back
Room disco. On one side, having a vagina was strictly verboten; on the
other, women could cavort as they had in the past. Although this
degree of segregation was unprecedented in Ptown, the staff at the
Crown & Anchor took it in stride. Sorrentino was constantly remodel-
ing, repainting, and generally tweaking the ambience of the club. One
day they came into the club and there was a wall. They laughed,
shrugged, and got to work.

One local woman was not so accepting. Barbara Rushmore, who
was famed in town for her gadfly activism, heard about the new wall
and decided to test it. She was denied entry. The walled-off area was a
gym, she was told. It was private and only for men. Rushmore, incensed,
took the matter to the Provincetown selectmen. "It's not lightly that I
ask you to hold a hearing to lift their license," she said, "but the reason
I'm here is because I don't believe in gay bars. I would like to feel at
home going anywhere in this town." She questioned whether there
really was a health club behind the newly created wall. "What health
club has disco music, dark lighting, and high walls?" She was joined by
many in Provincetown in her concern that nightlife would be segre-
gated into gay bars or straight ones.

Mary-Jo Avellar, chairperson of the Board of Selectmen, agreed, saying that competition for gay business in Provincetown had grown so
extreme it was leading to sex discrimination. Avellar continued, "I
don't like it one bit, and it just won't be tolerated. . . . I don't care
whether more gay people come here because of these businesses. What
I'm objecting to is the exclusion of the very people who made it possible for gay people to come here and be comfortable."

Stan Sorrentino defended his club, saying it was a "semantic mix-up" to say women weren't allowed on the premises. "They *were* allowed in the pool area and bar area, but because of the common showers and bathroom facilities, the gym was off limits." If enough women expressed interest in working out, he said, they would be accommodated. He also said that while no liquor was served in the gym, men could get a drink at the bar and bring it back to the gym. The selectmen weren't convinced. They set a date for a hearing on Sorrentino's liquor license. Ten days before the hearing, the wall was dismantled.

This was not the first nor would it be the last skirmish between gay business owners and townie straights.

Equally unorthodox was Stan's decision to hire town cop Freddie DeSousa as one of his bouncers. A local Portuguese, DeSousa stood at the door alongside Lisa Motherwell, the daughter of the famed painter. DeSousa was a maverick, a good-hearted, ribald soul who knew everyone and rarely, if ever, passed judgment.

"Stan hired me in seventy-six, I think it was, and, you know, gays were still getting a lot of abuse from local kids. That was an era when gays and straight were not too mixed. It was like oil and water. But that was one of the things that was so special about the Back Room," he said. "It was all kinds of people, and it was that combination of straights and gays that gave the place its energy. People were getting fucked in the bathroom, on the beach out front, right in the main room up against the walls, for Christ's sake. I mean, if you didn't get laid in that place something was very wrong with you, pal."

The relationship between the C&A (and the A-House, too, for that matter) and the chief of police, which is to say the law in general, was a little more complicated. Undercover cops appeared every once in a while and would try to get somebody to ask the waitresses where they could score pot. Staffers responded by sending these Quisling stooges back to the cops, telling them, "Ask that guy, he might know."

"Every year on Cheney Marshall's birthday, which was around Labor Day," says one bartender, "they'd have a big bust and round up maybe forty people, and out of that forty maybe three arrests would stick. But it wasn't for locals. It never was. There was a live-and-let-live attitude if you lived here. We knew the cops who were in the room.

They weren't looking for us; they knew we knew who they were. It was for all those who came here."

But it was simpler than that, really. The cops felt free to walk into the Back Room not to freak anyone out so much as to partake of the action. Like DeSousa, they were small-town cops and were impressed by Stan and the big boys from Boston.

"I think they were almost enamored," says one staffer. "Gangsters were in. It was cool. They liked hanging out."

Few of the summer people at the East End had the slightest idea what was going on, and except for the fuel-oil truck drivers and assorted service personnel, few of the Portuguese community knew either. The Crown & Anchor was a world apart. But that's exactly how Stan and his partners wanted it. When DeSouza first took his job, he'd been told to take care of any disturbances quietly, without calling the cops. But often the problem wasn't the patrons. It was Stan. "I liked Stan," says one of the club's musicians, "everyone did. But Stan was sometimes really out there, like *gone.*"

Staniford Sorrentino was cursed with a reckless boldness that undid him in the end. His fatal flaw was his addiction to speed and cocaine, but beyond that, he just wasn't practical. He couldn't even launder his money properly. Yet it didn't seem to matter. The money kept pouring in, and Stan would skim shamelessly. He paid the staff once a week in cash. Some employees would show up on the books for six months, then go off the books, even though they kept working. By hiding their income for them, Stan, who could be as generous as he was reckless, left them free to collect unemployment.

At midnight every night, an hour before the Crown & Anchor closed, all the tapes in the cash registers would be replaced with new ones. By the late seventies there were over a dozen cash registers on the premises—in the Back Room, the Cellar Bar, at the Inn desk, at poolside, at the Ms. Bar—but even today no one knows which tapes were being used to show taxable revenue. What is known, however, is that at least half the gross was not being declared. According to former employees, Sorrentino had an "upper" and a "lower" safe. The money was taken from the registers by various authorized hands, then put into sealed envelopes marked "special," then locked in the lower safe allocated for payroll or "other purposes."

A great portion of the money was used to support Sorrentino's lavish lifestyle. He built a home high on a bluff in North Truro, which included an indoor swimming pool. He frequently vacationed in Europe and bought any number of cars, including a vintage Rolls-Royce, which he kept registered in the name of his longtime boyfriend, Chester Warner. He also had his insatiable appetite for fine-grade cocaine and for chicken hawks—young boys with whom he surrounded himself.

"Stan liked having money. I mean here's a fat man, a really fat man. And he liked the younger boys, not teenagers, but, you know, *kids*," says Carolyn Tacke. "He liked their antics and energy, and how was he going to get their attention if he didn't spend money? There was a young guy, Robert, and his girlfriend, Margie, and they hung out with him quite a bit. Robert came from a really tragic family—both parents died when he was quite young—so he was really looking for a father figure and Stan provided that, and when Robert decided he didn't want to be a gay boy anymore, that was fine with Stan. Because Stan and Robert already had a father-son relationship.

"Chester was trying to get these guys thrown out of the house all the time, but what could he do? Stan liked their company. And these were for the most part not pretty gay boys. They were straight guys who would do whatever it was he liked them doing, which may have just been watching porno and jerking off, I don't know. He liked the companionship, he liked their wild lives. It was vicarious stuff. He may have gotten sex at all the coked-up parties anonymously, who knows? You have to consider the fact that he was fat—he may not have been able to have sex. He looked like Marlon Brando when I last saw him. That kind of fat."

Stan was never able to set limits with the young boys, and once, when he was out of town, two of them who were staying at his house made off with his Mercedes. Driving naked, they slammed the roadster into a telephone pole at about a hundred miles an hour, hitting it six feet off the ground. Everyone was just sitting down to dinner when the power went out all over Ptown. One boy, sixteen, died instantly. The other, who was critically injured, did survive, but he was badly scarred.

Stan was skimming from every corner of the Crown & Anchor operation—the bars, the door, even the food concession at the swimming pool.

He skimmed especially from the Cellar Bar, which opened at the crack of dawn and served all day, providing a little bit of Miami not just for hotel guests and town regulars but tourists who might stop in for a drink while downtown shopping. Some people came by just to watch the freaks. "You were in the movie and above it," said one employee, "and that's why the drink prices on the patio were higher."

And indeed, the amount of money flowing through the C&A was huge. Over the July Fourth weekend each of the half-dozen registers in the Ms. Bar were worth $5,000 to $6,000 nightly. The Back Room, according to most estimates, brought in $200,000 every week, perhaps $1 million monthly. Even off-season—September, October, and November through Thanksgiving—the place was packed, and during the winter months the Back Room and Piggy's were the only action in town.

No one knew precisely how much business was going on, nor could they, since Stan and his partners were, according to most estimates, skimming a minimum of thirty percent.

This larcenous behavior was mimicked by Stan's employees. Everyone stole, the bartenders most of all. "You could take a certain amount," recalls a former waitress, "as long as it wasn't outrageous." But there was also an element of fear. If anyone crossed the line, things could get ugly. Periodically the Vara brothers came up from Boston in their open convertible to collect the club's profits—Jackie Gleason and Art Carney look-alikes, high socks, Bermuda shorts, and all—and the staff would just tremble. Everyone, but everyone, was skimming. Everyone knew it. But so what? In later years the standing joke was that longtime Crown employees came away with at least a house in which to spend their senior years—those who managed to make it to their senior years, that is. At the time, most everyone was not only living on dope but indulging in sex indiscriminately and AIDS hadn't yet been heard of.

Mae Bush, who had convinced Stan to open the lesbian bar on the premises, the so-called Ms. Bar, once heard Henry Vara laying into someone he thought was stealing. "Henry was out of control," Bush says, "and all I could think of was darkness and death, so I said to myself, 'You better get your ass out of here.'" She went to Bob Hedrick, Stan's underboss, and, addressing him by his nickname, said, "Ms. Hedrick, you'll be getting a new bartender. I'm gone." On the streets, rumors were flying, rumors of people having "accidents." The Varas were an

unknown quantity and in that strange void between the Cape and
Boston's Combat Zone stories took on sinister dimensions.

On January 1, 1979, Bob Hedrick quit, supposedly because Sorrentino had accused him of stealing a five-hundred-dollar check.
Hedrick, angry, went to the IRS.

When Stan realized he was under investigation, he offered
Hedrick $20,000 not to talk, but it was too late. Hedrick told what he
knew, whether for revenge or the IRS informant's fee of ten percent of
the unpaid taxes they collect.

According to prosecutor Rosemary Paguni of the Justice Department's Tax Division, in 1975–78, Sorrentino had failed to report an
estimated income of $311,281 and owed the government $145,911
instead of the $1,576 tax liability he had reported. Many employees felt
that the feds' numbers seriously underestimated the Crown & Anchor's
cash flow. Neither of the Vara brothers were defendants in the case,
though they were implicated by Hedrick. Many people in town, Mae
Bush included, thought it was actually the Mob who'd first snitched on
Staniford Sorrentino, but no one could really be sure.

In retrospect, it may seem incredible that Stan thought he could get
away with it, but in those days, everyone in Provincetown was skimming. There were more than twenty leather shops within a half-dozen
blocks of one another in the downtown area alone, numerous new
cafes and sport fishing boat operations, and according to the most persistent anecdotal evidence, most were financed with drug money and
their principal function was not to generate cash so much as to launder
ill-gotten gains.

If, to Stan and others, Ptown seemed to be a world unto itself, the
IRS was relentless. The feds spent three years and hundreds of thousands of dollars on the investigation and trial. Even with the things
Hedrick had told them, no one knew exactly how much money had disappeared. They had to make rough estimates. During Sorrentino's trial
in Boston, Wendy Collins, the special attorney for the government,
asked one witness, "Are you aware, also, that there was a skimming operation going on with the door receipts from the cocktail hour or cocktail
shows that were being run at the Crown & Anchor?"

The witness, who had been granted immunity, was circumspect. "I
know that there were door charges."

The prosecuting attorney tried a different approach. "Do you know if the door charges ever went into the corporate accounts?"

"Not to my knowledge."

Sorrentino had paid in cash for his house in Truro. "Where," the IRS would later ask him, "did you get the money to build such a palace?" And where did he get the income for the white Rolls-Royce, the trips to Europe, and his impressive antiques collection? When he was finally brought to court, he mounted a "dead-man's defense," saying he'd been given the money by his father, who, the IRS duly noted, had died penniless and on welfare in Florida.

Sorrentino was convicted on all eight counts of tax evasion and sentenced to three years in prison and fined $40,000 in addition to the back taxes he owed. The judge, prior to the sentencing, said, "I can think of only one other case where I heard such obvious perjury from the defense." Sorrentino, who was out on bail, immediately began his appeal. He sold the big house he'd built in Truro, and in early March of 1984 he quietly sold his interest in Province Realty Trust, the owners of the Crown & Anchor, to Henry Vara. Later that same month Staniford Sorrentino fled to the Bahamas.

"Stanley fought the IRS," a friend recalls, "and that was bad judgment. He became a fugitive with the money he had stashed, with the coke, with the boys. That was how he lived."

Shortly thereafter, the Crown & Anchor was declared bankrupt by the feds and a huge padlock was put on the door. Former employees were crushed. It was the end of an era, recalls one former waitress. "The real critical point for me was when the IRS put big chains on the door and the whole place stopped functioning. It was like a big dinosaur sitting in the middle of town. It was sad. . . . When it finally opened again, it was exclusively gay. We were pushed out."

Sorrentino had fled to the Bahamas with one of his boyfriends, David, but David had a family and returned. In the Bahamas, Stan was having coke delivered to his door by taxicabs. He hosted a number of wild parties that, back in Ptown, were talked about as orgies. He also gambled and, as Chester remembered, he'd "always come back with money as if he'd won," even if it meant stopping at the bank on the way home to withdraw funds. "He was throwing money away. He'd lose two thousand dollars, then go to the bank and get more. And this was on a daily basis. He was paying people's ways. . . ." Eventually his behavior got so scandalous that the Bahamian government invited him to leave.

Sorrentino spent five years on the lam, living in Belize, Mexico, Italy, and the Netherlands. He was once almost caught in Belgium, but he talked his way out of it. He was almost nabbed in Rome, but again he slipped away. He then went to Holland. After five years, when his money had run out, he chartered a jet to America. When the small plane landed at Boston's Logan Airport, he was promptly detained by Customs officials and subsequently sentenced to two consecutive three-year terms.

After he got out of prison, completely broke, in the late nineties, Stan fell ill. Friends and former employees from Ptown visited him in the hospital. He was impossibly fat and blasting opera on a sound system he'd installed in his hospital room.

He died in the summer of 1998.

"You know, what pissed me off," said Carolyn Tacke afterward, "is that they never put an obituary in the *Advocate* or the *Banner.* I mean, this man changed the face of Provincetown."

CHAPTER 15

REGINA BINDER: CITY PLANNER

During the 1970s, Provincetown's Pied Piper was the foremost lesbian bar on the eastern seaboard, if not in the whole United States. During the summer season, lines snaked around the block, women bouncers guarded the entrance, and inside, women who had come from such faraway places as Montreal and Kansas City flirted, drank, danced, and, on occasion, got into violent fistfights.

The Pied Piper is where Regina Binder and her twin sister, Cindy, spent their adolescence. Now forty, Regina, a historical preservationist with a master's degree from Columbia, fights to save Provincetown's traditional architecture and community structures. She is also one of the town's most outspoken advocates of affordable housing.

But in the wild seventies, she and her sister were perceived only as the daughters of Linda Gerard, the most talked about cabaret singer in Ptown and the girlfriend of Pam Genevrino, who, as the Pied Piper's owner, was the reigning "Don" of Ptown's lesbian community. When the twins were on the premises, Pam was often heard to yell over the microphone, "If I see anyone talking to them, I'll break your legs!" The twins were protected. Like their mother, they grew up to become lesbians.

"There must have been a legion of women who felt it was part of their job description to make sure my sister and I were kept occupied,"

Regina recalls, smiling at the memory of the many bartenders and bouncers assigned to look after them. "Surprisingly, the Pied Piper was a world that I felt comfortable in. For me, it was the most natural thing. I didn't think of it as different."

Most of the women who gathered in the Pied Piper didn't have children and never would, so everyone nurtured the twins and sheltered them from some of the more wanton aspects of the courtship rituals played out on a nightly basis there. Many in the inner circle were hard-drinking, fast-living women, but around the children of Pam's partner they were on their best behavior. Not for nothing were the twins known as "the Vatican Children."

Regina Binder and her identical twin were born into an upper-middle-class Jewish family in Trenton, New Jersey, in 1962. There was nothing odd or bohemian about their background, until their mother put them second to her pursuit a singing career, which took her not only to the Cape but also to Broadway as Barbra Streisand's understudy in *Funny Girl*. Linda Gerard was clearly born to be a star. The girls' father, the owner of a chain of piano stores in the greater metropolitan area, was left to take care of them, and at age eight, the blond, blue-eyed twins began to do television commercials. They were in great demand: Campbell's Soup, Trident gum, Kentucky Fried Chicken, and Kodak all used the youngsters, and Regina, younger-looking than her twin sister, had a part in the Broadway show *All God's Children Got Wings*. Their acting careers, which lasted until they were seventeen, generated tens of thousands of dollars.

At the age of three, the twins had already been taken by their maternal grandparents and brought to New York City, where an apartment at the Essex House was rented for them. With their mother and their governess, they lived there until their apartment was ready on East Seventy-seventh Street, and it was in the lobby of the Seventy-seventh Street building that, in 1969, Linda met a man who would live with Linda and the girls until 1976. He was violent and unemployed, relying upon the twins' income for his livelihood. Linda, needy if not enamored, let him have his way.

"We are talking about a woman who never wanted children," Regina says of her mother, "who ended up with two who were marketable. I mean, my mother is not a bad person, but it was never in her formula to have children. So she did what she could to further herself, not at our expense, but without our consideration."

In 1975 this took the form of a move to Provincetown, where Linda was hired to sing at the Post Office Café. That, in turn, led to a gig at the more popular Pied Piper. The twins, now thirteen, were returned to New York to go to school and, largely, to fend for themselves, living off their residuals checks and eating TV dinners. As they had for the past several years, they lived mostly without adult supervision. Their grandfather, a wealthy manufacturer of industrial rubber products, came to take the girls to his home in New Jersey and to take them shopping at Bloomingdale's and pay the bills, but, basically, "We had each other," says Regina. "And we weren't unhappy. Honest."

In Provincetown, Linda was building a career, or at least a devoted following. A Suzanne Pleshette look-alike, she was lithe and of medium height with dark skin and raven hair. To perfect her "look," she had had her nose done a year or so before coming to town, taking the twins with her to the plastic surgeon. Ginny remembers her mother saying, " 'I want that nose,' pointing at me, and she got it. So my mother has my nose."

From the very first minute Linda set foot in the Pied Piper, Pam Genevrino was smitten. Looking back, Regina says that it wasn't a case of her mother's suddenly going from being straight to being gay. Pam "worshiped" Linda, Regina explains. "She took care of her, which was all my mother had ever wanted. If a man had come along and done the same thing, perhaps she would have gone with him."

In October of 1976, after her second headlining season at the Pied Piper, Linda informed the twins that she was moving in with Pam. The kids, fourteen, were delighted. Linda brought her new partner to New York, and Pam became a welcome addition to the household. In Ptown Pam was known as a harsh taskmaster, as the "godfather," but in New York she was more nurturing and supportive of the girls than Linda had ever been.

Two years later, on New Year's Eve, the Pied Piper burned to the ground. Pam and Linda rushed back to the Cape, leaving the twins behind in New York. Linda borrowed $50,000 to help rebuild the bar and became Pam's business partner. In 1987 the two women would sell the business for over a million dollars.

The seventies passed like a delirium. At night, after the bars closed, Commercial Street was something out of Fellini's *Satyricon*, and a local rock band, Moulty and the Barbarians, briefly enjoyed international acclaim after appearing on *The Ed Sullivan Show*. A local druggie by the name of Anthony "Tony" Costa was convicted of the murder of a series of young runaways, whose severed arms and legs were found buried at widely scattered sites on the dunes. At his trial, Costa was asked if he had anything to say before sentencing. The man's terse reply was "Keep digging." Another townie, Durand "Ziggy" Janard, was arrested for shooting two sunbathers he'd never seen before and was held for psychiatric observation at Bridgewater State Prison. A serial rapist assaulted six women over a period of three months, forcing locals to lock their doors for the first time ever. Dr. Daniel Hiebert, the town's revered eighty-three-year-old general practitioner, was attacked in his office by a knife-wielding assailant looking for drugs. Then, as though to cap it all, in 1975 a middle-age woman, her body half decomposed, was found in the Province Lands with both hands cut off to prevent identification; her body lay facedown on a neatly folded pair of dungarees in a patch of scrub pine; despite forensic help from state and federal agencies in Boston, the crime was never solved

The town's most dedicated potheads were gathering for debaucherous, Woodstock-like jam sessions, the so-called Dump Concerts, that lasted until dawn at the site of the town's garbage dump off Race Point Road. Nudity was also in vogue and when the Cape Cod National Seashore started arresting people for sunbathing in the buff at Brush Hollow Beach, the Massachusetts ACLU jumped in. John Waters, an unknown clerk at the Provincetown Bookstore, generated a new level of camp with his underground film *Pink Flamingos*, starring the transvestite Divine, who managed to drive a Cadillac convertible through the window of Land's End Marine Supply while absorbed in reading a billboard announcing his appearance at the Pilgrim Club later that evening. Pop, as an artistic style, was on the ascendance and the abstract expressionists in decline. Pollock died in a car wreck far away in the Hamptons, and Andy Warhol, who used to hang out so quietly at Ciro & Sal's, was suddenly an international superstar.

It was into this milieu that the twins arrived from New York. Their mother was now co-owner of the foremost women's bar on the East

Coast, and the Pied Piper, like the A-House and the Crown & Anchor, was thriving as a safe harbor for lesbians who came from all over the country. No cameras were allowed. No men were tolerated; if any tried to get in, they were turned away by Pam's bouncers with the explanation that house rules required everyone to produce *six* pieces of personal identification.

Like many businesspeople in town in the seventies, Linda and Pam were awash in cash. "All the businesses were cash," Regina remembers. "I mean, I would wake up in the morning and there would be cash everywhere in the house. At the Pied Piper, people lined up outside the building and down the alley. On holiday weekends, they charged two dollars to get in. There were so many people who wanted to get in that this is how they tried to control it."

The bouncers at the Pied Piper were a tough, broad-shouldered lot, and Regina remembers one woman in particular, Austin, who was assigned as her roommate-cum-caretaker that first summer. Austin always wore impeccably ironed shirts with knifelike creases, "perfectly starched with a can of starch each time." The shirts, she remembers, were tailored men's shirts of the finest cotton, and she also wore men's pants, cowboy boots, a belt, and a vest. One of her front teeth had been capped in gold. Austin's father was a colonel in the military. She was a force. She also played drums for Regina's mother.

Pam Genevrino, too, dressed hard. She wore her hair short, sported aviator glasses and gold chains, and seemed to live in bell-bottom Levi's. On one occasion, when a drunken woman broke into Ginny's room next door to the club late one evening, it was Pam who dragged the woman back outside and beat her up.

Nightly, Linda went onstage at eight o'clock to present her repertoire of ballads that included "Cry Me a River," "Yesterdays," and "My Funny Valentine," always swathed in full-length gowns and jewelry. After finishing, she'd change out of her costume and circulate among her fans in the long, narrow room or outside on the deck. She basked in the attention. Usually she didn't leave the club until two in the morning. Pam always knew where the girls were and whom they were with. Pam was their first real parent.

To this day, Ginny's voice drops when speaking of her surrogate mother: "I think we let her be softer than she had ever been before, or thought she could be."

This, of course, stands in sharp contrast to most people's view of Pam Genevrino, but so great was her nurturing that a year and a half later, in the fall of 1978, when Ginny went to interview at Vassar, it was Pam, not Linda, who accompanied her with Betty Vilari, one of the club's bartenders. The pair were distinctly different from all the other parents present. They wore button-down shirts, open, of course, since that was the style of the day, with T-shirts underneath and pants. They looked "like two men," Ginny recalls, grinning. Everything went smoothly on her tour of the campus, but back in the admissions office Regina began to get nervous when the director of admissions, a bright, imaginative man, went out of his way to ask about her theatrical career, which interested him more than her grades and extracurricular activities at the Lycée Française in New York. When the interview was done, he accompanied her back outside into the waiting room, where he asked if her parents might have any questions. Regina, looking pointedly at a normal-looking hetero couple, shook her head. "No," she said, "they don't have any questions."

It was an awkward, cowardly move, Ginny admits now, and, later, the whole way home she feigned exhaustion in the backseat so she wouldn't have to explain. Sitting up front, Pam and Betty seemed oblivious to what had happened.

In the end, Regina was accepted at the Poughkeepsie-based school, and what struck her when she matriculated the next fall was that even though straitlaced and traditional, Vassar was an intellectual rocket ship. This was the first opportunity she'd had to be by herself, really to find herself, and from the very beginning, she read writers like Edmund Husserl and Roland Barthes in the original French, as well as the philosophers Georges Poulet and Immanuel Kant, who fascinated her. She spent hours of her free time in the school library, poring over drawings of Renaissance architecture. She tangled with some of her professors, speaking up in her classes in a way that made her stand out, even at Vassar, as bright and "different." She also kept a diary, and for the first time sensed that there was not enough time to do everything that needed to be done in a given day.

She was, she now realizes, "pretty sure" that she was gay at this time but as yet hadn't come out. Her sister, Cindy, after dropping out of Smith in the middle of the year, had returned to Provincetown, where she was working at the Pied Piper and was openly lesbian.

Another thing that separated her from her classmates was that Vassar was easily as expensive as Harvard or Yale, and she was paying her way with money she'd made over the summer—working mornings as the desk clerk at Gabriel's Guest House, one of the first all-women guest houses in town, shucking clams and oysters from three to five-thirty at the raw bar at the Pilgrim House, and then later waitressing in the cocktail lounge at the Pilgrim House upstairs. "I would sometimes come home with a hundred dollars, hundred and fifty dollars. . . ." Her savings covered about half her expenses at school, the rest she was financing with student loans. Linda hadn't wanted her to go to college in the first place and only the intercession of one of Pam's bartenders, a Ph.D., had made it finally possible, albeit without financial support from home.

It was toward the end of her freshman year that Ginny went into therapy, largely because she was still trying to figure out where she fit in. In her dorm, after only a couple of months at school, she'd become a steadying influence for a number of the other students, but she'd grown tired of dispensing advice and dealing with needy people. Another factor, at the start of the year she had chosen to major in philosophy but more and more was coming to see this as a mistake. Philosophy was too ethereal, too insubstantial; given her propensity for abstraction, it could turn into a trap. What she really wanted, she felt, was to study art history.

By midyear she'd also begun an affair with an impossibly rich debutante named Mariel Clinton, a stunning blonde who wore leather, rode a motorcycle, and came from a home with "at least sixteen bathrooms." Mariel never took no for an answer. One day Regina came back to her dorm to find the word *want* scrawled on her door in Chanel Red lipstick. For Ginny, it was an eye-opener. "She took me into New York and dressed me in a little Chesterfield suit and took me out. . . . I was like her little doll."

The Mariel affair raised other issues, naturally, which were only exacerbated by the fact that they were carrying on in secret. Why were she and Cindy *both* gay? Ginny asked herself. What did this have to do with Linda? With Ptown? Was it environment or genetics?

Her therapist, a middle-aged woman whose office was in Manhattan, encouraged this questioning, and by her second year Ginny had found a new group of friends, a superbright brat pack, all of whom were, nominally, straight but later came out as gay. On weekends, weather permitting, the group would rent a car, drive down to Zabar's in Manhattan to buy bagels, lox, caviar, and champagne, then disport themselves with picnics out in the countryside. The whole thing was "distinctly *Brideshead Revisited*." Ginny laughs, recalling how they'd talk, argue, and pretend to a sophistication that none of them really had. Although she was chronically short of money for clothes, Ginny wore wool slacks and always had a scarf around her neck, tied off to one side, French style, which looked perfect since people were always telling her she looked like Leslie Caron. Like the French actress, Ginny had a small frame, big sparkling eyes, chiseled cheekbones, and a high nasal voice that could easily spill off into a giggle.

From the time she'd first arrived at Vassar she hadn't wanted to acknowledge that she was from Provincetown, but now she not only confessed to her new pals but later that spring took the group to the Cape over Memorial Day weekend. "You couldn't imagine two more dreamlike worlds to go between," Regina recalls, expressing her happiness or what passed for her relief. "Everyone stayed with Pam and Linda, who were delighted to have them. My friends loved Ptown. They thought it was cool," she giggles.

Regina carried her new, quirky style with her to Provincetown, wearing an elegant string of pearls, a gift from her grandparents, with khaki Bermuda shorts and a red sweatshirt with the neck cut out. "I wore pearls, which really set me apart. That was my trademark. Just that one strand. I thought it looked nice on me."

By the beginning of her third year she was out of the closet with her first real girlfriend, a woman named Kathleen whom she'd met at the Crown & Anchor, where she'd worked over the summer. Kathleen was seven years older. She came from a blue-collar family, was a chemist by training, and worked in sales for a large industrial firm in New Jersey. Regina's friends reacted strongly: Before Kathleen they'd been a tight little group; Ginny had broken the circle by getting involved with an outsider. Worse, Ginny had publicly acknowledged she was a lesbian, something none of them had bargained for. Nobody liked Kathleen, and

Kathleen made matters worse when she came to Poughkeepsie on the weekends, got high on cocaine, and became aggressive.

"I was drawn to her because she saw that I needed a pair of boots, that the reason I was getting sick all the time was that I only had sneakers, which I wore in the snow. I thought Kathleen was taking care of me," Ginny explains.

"Her father was an ex-cop who beat her up very badly, actually tried to strangle her, when he found out she was gay. I nursed her during my final exams, during the last two weeks of my junior year. It was very, very difficult—she wouldn't go to the doctor, even though she probably had a skull fracture. She never went back to work. I wound up taking care of her."

CHAPTER 16

THE DROP-IN CENTER

It was Ciro's second wife, Patti, who first turned Norman Mailer on to psychedelics. Like most Provincetown wash-ashores, Patti had an interesting history. Originally from the rural Midwest, she had gone to San Francisco to study Gurdjieff and tantra, the latter under the philosopher Alan Watts. She spent time in New Orleans, where she had a TV show reading palms, and a boyfriend who was a graphologist and told fortunes as part of a nightclub act. Patti was into EST, primal scream therapy, bioenergetics, hypnotism, holistic medicine, meditation, tai chi, and Silva mind control.

Arriving in Ptown almost penniless, she had gone to work with Dr. Daniel Hiebert, who, since 1919, had been the town's all-powerful general practitioner. There was one other doctor in town, Dr. Thomas Perry, but it was Hiebert who delivered most of the babies, cared for injured fishermen, counseled the aged, and supplied medications to people who didn't have the money to pay for them.

Stories about Hiebert number in the hundreds, and it would take Neil Simon or Mel Brooks to do them justice.

Patti recalls getting a frantic call from a friend whose boyfriend had cut both his wrists attempting suicide. She told them to go to Dr. Hiebert. Half an hour later, her phone rang again. "Richard is sitting with his arms over a garbage can, and the garbage can is half full of blood."

Patti asked where Dr. Hiebert was. "He's sitting here, talking to
Richard. Please come down and do something."

When Patti walked into the office, Hiebert looked up and said, "Hi.
Want to see something?"

He pulled both the man's wrists open like an accordion, showing
her the gaping wounds.

"I don't need to see those," she said. "Let's try to cut down some of
this blood loss with vitamin K. At least it'll help the clotting."

"Good idea," Hiebert agreed.

He remained motionless, though, still looking up at her.

"You realize this is a very important case?" he asked. "This young man
is despondent because he can't get on with his mother, and I think the
reason he did this is because his mother works in a mortuary, and he's
trying to get close to her."

"Dr. Hiebert," Patti tried to cut him off, "I don't think that's really
an issue here. What we ought to do is bind these wrists and take him to
the hospital."

"Good idea," he said in the same tone as before.

As Patti administered the K shot and started to wrap the man's wrists
in bandages, she asked Hiebert to call the ambulance. "Oh, no, no,"
Hiebert replied. "Because then we'll have to report this as an attempted
suicide."

"That's okay," she said.

"No, no. I don't want to report those things. This young man said you
can put him in your car and just drive him right straight to the hospital."

"At ten o'clock at night in the middle of winter, in February? I'm
not driving anybody with lacerations like that to the hospital. Call the
ambulance."

Finally, after the man had been taken off to the hospital in Hyannis, an exhausted Patti walked back into the office. Hiebert turned and
looked at her with surprise. "Well, hi, Patti. Haven't seen you in a long
time."

"His sanity was okay," she said later. "The reason that he was sitting
there in his pajamas was because he had taken a couple of Seconals. He
had a sleeping problem, because he was on call twenty-four hours a day.
If somebody brought him a dog with a hook in its foot at three A.M.,
Dan Hiebert would take care of it. The only problem was, he wasn't

always in touch. He'd do things like give Mrs. Sousa the pills that were supposed to be for Mrs. Costa, and often Mrs. Hiebert would be right behind him, saying, 'No, Dad, those go to Mrs. Costa. Come on now, Dad. Those pills are not hers.'"

His absentmindedness led him into all sorts of situations. Once, at the scene of a car crash, he jabbed his syringe into the arm of the paramedic instead of the victim. In the course of suturing a patient's arm, he wrapped his necktie into the gauze dressing. In another incident, when he made a routine house call to see a pregnant woman, he decided she was in the midst of a spontaneous abortion. "Oh, here it is. Yes, you did. Yes, you did," he said. "Well, we'll just keep that as a specimen." The woman looked down and said, "Dr. Hiebert, that's not a fetus. It's a peach pit!"

Another patient, waiting in Hiebert's waiting room, witnessed the Rescue Squad bring in a man who'd been shot through the middle of the chest. Hiebert jumped on the situation right away. He shuffled out of his office, knelt down, and shoved his finger inside the wound to find where the bullet went. After a moment he exclaimed, "I got it. It didn't hit nothing." The patient witnessing this frontier-style exam, a grizzled old fisherman, later said he nearly fainted. "He just put his finger in there, I couldn't believe it!"

Thanks to his nonstop work schedule, Dr. Hiebert was rarely fully awake, and if he got to someone's house when the television was on, he was likely to plop himself down in front of the set instead of going upstairs to see his patient, often sitting there sipping a brandy. Sometimes he'd sleep for fifteen or twenty minutes, just enough to get going again. Some evenings he made house calls in his PJ's. Families fed him and named kids after him, and since it was known that he was a little henpecked, if his wife called while he was at someone's house, people did as he instructed and told her he'd already left.

He may have disregarded standard operating protocol, but he could always be counted on to show up. When the painter Nanno de Groot was dying of cancer, he'd spend hours sitting in the john, counting the tiles on the bathroom floor. Hiebert would talk to him through the locked door for as long as it took to get him out. Phil Roeber was another artist Hiebert cared for. When Roeber fell off the wagon, Hiebert, complaining that it was "all a waste of time," would show up with his syringe to give Roeber a shot. "Who knew what was in that black bag of his," Patti says, pointing out that when Roeber was on a suicidal bender, he'd sit in a blackened room, drinking aftershave lotion, while talking to himself about Malcolm Lowry's *Under the Volcano*.

According to Jean Bultman, Fritz Bultman's widow, Hiebert also regularly retrieved the drunk Franz Kline from jail. In later years, before the full effects of drugs like Dexatrim and Benzedrine were known, he thought nothing of writing prescriptions for anyone who walked into his office, including filmmaker John Waters, then working at the local bookshop. Six feet tall and weighing only 138 pounds, Waters told Hiebert he needed the pills because he had to diet. Other people got onto Hiebert's scale wearing raincoats in the middle of August with their pockets filled with rocks. Hiebert didn't care. It didn't even matter to him that some of his patients were selling "bennies" on the side, something he must have suspected, given the patients' repeated visits.

His goal, as always, was to help out.

One patient, a year-rounder, was a big, tall Portuguese who wasn't all that bright, a man with an enormous head who used to sit on the Town Hall benches where the local kids teased him mercilessly. To keep the man from getting overly agitated—indeed, to keep him from harming his tormenters—Hiebert prescribed Seconals. This seemed to help things until the kids started giving the man beer on top of the tranquilizers. The combination made him crazy, and the police were forced to put him in jail. This happened repeatedly, and the guy was in and out of the jail in the basement of Town Hall like a yo-yo, until the ever-resourceful Hiebert got on the phone to his old friend Police Chief Cheney Marshall, the renegade redneck himself, who agreed to put the man in the county jail in Barnstable for the whole winter, so that he would be fed, clothed, and taken care of.

When Hiebert wasn't being the disaster, he was the bulwark against it. Sometimes he refrained from billing people; other times he tried to take patients' property when they were on their deathbeds.

"Dan was always there," says Patti. "It was his town and he was going to take care of it."

Patti stopped working around the time she moved in with Ciro in 1964, two years before their marriage. But no sooner had she settled in than the restaurant alley became a mini-Lourdes. People arrived with headaches, rashes, allergies, and vaginal infections. There were the depressives, the hysterics, those about to commit suicide. Patti administered herbs, advocated meditation, talked about the importance of diet, and passed on local Portuguese home remedies. In no time, she became one of the town's major health resources, not only during the summer months but for the community's year-round and ever-growing counter-culture population.

With her bobbed blond hair and easygoing, pixielike smile, Patti reminded people of Doris Day, but Patti was far from being Hollywood's innocent girl next door.

Like Berkeley and Woodstock, Provincetown was in the forefront of the "cultural revolution." Fifteen- and sixteen-year-old kids with babies in papoose backpacks were wandering the streets; there were run-aways with rotting teeth, unkempt middle-aged alcoholics babbling to themselves out on the town pier, ambulatory schizophrenics hanging out at the bars when everybody knew they should have been in institutions. For years, local services for handling "social cases" had been marginal. Hiebert, who died in 1972, was on his last legs but even in his prime he wouldn't have known how to handle a drug overdose. AIM, the medical clinic in Wellfleet, was worse than useless; its WASPy staff sneered at Ptowners, just as the upper-Cape Yankees had sneered at the Portuguese, the artists, and Ptown's gays for years. Word was, if you went to AIM you'd just be passed on to the emergency room at Cape Cod Hospital in Hyannis.

In the spring of 1971, after two local teenagers died of drug over-doses, Patti started the Drop-In Center.

"We had to do it. There was just no other way we could get through," says Patti. "There were all kinds of problems, but mainly a lot of hard-core addicts, and they were our number-one priority. The town was doing nothing except putting these kids in jail, which was no good at all, since a lot of them were seriously *sick*."

The original Drop-In Center consisted of seven directors: Patti; Barbara Ellison, a candle-maker, hippie type who eventually moved to rural Vermont; Ruth Hurd, a registered nurse from Truro; E. J. Kahn III, the young Harvard-educated editor of the *Advocate* and son of *New Yorker* writer E. J. "Jack" Kahn; Janine McMichael, a concerned community

member; Lenore Ross, a local Provincetown artist; and Maureen Sullivan, one of the early practitioners focusing on women's health. There
was also a psychologist, whose role was to deal with the addicts.

Initially, the group set up quarters at the Methodist church on
Shank Painter Road, where six to eight patients were treated daily. To
defray expenses, Patti had fifty-six people take the Silva Mind Control
course under the guise of doing a "study" of the town's addicts. Later, she
would pull a similar stunt with EST.

Like Hiebert, making do was very much her thing, yet after a
month it was obvious that the group's resources were being stretched too
thin. The problems with quaaludes alone, not to say marijuana, and to
a lesser extent heroin, cocaine, PCP, speed, and God knows what else,
were of epidemic proportions.

Patti rented an empty beauty shop at the West End of town for fifty
dollars a month and brought in additional staff, including a full-time
general practitioner from Chatham, who volunteered his services.
There were clinics for unwed mothers and their babies, many of them
malnourished because they were ineptly following a macrobiotic diet.
When a vast majority of the walk-ins turned out to have gonorrhea and
other forms of VD, the Center began giving free shots; the bathroom in
the beauty shop was so tiny that when the patients bent over, their bot-
toms would stick out.

By the end of that first summer, the heavy flow of traffic had overwhelmed the small storefront.

The Center's board held meetings with the police and the town's
Rescue Squad, asking for the right to use an abandoned, ramshackle
two-and-a-half-story building on Gosnold Street right around the corner from Town Hall. The property, which dated back to the Civil War,
was owned by the Massachusetts Red Cross Council and hadn't been
used in years, largely because there were holes in the roof and rain had
short-circuited the wiring. Instead of responding to an opportunity to
help control the town's drug crisis, town officials accused the Center's
staff of "writing letters to California," telling the kids to come to
Provincetown for treatment of their gonorrhea.

The official turndown came from the conservative elements in
Town Hall, the ones who made up the VFW and the Knights of Colum-

bus and had encouraged Police Chief Cheney Marshall in his fight against the gays.

"You know how the Portuguese kids beat up on the kids who aren't Portuguese in school?" Patti asks. "It was the same kind of thing. 'You're not one of us, we don't want you here.' That's always been the Portuguese thing—they couldn't get all the Yankees out, because the Yankees were here first, so now they were going after us."

The "us" in this instance were the artists, the hippies, New Agers, and rich summer visitors in general, and the druggies in particular. Despite the resistance from the town, Patti and her fellow directors got the building by going directly to Red Cross headquarters in Boston.

For the first half-dozen years of its life, the Drop-In Center thrived under Dr. Eric Chivian, a longhaired, bespectacled John Lennon lookalike who would eventually receive the 1985 Nobel Peace Prize as cofounder of the worldwide physicians group International Physicians for the Prevention of Nuclear War.

Like many clinics around the country, the Drop-In Center took as its model San Francisco's Haight-Ashbury Clinic. Its services were free. Patients were guaranteed complete confidentiality and help was not limited to crisis intervention, drug counseling, and medical care but also included employment referrals, a housing bureau, and a suicide hot line, which was manned twenty-four hours a day by volunteers. There was an acupuncturist, an internist, and an expanded team of psychiatrists, as well as the staff of several lay counselors, who handled clinics and workshops and, when necessary, retrieved kids from jail.

There were two high-energy Jewish women from New York, both in their early twenties, one a certified RN like Patti, the other handling administration. There was also an ethereal girl, who wore a slip instead of a dress, who did the filing.

Patti presided over them all.

"I spent a lot of time with everybody," she recalls, "making sure that the schedules were right. Some people were on the phone, and some people were out seeing patients or counseling. It was nonstop. There was always somebody doing something that they shouldn't have, or some kid who had been caught with drugs, or been found unconscious. Sometimes you'd have to let them sleep there overnight," she adds.

During this time, Patti also had a health food store and, naturally, she hired the Drop-In Center kids to work there. Another part of her network was a year-round cooperative restaurant called the To Be Coffee Shop, which had been set up in the spring of 1971 by a graduate of the Wharton School of Finance who drove around town in a government-surplus mail truck with a psychedelic paint job and the steering wheel on the wrong side. The To Be Coffee got its brown rice—used in great quantities—wholesale through Patti's store and Patti even supplied a mill so the restaurant could make "rice cream."

In 1975 Jay Critchley, an ex-VISTA volunteer from Connecticut, was hired as program coordinator for the Center's social service programs. Frank Zampiello, a GP, became a member of the Center's board and joined Patti in starting another medical group, Health Associates of Provincetown, Incorporated. This was a pay-for-services clinic designed to fill the void left by the death of Dr. Hiebert. It would offer such day-to-day services as pediatric and geriatric medicine, a woman's health clinic, laboratory and X-ray facilities, mental health counseling, and even dentistry. HAPI, or its descendant, Outer Cape Health Services, remains the town's principal medical facility.

By the late seventies, the Drop-In Center was experiencing hard times. Understaffed and underfunded, it had never completely overcome local bias, and town officials continued to charge the Center with promoting dope. Patti's strongest allies were the cops and members of the town's Rescue Squad, who were aware of all the drugs on the street, and occasionally she managed to squeeze grants of $5,000 or $10,000 out of the town health department.

The task was Sisyphean.

The summer people didn't care all that much. They might pony up for the Art Association, say, but the Drop-In Center and what was happening downtown didn't much concern them. For godsake, it was *summertime*. They were on vacation.

Despite her New Age ideas, Patti was practical. The *Advocate* of March 8, 1979, quoted her as admitting that they were "skating on thin ice, going after all kinds of crazy funding." In order for the state to continue their accreditation, Patti says, "They wanted new stairs. New bathrooms. New doorways with special handrails for the handicapped."

For years afterward people wondered if the Drop-In Center could have been saved with a sudden last-minute infusion of cash. The answer was yes. But if the cash was not forthcoming—Jay Critchley scrambled like crazy, along with various board members, to raise the needed $75,000 to $100,000—then the need for the Center itself wasn't as pressing as it had been in the past. Times had changed. There weren't as many runaways. The kids weren't coming in crazy on quaaludes like they had before.

"Ptown is where all these experimental things start and in the end we educated the town—the Rescue Squad, the doctors, the police chief," Patti says. "A lot of the old-timers hadn't been able to see what was happening in the world because of their isolation. We helped change that."

"Ptown is a place where people take care of one another. They may tear you apart with all kinds of vile gossip, but in the end they're there for you."

CHAPTER 17

JAY CRITCHLEY

There is a modest little house in the West End surrounded by fifteen-foot hedges that enclose a charmingly disheveled garden. The house, a tiny New England bungalow with low ceilings, bric-a-brac and books, papers, cassettes, and flyers everywhere, is the home of Jay Critchley, artist and activist.

He has invited several guests to an impromptu dinner party to celebrate the Fourth of July. There is Jay's friend, a young man named Billy; a slender, somewhat reserved man named Will; Isaac, thirtyish with curly bleached blond hair and an iridescent blue-gray shirt that shimmers as it catches the light; and Damien, a waiter who has taken to hanging out with the artsy set and who is one of Jay's straight friends.

They are discussing the parade and what they consider the invasion of the muscle queens. Jay finds their distended muscles an exaggerated burlesque. "They're like blow-up dolls," he says.

Will is offended by their elitism. "They won't even look at you unless you look a certain way."

There is a deep schism in the gay community regarding the deification of the body and the party/drug ethic. "They're not political; they're corporate," Jay says disparagingly of these men who have forgotten the struggle it took for them to be allowed to live openly as gay men. His concern is the commodification of the body and its marketing in the gay community.

"What's strange," says Will, "is that even though these men have transformed themselves into sex objects, many of these guys don't really fuck all that much. They're too wasted on drugs at all their parties. Many people, in fact, have just stopped having sex because of AIDS. They're scared. I haven't had sex in four or five years," says Will, who is HIV positive.

The men begin to argue about promiscuity—love versus sex. Jay is stubbornly libertine. "Love is love and sex is sex," he says firmly. Will disagrees. "I don't want to have sex with someone I don't love. I've always been that way. Many straight people, when you tell them you have AIDS, they think to themselves, 'He must be a promiscuous fag.' I'm tired of that, because it isn't true. I think a lot of gay men are oversexed, they become distorted, a bit one-dimensional."

Jay interrupts, "Oh, come on, Will. You're just bitter because you haven't been laid in five years. Stop with this puritanical shit. Love is love and sex is sex. The straight culture is always trying to conflate the two, and that's where it runs into problems. American culture is very backward when it comes to sex."

Isaac agrees with Jay. "In the ideal, I'd like to be in love with the man I'm fucking. But until I find that, it's going to be sex without love."

Damien says he agrees that love and sex are separable, then adds, "But the promiscuity I've seen in the gay community sometimes seems over the top."

"Well, I'd be willing to bet," Jay says with a smile, "that if you asked your average straight man, he'd like to be having much more sex with many different women. But the straights are so hung up on sex, they don't quite get it—or at least don't have the courage to cop to it like we do."

It is getting late and Jay stands up. "Let's go, we're missing the fireworks!"

The beach in front of the Boatslip is packed with people, gay and straight, sitting around and drinking, watching the fireworks explode over the harbor. There are falsetto cries of appreciation, a good-humored element of camp to all the gasps of wonder.

Inside the Boatslip there is the usual collection of writhing bodies, and Jay, who often has a preoccupied air that keeps others at a distance, dances with abandon as the strobe lights flash, the music blocks out other sounds, and a bunch of sweaty shirtless gay men, bathing in their testosterone, celebrate freedom.

Jay Critchley, who first arrived on the Cape in 1975, was the perfect Ptown candidate: As a child he was an altar boy, a straight-A student, and one of nine children in an Irish Catholic family so exemplary that it won the 1958 Catholic Family of the Year Award for Connecticut. The Critchleys lived on a tree-lined street in Forestville, Connecticut, southwest of Hartford, only three houses away from the house in which Jay's father was born and three blocks from the family church. His maiden aunts still lived down the street with his grandmother, his sister's family was three miles away in Bristol, and his mother's cousins were in neighboring Thomaston.

Jay can't help smiling as he recollects "an idyllic childhood" in a town that was "ninety-nine percent Catholic and exclusively white." There was a Polish Catholic church, an Italian Catholic church, an Irish Catholic church, and even a French Catholic church in nearby Bristol.

Jay's father was a modest man who worked his entire life as a patent law secretary at the local General Motors plant, a man who loved to sing, play baseball, and putter about fixing things in the family's eighty-year-old row house. The most unusual thing Jay mentions about his father is his hobby: He raised and trapped minks, which he often told the children is what got him through the Depression. Like many Irishmen of his generation, Jay's father thought John F. Kennedy was the prince of light.

Jay's mother, a high-strung and demanding high school English teacher, was deeply religious. Her own mother, an immigrant from County Limerick, had worked as a maid and managed to put all three of her children through college. Jay's mother shared this determination to make much out of little and follow always in the Lord's path.

Jay's parents often attended Mass in the morning with the children and also led the family in a nightly rosary. "Today my mother thinks she's a total failure because none of us go to church on Sunday.

· "You can imagine all of us parading in." Jay laughs, looking back forty years. "I'd have a jacket and tie on—my little blue blazer, secondhand. Brass buttons and all. A white shirt. Gray flannel pants and penny loafers. My two brothers, the same. My six sisters, the dresses that my mother was always altering. She was always raising and lowering hems on skirts. It never stopped."

The children were taught to help others—volunteering at soup kitchens and the local hospital, collecting clothes for the needy at Christmas, and caroling for shut-ins. They were also expected to earn straight-A's in school.

While in the sixth grade at St. Joseph's, Jay won a national essay contest sponsored by the American Legion, "What Democracy Means to Me." "They came into the classroom in uniform, I remember, and in front of all the students gave me an award." That same year Jay and five of his sisters appeared twice on the *Ted Mack Original Amateur Hour*, singing a Maguire Sisters number called "Sugartime." Jay remembers the group being introduced as the Critchley Girls or the Critchley Sisters. "And then I'd show up onstage. They'd go, 'Oh, what do we do with this?' "

The family's all-American enthusiasm extended to the *Lawrence Welk Show*, which they'd watch together on Saturday nights on the tiny Dumont television. They were *a family*, even when Jay's father couldn't be pried from the set during weekend sporting events. At those times, Jay, who would have gravitated outside to shoot marbles, would be called back to sit beside his father and watch the Yankees.

With Jesus perched happily on everyone's shoulder, there was no room for unhappiness in the Critchley household. Jay's childhood was remarkable only in its absence of dysfunction. Jay's father tried alcohol only once, at his thirtieth wedding anniversary. "That was the first wine he'd ever tasted outside of Communion," Jay says. "I mean, it's incredible—Irish Catholics. No one was alcoholic, there's no child beating that we know of. No abuse. No extramarital affairs."

Regularly, he and his siblings attended services at St. Matthew's, where Jay was an altar boy. They piled into the family station wagon for the short drive to the same small frame structure where Jay's father had worshiped as a youngster. It was the priests at St. Joseph's in Bristol, where Jay's sisters attended school, who had underwritten Jay's mother's tuition at college just as the priests at St. Matthew's supported his cousin Mary Therese, when she became a Benedictine nun.

"I knew the Latin Mass when I was in third grade. Once a week I would serve at a Mass, in addition to the holy days. I did it through high school. It was expected," Jay adds.

There were other rituals in Jay's childhood, the nightly prayers, with the children gathering with their father at the top of the stairs: Betsy, the oldest, who would later be found dead in the New Hampshire woods, the victim of a suspected serial killer; Eileen, Anne, Jay, and Jay's "Irish twin." Geri; Cece, Donny, Mark, and Kathleen, or "KC." Cece and Geri were sister-best friends, and so were Lee and Anne.

Jay, the oldest son, was more intellectual, more artistic than the others. At eight and nine, he showed little enthusiasm for baseball. By the time he reached high school, his father had taken to calling him "Sissy." Jay decided to go out for soccer—this "other" sport that still might validate him as a man.

"I was scared, because soccer's such a rough game," he recalls. "But I still didn't get my father's approval. He came to watch me play a few times but just shook his head, 'You know, I don't get it.' Soccer wasn't an American sport, and he could just never figure it out, even though I stuck to the team for the full four years."

Ask Jay what influenced him as an artist, and he talks about Uncle Cliff, the family's "virile one." Uncle Cliff drank beer, he skied, and, as a veteran of World War II, loved to tell stories about his military exploits on Saipan and Tarawa. He was handsome and muscular, had a great sense of humor, and tended to brag a bit. He was a salesman for Pittsburgh Plate Glass and, like so many other relatives, he lived nearby. But Uncle Cliff also owned property on a small island off the coast of Connecticut where the family vacationed every summer.

"The house on the island had to be rebuilt, and every summer, from the time I was five years old, I worked with him, holding wood, cutting, whatever. There was no electricity, so I learned to use tools. I got to work with rocks and sand, and, of course, I started collecting shells, rocks, and Popsicle sticks, and started to make things with this stuff."

At home in Forestville, Jay spent time in his room (of all the nine kids, Jay was the only one with his own room) doing his "thing," while his sisters flitted around the house chitchatting, trying on clothes. "I think partly it was survival—there were nine kids, remember. I was making things like altars and little model homes, Halloween costumes and Christmas Santa Clauses and sleighs. I also had this little nativity that I made out of shells and gave my grandmother when I was ten.

Every year my two maiden aunts would say, 'Look at this wonderful thing Jay made,' and they'd bring it out and everyone would go, 'Oh, we can't believe you made this, Jay.'"

It was "the only real attention" Jay got, "like I was the artist in the family." He won poster contests. He did extracurricular projects at school—maps, hand-lettered signs, illustrated charts. He often had the lead role in the annual spring plays—*Pajama Game, South Pacific,* and *The Sound of Music.* He continued to excel scholastically and was the teacher's pet, always ingratiating himself as the volunteer, the eager, smiling winner. He knew that he was "different," and like a lot of other kids, he felt intimidated by the jocks and roughnecks around him.

"That's one of the reasons why I made sure that I was popular, so they wouldn't discover my secret," he said years later, after a decade of psychotherapy. "At the time, I didn't know what the secret *was.* I just knew that I didn't fit into what other people were feeling and thinking. Again, we're talking about a small Catholic school in an isolated little town, and, even though I graduated in 1965, it could have been 1955. I mean, when I was a senior I went to *six* proms. I was Mr. Popular. It wasn't until I went to college that everything fell apart—or I should say, started to open up."

Jay wouldn't understand why or precisely how he was different for another ten years. But he had faith. Like his father, he believed that the Lord provides.

In the fall of 1965, Jay Critchley entered Fairfield University, a small all-male Jesuit school located in southwestern Connecticut, where he majored in English with a minor in theology. It was only two years after the Kennedy assassination. Lyndon Johnson had recently ordered raids on North Vietnam; Dr. Martin Luther King had led his voter-registration marches from Selma to Montgomery, Alabama; the Watts riots erupted in L.A. and Malcolm X was shot in Harlem, allegedly on the orders of Black Muslim leader Elijah Mohammad. With the Vietnam quagmire deepening daily, Jay joined the small campus minority in antiwar demonstrations, then the Eugene McCarthy presidential campaign. He read Frantz Fanon, as well as Faulkner and Flannery O'Connor. He went to foreign movies in New York City, where he'd been only once or twice in his life, and one of his classmates introduced him to the amazing Bob

Dylan. His grades, which had always been beyond reproach, went to hell in a handbasket.

Jay didn't care. He was alive and going places he'd never been before.

The first confrontation with his mother took place that Thanksgiving, when he came home for the holiday sporting a mustache. Despite his mother's repeated requests, he refused to shave it off. When he returned to school, he received a letter from his father: "Dear Jay, you're making my life miserable. Please shave off your mustache."

Jay refused. He was now "the renegade." He let his hair grow to his shoulders, smoked pot, and, under the auspices of a favorite history teacher, began broadening his knowledge of the past. In the process, he lost interest in art.

Sometime during his freshman year, Jay stopped going to church. At first it took the form of skipping a few Sundays. Then he missed a few more. Finally he realized that, tacitly, he'd made the decision not to go to church. He found his desertion of the church both bizarre and scary; he also found that God wasn't going to strike him dead.

"The world was much bigger than I'd ever imagined," he says, remembering that at the time he'd found it all "*very, very* exciting."

In the summer of 1968, after his junior year, Jay flew to Chicago with a classmate to join the thousands protesting the nomination of Hubert Humphrey at the Democratic National Convention. He was tear-gassed in Grant Park with Allen Ginsberg, Jean Genet, and others speaking out against the Vietnam War. This was Mayor Richard Daley's famous "police riot," and it left an indelible impression: Power, Critchley realized, *could* come out of the barrel of a gun.

After graduating, Jay signed up as a VISTA volunteer, starting a youth center and doing drug counseling in a rural lumber town in Oregon. During his two years there, his good humor so endeared him to the locals that they asked him to stay on and run for mayor.

The time on the West Coast with its seductive, fog-shrouded topography, the laid-back easiness of the people, and, yes, the smoking of pot confirmed Jay in his new acceptance of life *as it is*. Now he was driving a VW Microbus, had a long, scraggly beard, and was playing the guitar. At six feet one and 170 pounds, he looked like any run-of-the-mill emaciated hippie from Haight-Ashbury or the East Village, indistinguishable from the millions whom Richard Nixon had started to call the enemies of the people.

When he returned home to Connecticut in 1971, he moved in with his future wife, Alva Russell, a shy, quiet-voiced RN whom he'd met before going west. Alva had, in fact, driven back east with him, having joined Jay for the last several months of his stay in Oregon. Critchley's mother was in anguish. Alva and Jay were "living in sin." In short order, Alva was barred from the Critchley home, the couple was forced to move to nearby Plainville, and then, in 1974, they decided to get married. The ceremony, which took place on Cape Cod, where Alva's parents had a summer cottage in Truro, was, in Jay's words, "a sweet little hippie wedding" on a hilltop overlooking the quiet Pamet River marsh. The service was Episcopalian, not Catholic, and no sooner had the couple exchanged vows than Mrs. Critchley, unwavering in her beliefs, loudly yelled, "This isn't a real wedding! You haven't gotten married at all!"

Married or not, in February 1975, Jay got the job of program coordinator at the Drop-In Center, and he and his bride settled in Provincetown. The second-floor apartment they'd taken near Duarte Motors behind Bradford Street was adequate, but if they didn't have much money—Jay's salary was $6,500—they did have friends. In the mid-seventies, Provincetown's usually desolate winter community was thriving. Many of the shops along Commercial Street, which were usually closed and boarded up after Labor Day, had remained open. Every Saturday night, the To Be Coffee Shop, which wasn't so much a coffee shop as a folksy crash pad/community center, had a guest chef who would cook for the crowd of several hundred regulars. During the day people gathered to play chess, read newspapers (even the London *Sunday Times* was among the house selection), sip herb tea, and enjoy human fellowship out of the blast of the Cape's winter winds. The music leaned more toward Bartók than The Doors, which may have been odd, given the times, and there were free films shown in the evening, projected onto a stretched bedsheet. The coffee shop's majordomo, the Wharton School graduate, was able to keep the place packed.

One of the reasons so many people were able to stay on in Provincetown after the summer jobs had ended was that President Jimmy Carter had extended unemployment benefits. The chief beneficiary was the Provincetown Theater Company, which, with the aid of these government stipends, was able to put on a winter-long production of *Marat Sade*.

It didn't take Jay long to become part of what he realized was Provincetown's "island" mentality. People clustered. Being part of the community meant mixing not only at the A&P or post office, where you could always count on running into friends, but at places like Cookie's Tap, the fishermen's bar at the West End, or the Mayflower at the foot of the pier, where the walls were covered with charcoal caricatures of Ptown's greatest legends: "Fat Francis," the 350-pound Harvard-educated town tramp who walked around in top hat and tuxedo; Howard Slade, Tex Slade's hunchback, bulbous-nosed brother, who unloaded baggage from the Boston steamer; and "Clark Gable," a commercial fisherman of Portuguese extraction, who bore such a striking resemblance to the famous movie star that no one in town could actually remember his real name.

There was also the Patrician Shop at the East End, which had a reputation for the best Portuguese soup on all of Cape Cod, and farther downtown, a cluster made up of the Wharf Luncheonette, the Meeting House, and Adam's Pharmacy. Adam's, the oldest of the three, had a sign over the doorway announcing that they'd been in business since 1875; there was a soda fountain where you could sit for hours reading the paper and nursing a single cup of coffee. In the evenings, you could pass the time at the upstairs bar at Ciro & Sal's.

It was the dole that was keeping all these places open and sustaining the town's winter economy, so it was natural that one of the liveliest meeting places was the weekly unemployment line that formed at the basement entrance to the Community Center. Here, at eight A.M. every Monday, as many as five hundred people, roughly a sixth of the town's off-season population, formed a line that stretched clear out to Bradford Street, young and old, straight and gay huddling against the cold in mangy combat jackets, foul-weather gear, and even thrift-shop Brooks Bros. The standard query up and down the line was "Where'd you work last week?" It was an insider's joke, since many people were actually working off the books, doing housecleaning, cutting fish, and banging nails. It was in violation of the law, of course, but violating the law was the Ptown way.

From the start, Jay had a romance with the town, with the dunes, the feel of the streets off-season, and with the people, who never judged and accepted you for who you were and what you had to say. Jay loved the energy of the place, though what it would be like in summer he couldn't imagine; many of his new friends warned him to brace himself, that August would be another scene entirely.

Jay's life revolved around the Drop-In Center. As program coordinator, he expanded the clinic's suicide hot line, helped to reorganize its job referral service, and eventually got involved with fund-raising, which threw him into Provincetown's perennial political fray.

Because the clinic's clientele and staff consisted largely of non-mainstream types, the old-timers charged that the Center was a magnet for undesirables, the staff barely distinguishable from the patients—the men with their beards, cutoffs, and sandals, the women braless. Local Portuguese were also angered by the fact that many of their own sons and daughters were becoming hippies, and although this was happening everywhere throughout the country, they felt that it was directly due to the presence of the Drop-In Center.

If the Drop-In Center served the town as a political lightning rod, it also had its own internal friction. It was organized as a co-op and run by consensus. The coordinating committee was made up of seven people who, through more meetings, conferences, and planning sessions than anyone cared to acknowledge, had a hard time agreeing on anything.

There was also an ongoing competitiveness between the Center and Health Associates, a local for-pay clinic, which was exacerbated when the Women's Clinic was formed in 1974–75 and, almost overnight, turned into ground zero for the community's most ardent feminists. At one point, there was a big and very public meeting at the Community Center, a showdown that drew hundreds of people over the issue of whether the Women's Clinic should continue as an adjunct of the Drop-In Center or whether it would become independent.

Jay, who had been in town for less than a year, found himself eyeball-deep in all of this; he embraced it as if he'd found his New Jerusalem. Then, only several months after his son Russell was born on October 6, 1975, Jay's marriage fell apart. He had discovered he was attracted to men.

CHAPTER 18

CIRO LETS
THE GOOD TIMES ROLL

Through the sixties and into the seventies, Ciro & Sal's continued to do a booming business. One year Ciro estimates that he cleared $1.2 million, roughly equivalent to $2.5 million or more in today's currency.

His bookkeeping methods were spectacularly unorthodox, but it didn't seem to matter; he was awash in money, driving a white Mercedes roadster, and keeping at least $25,000 in cash on hand in his home wall safe. He never used a credit card because he didn't need one. Everyone in town knew him.

He expanded the restaurant's kitchen and added an upstairs dining room, and as the cash poured in, he bought the property at the head of the alley. Patti moved her health food store there, and Ciro used the rest of the place to create three more apartments for the restaurant's staff.

He also bought the house across the street. Busy as he was, he maintained his involvement in the Art Association, where he'd already served two of his eight years as president. Because the main gallery was inadequate, the museum's permanent collection was stored in a leaky little shed. Ciro organized a barn raising, except, because it was Provincetown, what was being raised was an art gallery.

Local architect and historian George Bryant drew up the plans, and on a sunny spring weekend the new structure went up piece by piece on the west side of the existing gallery, first the frame, then the roof sheathing and the walls—a community enterprise if there ever was one. In addition to the artists, there was a local contractor named Bill Fitts as well as the Meads brothers, who were the town's Portuguese plumbers. There was also food, tons of it supplied by wives and girlfriends. With the volunteers working nonstop, almost miraculously the addition was done in three days.

Ciro and Larry Richmond, a longtime summer resident from Great Neck, underwrote the cost of all the construction materials, just as they paid the electric and heating bills for the Art Association over the next few years when times grew tight. One month Larry paid; the next, Ciro. When Richmond died in 1978, Suzanne Sinaiko, another affluent New Yorker who'd been summering on the Cape for years, took up the slack. The museum's collection of early-twentieth-century American figurative paintings by such artists as Gerrit Beneker, Charles Hawthorne, Edwin Dickinson, Marsden Hartley, Ross Moffett, and John Whorf, and modern works by Milton Avery, Fritz Bultman, Chaim Gross, and others were removed from the leaking shed and preserved as part of the town's heritage.

During July and August, Provincetown seemed to be at the center of the world. Everyone was there and most of them came to Ciro & Sal's. Edward G. Robinson showed up at the restaurant one night with his weekend host, public relations wizard Benjamin Sonnenberg. Henry Morgan, the TV figure, smashed a bottle of wine in the garden when the maître d' wouldn't put him at the head of her reservation list. Lily Tomlin, Bette Davis, Faye Dunaway, and Peter Wolf were in town. Moviemaker John Waters recalls seeing Judy Garland weaving down Commercial Street, drunk and in terrible shape, with hundreds of gay men following her. There was also a spotting of Elizabeth Taylor and Richard Burton at the Atlantic House.

Even Jackie Kennedy had her eye on the place. During her husband's presidential run she told an interviewer in Hyannis Port that Province-town had always fascinated her but that "Jack didn't think a trip was a good idea now." In later years her sister-in-law Pat Kennedy Lawford came and toured the town from one end to the other by private motorboat. What interested her most was the late afternoon Tea Dance at the

Boatslip, the hundreds of scantily clad men flouncing on the beach to loud pulsing disco music. Her tour guide was Norman Mailer.

Throughout the seventies the restaurant continued doing gang-buster business with the kitchen going through 20,000 pounds of veal during high season alone, plus another 100,000 pounds of pasta, which translated into more than 500 meals a night. The waiters were, of course, delirious. They had the best jobs in town. Tips amounted to $1,500 a week, and only a slim fraction of that ever got reported to the IRS.

The cooking was better than it had ever been, even though there was basically no competition in town—no *need* for the special effort, the quality ingredients. Everything was made from scratch, in-house, except for some of the desserts and the Portuguese bread, which Ciro, sentimental about all things local, considered far better than most of the regulars did.

"We never threw anything out and it wasn't a question of economy," says one of the cooks. "We'd boil down bones for stock, we used meat cuttings that other places would throw out for our marinara, we even seasoned the old bread for bread crumbs and the leftover eggplant went into the Filomena. In fact, we kept trying to take things off the menu. But Ciro wouldn't hear of it. The Arrabiata and the brodetto, and we had fights about it. These things were very labor-intensive. Everybody thought he was out of his fucking mind."

Out of his mind or not, Ciro had his vision, and by the mid-seventies, Ciro & Sal's was rated as one of the top half-dozen Italian restaurants in New England.

Late in the evening, after the restaurant closed, he'd bring friends, friends of friends, and total strangers across the alley to the house he and Patti had bought in 1972. Two doors east of the restaurant on Com-mercial Street, it was the former residence of Charles Hawthorne, the man whose art school had turned Ptown into an art colony in 1899. A three-story white clapboard Georgian house, it had two-story-high columns in front, and though it was in fairly good shape when Ciro and Patti bought it, Ciro felt compelled to make improvements.

An army of carpenters, electricians, painters, and craftsmen descended on the place. Mahogany, maple, and yellow pine were used to repair the chipped moldings and wainscoting. Ash was lathe-turned for the billet molding and new balusters for the center-hall stairway. The two-hundred-year-old beams were stripped, sanded, and stained, then sanded and stained again. The windows were replaced with new double-hung units, each featuring twenty-four panes to replicate the originals. The wide-board floors were renailed and treated with repeated coats of polyurethane to ensure depth and luster. Local sculptor Conrad Malicoat, the man who'd done most of the structural work for the recent Art Association "gallery raising," was brought in to rebuild the fireplaces. When Malicoat was done, the walls were painted in colonial blues and light pewter grays, the trim boards carefully detailed in a matte buff. Then, after filling the house with Shaker furniture and braided rugs, sailing ship models and his considerable art collection, Ciro and Patti moved in.

The complete restoration had taken two years, and the high point of the project had been the country kitchen. Here, consistent to the end, Ciro had insisted on custom cabinets and marble countertops. He had designed an L-shaped maple chopping-block island and installed a big eight-burner Garland range, complete with salamander, as well as the largest refrigerator available. In addition to a regular dining table and chairs, there was a desk, a couch, and several easy chairs, making it not simply a cooking-dining area but a place for people to gather. It was here he did his entertaining. People came for two A.M. scrambled eggs or vats of pasta. People drank. People argued, while Ciro held forth on Matisse, his favorite modern painter.

Ciro had even built himself a studio up on the third floor, though he hadn't painted in years.

"He'd already stopped about fifty-seven, I think," says his close friend psychologist Mel Roman. "Sal was always painting. Ciro talked a lot about wanting to, he still does, but he didn't do it. He should have kept painting, because I think he dismissed or destroyed a part of himself.

"It represented a lost identity, which he tried to keep. He always talked about himself as an active painter—not 'I used to be a painter' or 'I was interested in being a painter,' but 'I *am* a painter.'"

Roman, who has been close to Ciro for forty years, has never seen him display the real drive or vision of the artist. And certainly the rewards and gratifications of money and success, of being a celebrity in

Provincetown, had "overrun everything else." For Ciro, to be around young kids or other artists, to be a friend of artists, to buy art, to help the Art Association and be identified with the art community, that was compensation for a forgone career.

Until the problems began. "But, Christ," Roman says, "part of Ciro's character is to *bask* in denial. I joke about him to friends, shrink friends of mine, that he's one of the few guys where denial seems to work. He'll deny anything. He's going down the tubes. 'Nah, it's no problem. I'm going to get a million next week.'"

CHAPTER 19

OUTLAWS

Transgression has a long and hallowed tradition in Provincetown. During the nineteenth century, not everyone practiced "mooncussing"—using false lights to lure ships onto the shoals and then, once the ships had run aground, looting them—but no one turned down a chance to strip a ship. The Reverend Isaiah Lewis of Wellfleet once dismissed his congregation in the middle of a sermon because he saw a ship in distress through the window. According to the diary of the Reverend Dr. William Bentley, his last words in the church were "Start fair," as the whole congregation rushed for the beach, pausing only long enough to grab their pry bars.

When the *Fortuna*, a fully laden fishing schooner, ran aground at Race Point in 1894, two famous wreckers, Barnabas and Watkins, were there, waiting, and they had the craft stripped "of everything of value but the rigging" by dawn of the next day.

The outlaw tradition continued with the Portuguese, who arrived in large numbers in the nineteenth century. Disdained by the Yankee community, they returned the favor by ignoring the community's laws. This disregard of the rules has, over the years, spread to most everyone who lives in Ptown.

No one gave a second thought to whether it was illegal when, in 1971, some of the staff at Ciro & Sal's began a bookie operation that was soon "handling" tens of thousands of dollars in football bets every week-

end. By its second season, the betting service had grown so big it drew
the attention of the Boston mob, which decided that the amateurs were
taking business that belonged to the professionals. In November 1971,
a man arrived in Provincetown driving a dark green Lincoln Town Car.
Laughably out of place in a suede trench coat and Gucci slip-ons, the
Mafia torpedo, who had presumably planned to deliver a frightening ultimatum to a meek, compliant local, found himself in an argument with
one of Ciro's waiters, the rambunctious former football player Mike
Milewski.

The dispute began in the bar upstairs and quickly escalated. Both
men were big, although Milewski, the archetypal Polack, was bigger.
With furniture crashing, the two managed to career out of the upstairs
bar into the dining area, knocking over more chairs and tables. Soon
they disappeared, tumbling down the narrow stairway, locked in a
loud, thumping embrace. As they hit the bottom, they crashed through
the window to the garden, where they continued going at it. Shards of
glass lay scattered everywhere and dusted the men's hair; Milewski, in
a T-shirt, was bleeding from his left biceps. Ciro and several others stood
by, stunned. Finally the torpedo from Boston, more winded than hurt,
backed off and held up his hands.

"No more," he said in a guttural bark. "It's yours, I'll tell 'em. . . .
Fuck the whole thing, ya hear?" he added, his chest heaving.

Milewski nodded but said nothing, his shoulders still pumping
rhythmically, keeping himself on guard. The winded muscleman pointed
at Milewski's bleeding arm, and Milewski nodded again, as though to say
it was nothing. Then he suggested that they both go back upstairs to have
a martini.

"And that," says Ciro, "is when I put bars on the window. That
S.O.B. Milewski, he never paid for the damage. Not a dime."

The gambling operation flourished over the next three or four sea-
sons. It helped locals get through the long, gray months of winter, and
they began a flurry of Sunday football parties that lasted from lunch to
early evening, when the West Coast games wrapped. Soon Milewski was
covering college games in addition to the pros, and he started offering
perfectas, trifectas, and exactas. His business expanded. Though most of
the bets were from locals, carpenters and waiters making it through the
winter on unemployment, some came from those up-Cape businessmen

who weren't on vacation in the Keys or the Caribbean. But the biggest dollar action was from Norman Mailer and Ciro himself. Mailer, who in those days was not living in town year-round, phoned in upwards of several thousand dollars' worth of action every weekend from his place in Brooklyn Heights. Some Sundays he'd call several times, piggy-backing his bets. Ciro proved to be just as big a fish, if not bigger. Week after week, he lost in the thousands, and by Sunday evenings he'd have given up any hope of a face-saving comeback. He'd pace up and down, yelling at Milewski, who'd be sitting there, his betting pad propped up in front of him on the bar, doing postgame accounts. Half a dozen of the crew would be at the bar, too, including Carl Cummings, the restaurant's manager, since on Sundays he served as Milewski's assistant and, indeed, his accountant, despite the fact that at the time Cummings was a duly-elected town selectman. Cummings was rarely able to calm Ciro down and, being a tactful politician at heart, he usually paid Ciro's losses straight out of the restaurant's till, so as to spare his *patron* the agony of having to hand over the money personally.

What irked Ciro most of all, of course, was not that he was losing so much as that Milewski was winning. It *killed* him.

"You cocksucker!" he'd rave. "You get money from me in salary, then you and the rest of your filthy crew take food outa here when I'm not looking, and now you're living rent-free, you bastard!"

Milewski, saying nothing, would smile. What pleased him most was that Ciro was right—he was renting the biggest apartment above the restaurant, the one with the deck and the bay view, and given Ciro's losses on the Patriots alone, Milewski was living rent-free and then some.

Town authorities ignored the gambling operation, even though it was a secret known to everyone. They looked the other way when Milewski left town to open a saloon on the West Coast in the late seventies, and the business was taken over by a waiter from another restaurant, Phil Castellano, who, perhaps based on nothing more than the coincidence of name, was said to be the nephew of Paul "Big Pauly" Castellano, the New York Gambino family crime boss slain by John Gotti in 1985.

Nobody could figure it. Nobody wanted to. If pressed on how the town could possibly allow gambling in its midst, knowledgeable types chalked it up to Chief James Meads's altogether intelligent policy of live-

and-let-live-so-long-as-nobody-gets-hurt. Meads had run the local police department from the mid-sixties, and unlike the town's police chief today, Meads was autonomous. This was his attitude and it worked. The community got by.

Hard on the heels of the gambling came the smuggling. The Cape has always had a history of smuggling, whether it was during the American Revolution when fishermen dodged the British blockades to bring supplies into their communities, or during Prohibition when local skippers like the legendary Manny Zora, aka the Sea Fox, worked with Italian and Irish bootleggers out of Boston, making more money than they'd ever seen in their lives by off-loading the mobsters' oceangoing freighters.

As the fishing industry started to hit on hard times in the early eighties, a whole new cast of characters emerged, and their hauls were huge, literally tens of tons of marijuana or hash. The rewards for success were commensurate. Millions of dollars were made and millions were lost, and, just as notable, nobody seemed to get hurt, at least not as they did in other places. Provincetown was not Little Havana. The scene wasn't something out of *Scarface*. The accepted attitude was that if you were betrayed (even by a buddy), you just walked away, because with all the money to be made there was always a next time.

"The thing is, you knew that somebody along the line was going to break down," explained one veteran smuggler, pointing out that the real key was that in Ptown everyone knew everyone. "We were all brought up together," he said. "We went out with each other's sisters and married neighbors, so if somebody got out of line, we could make it hard for him. He got a punch in the mouth or something. But you don't take a man out and blow his head off."

In Provincetown, this same closeness included those who were supposed to enforce the law. Chief Meads was himself the son of a fisherman and was married to the niece of another fisherman, Richard Dickey, who, in 1972, was arrested in Jamaica for smuggling pot. Of the town's ten police officers, eight were Portuguese. Several were related through marriage, among them Ferdinand "Freddie" DeSousa, who was married to the sister of Sergeant Paul Mendes.

Mendes, at one point, was forced to arrest Frankie Rogers, who worked for the town's Department of Public Works and had reportedly been dealing heroin from one of the town's water trucks; Rogers's brother-in-law was Sergeant Robert Russell, the department's prosecutor; his father was the town's postmaster, and his lawyer was the son of the long-standing town moderator, John Snow.

It was no surprise, therefore, when Frankie Rogers, though dismissed from his job, was not prosecuted. In Provincetown, everyone—doctors, lawyers, bankers, businessmen, even the cops—looked out for their own. And why not? It was the Cape, sixty miles out in the Atlantic.

"The Portuguese, in general, are pretty tight, and they don't rat people out," says one veteran policeman, who wished to remain anonymous. "Jimmy Meads might have known so-and-so was doing drugs, but he probably wouldn't go out of his way to bust him unless it was a situation that had to be taken care of right away—like it was too obvious or people complained. But let's not kid ourselves," he added, "it always depends on who's complaining and what about."

The local smugglers fell into three distinct categories. There were the fishermen who concentrated on off-loading "mother ships," much in the same way their relatives had unloaded Prohibition-era whiskey boats; this generally amounted to an evening's work, a quick in-and-out run, although some of the more intrepid types off-loaded several hundred miles offshore, making them more vulnerable to the Coast Guard.

Another group was made up of yachties, who, as the name suggests, used fancy sailboats, not workaday draggers, to ferry shipments that generally went into Key West and other points south, not Ptown. These people lived and played in Provincetown but never did business there.

Finally, there were the counterculture, hippie types, some of whom had gone to college and/or were the owners of leather shops and other artsy emporia selling things like silver jewelry and tie-dyed clothing. Their activities ran the gamut from low-volume street dealing (pot, pharmaceuticals, hallucinogens, and cocaine) to elaborate importation schemes like the one foiled by federal agents in 1984 that netted one hundred tons of marijuana worth an estimated $80 million.

What they all had in common was an understanding of how Provincetown worked and, to a greater or lesser degree, a shared dream of striking it rich.

•   •   •

Chad Elsworth was anything but old-line Portuguese, but he was one who managed to make smuggling pay off. Women loved Chad: He looked like Robert Redford, dressed in peach- and pink-toned Lacoste tennis shirts, treated people with unfailing courtesy, and, when he bought a small house at the East End, no one thought it strange—after all, he was making good money as a bartender at one of the town's most popular restaurants, and he made extra diving for lobsters. What most people didn't know was that Chad was also making periodic cruises to South America for large loads of marijuana, which he would then sail into Florida. Chad quietly stashed his profits in art and in offshore bank accounts.

"You don't shit where you eat" was Chad's undeclared motto, and it served him well since the feds were unable to catch up with him for close to a half-dozen years. When they did, it was because a faulty rudder immobilized his sloop off St. Thomas. Even so, his time in jail was tolerable. He ended up in a minimum-security federal facility in the sunny south, where he read Melville and learned to play tennis. Today he's back on the Cape, still playing tennis but also playing the real estate market, most recently with a large four-thousand-square-foot bayside house that he's turned over for a million-dollar profit.

Another one of the sailboat smugglers was Joe Giovinno, a mentor of Chad's, who spent his last days cruising the Caribbean aboard his fine, teak-decked sixty-foot yawl, *The Viking*, and hanging out with singer Jimmy Buffet and other celebrities on St. Barts. One of Giovinno's more lucrative deals involved taking an oceangoing tug to Iran and filling it with hashish. He was delayed on his return when the tug's transmission gave out off the coast of Spain. Reportedly, that deal, which was sponsored by the PLO to raise money for their activities in the Middle East, netted Giovinno $2.5 million, and he made it his last.

Like Chad, Giovinno had always done summers in Ptown, winters in Key West and the Caribbean, and he was a smuggler who never got caught. June, July, and August, he courted women and tended bar at the A-House. Like Chad Elsworth, Giovinno never dealt dope on the Cape. Giovinno died in Guatemala, stricken by double pneumonia at forty-seven.

After Giovinno's death, Jimmy Buffett brought his float plane over from Martha's Vineyard and scattered Giovinno's ashes across the waters at Wood's End. Watching the ceremony from a nearby dragger, the crème de la crème of Provincetown's dope smugglers toasted their friend with an endless supply of Dom Pérignon.

Joey Lisbon was aboard that dragger, and he, more than anyone, was representative of the local Portuguese who chose to go outlaw. At forty-four, Joey was a man who had gone from hauling fish for three bucks an hour to driving a white Cadillac with tinted windows, usually with a Dolly Parton look-alike at his side. He wintered in Key West and Miami with Cape cronies, had a weakness for gold jewelry, like the $7,000 gold bracelet that said, in an understated sort of way, "Joey," and the thick gold chains that lay across his chest, visible through his unbuttoned shirt.

In the Old Colony and the Foc'sle, the drinks were always on Joey. He once took over the high-end Boston restaurant Locke-Obers, where a succession of $100 bottles of Burgundy helped to run up a $5,000 tab. Naturally, being a profligate kind of guy, Lisbon left a $5,000 tip.

Lisbon, from a desperately poor background, was legendary in his excess. His biggest gesture was to make a point of stashing his money under his mother's bed—piles of it.

"It was nuts," recalls Lisbon's cousin Francis "Rocky" Rego, another fisherman who was also into smuggling. "Joey's mother would go, 'What are you doin'? What are you doin'?' And Joey'd only laugh. It was huge paper bags filled with cash. Hundred-dollar bills just stuffed into A&P bags, spilling out the top."

Lisbon's parents may or may not have known where the money was coming from, but they regularly slept atop $200,000 in twenty- and hundred-dollar bills, as Joey went in and out, using their bedroom as his private bank.

Once Lisbon came into the house dressed top to toe in foul-weather gear. His grandmother, who spoke only Portuguese, asked why he was dressed like that on a clear August afternoon. Joey dropped his pants, releasing a torrent of cash. There was money inside his boots as well, and inside his shirt, and stuffed into the inner pockets of his slicker. He'd stashed the money there and carried it over on the Boston-to-Provincetown shuttle flight.

●   ●   ●

Lisbon's specialty was off-loading mother ships, though he also made several Caribbean runs. He was the kind of guy who'd take a boat into your backyard if there was enough water, and if there wasn't, he'd have a tractor drag it in.

He was also dealing, and he had a warehouse behind Bradford Street near the center of town where bales of cannabis were often stacked four and five feet high, as well as a separate store at his West End beach cottage, though it was next door to the U.S. Coast Guard Search and Rescue complex.

Lisbon thrived on danger. By late 1981, with law enforcement agencies tapping his phones, he went out of his way to taunt them. After bringing in a load of dope, instead of scuttling the vessel, he tied it up at a Boston pier, leaving a single, conspicuous bale sitting abovedeck—a "Catch me if you can" message to the feds.

He was "an arrogant bastard," says one of his cohorts.

Lisbon had all kinds of connections, from Boston mobsters to black street guys he'd met in Vietnam. He did business with the Sidewinders, the biker gang that controlled the New Bedford and Fall River waterfronts. They helped him put two "big ones" into Boston and another into Rhode Island. They supplied front money for drugs, and they knew exactly how to set up a deal down in the islands. "They'd send their man down to line everything up," says one local. "Joey told me that once, when he went down there, the cops were actually loading the boat for him."

Some say that Joey made over a dozen major hauls, and during one of these his boat's generator and batteries failed in a storm along the Nantucket Shoals. Joey was rescued when a workman from the nearby Texas Tower, the early defense warning installation run by the U.S. Defense Department, came alongside in a tender and supplied a boost to get his engine going. As the boat pulled away, Lisbon tossed a bale of marijuana into the stern, then set a new course for Scituate on the far side of Cape Cod Bay; he'd been sitting in open water for hours and was afraid he'd already been picked up on Coast Guard radar. Four hours later, Lisbon unloaded in Scituate Harbor, took the boat back out to sea, and sank it. He'd bought himself time by radioing the Coast Guard to report the marijuana in the boat of his rescuer.

It was only a matter of time before Joey got caught. Arrested in

1982, he was busted again two years later, when he was turned in by a girlfriend, who ratted on him after she'd been caught escorting a load of cocaine up from New York City. Lisbon served three years at the State Correctional Facility at Deer Island. When he came out of prison, penniless and in ill health, the friends he'd helped in his high-flying days did not help him in return. In 1993, at age fifty, Lisbon died of pneumonia and heart failure, too worried about his medical bills to take himself to the hospital until it was too late.

He had "the biggest set of balls ever," says Detective Sergeant Robert Melia, chief narcotics investigator for the Massachusetts State Police Cape and Islands Drug Task Force since 1976, who added that by the early eighties the Outer Cape was filled with a number of high-flying characters, not just in Ptown but along the Cape's lower belly and in the towns of Wellfleet and Truro. The reason was simple. President Reagan's "war on drugs" had been so successful in Florida that smuggling had moved north, much as a forest fire drives the wildlife ahead of the blaze. Even Long Island had gotten too hot. Rhode Island, Maine, and the Cape were where it was happening, and the Outer Cape, from Orleans to Ptown, was ground zero.

"My personal opinion, this was probably the number-two spot for smuggling in the entire country at the time," says Melia, comparing New England with California and the Pacific Northwest, where dope running had been a way of life since the sixties. "What we found was that there were more and more smaller loads coming in, as opposed to one big load, and that for every one we busted, we figured nine were getting through."

The ratio was awesome—a ninety percent success rate for the "bad guys" versus the authorities, who could barely maintain the status quo. For the twenty-year period of 1970–90, an estimated two million pounds of marijuana were smuggled into Cape Cod. As soon as it came ashore, most of it was trucked to places like Boston, New York, and even back down south, with the result that a whole network of subdealers, money men, and fixers came into being.

In June 1982, a task force was formed made up of the DEA, Coast Guard, National Park Service, Barnstable County Sheriff's Office, D.A.'s office, and all fifteen Cape Cod police departments. It was named

Operation Cranberry and the federal government spent huge amounts
of money to fund it.

There were many arrests but there was no end to the dope. One
after another, the smugglers kept coming, and their loads were huge.

In one bust alone the cops managed to lasso twenty-six locals out of
the Bradford, the saloon at the foot of the town pier. In another arrest, in
1983, ten drug-related counts were levied against twenty-five others,
who were charged with smuggling a hundred ton of marijuana, valued at
$80 million; among these was the majordomo of the town's art cinema.

The smugglers were having a field day, largely because Provincetown was hard to infiltrate. "It was like the Vineyard but worse," says
one law enforcement official. Another difficulty was that the town was
filled with "a lot of arty people with money that was hard to trace."

The thing is, nobody really cared. There was no denying the essential
romanticism of it. Running dope was a hoot, the sine qua non of cool.

"It seemed like a clean business to me," says one local, whose
unflinching approach spoke for the town as a whole. "Ever since I was a
kid, I wanted to be a diamond smuggler. Didn't hurt nobody, you
know? I wouldn't have done heroin or coke, I was a grass smoker, and,
basically, what I said to myself was that someday they were going to
legalize this shit because it ain't nothing but good, you know? Besides,
it was a kick in the ass to society, and I didn't have any qualms about that
at all."

It was no big deal, getting busted in Provincetown. You could even
say it was somehow *normal*, and even the town's assistant high school
hockey coach was arrested on coke charges in early 1980 with the son
of the commander of the local VFW.

David Salvador, the son of Louis Salvador, Tony Jackett's highliner
uncle, had gotten into the dope business early on with a modified crop
duster that he used to transport loads of sensemilla from Jamaica,
doing a sort of Lucky Lindy number, flying solo sixteen hours straight.
His routine was to fly down, load up, then fly back, landing at Provincetown's airport, which is little more than a single-strip affair located a
quarter mile from Race Point at the Cape's outermost tip. After dark,
even in the summertime, the area is deserted; with a car waiting at the
end of the runway there was nothing to it: "You'd just kick the stuff out

of the plane, maybe five or six bales, which amounted to three or four hundred pounds. We were getting a thousand dollars a pound even then, so there was real money in it. You wouldn't even shut the plane off, just dump the shit and then take off."

Salvador bought himself a Porsche and a couple of lovely sailboats. Unfortunately for him, he was caught and sentenced to seven years for what was supposed to be his last run, smuggling $18 million's worth of Moroccan hashish into Nova Scotia with his fifty-four-foot ketch, *The Sea Tern*. Once in jail, he was a model prisoner. The authorities took note and soon cut his time in exchange for David's agreeing to participate in the prison's Accent on Youth program—lecturing Canadian high school students on the dangers of drug use. "Kids," he had told the teenagers gathered at the Amherst, Nova Scotia, YMCA, "there are times when you have to say 'No.' When you have to be your own person and say 'No more'; when you have to do what in your heart you know to be *best*!" Then, David, who had six months left on his sentence, excused himself to go to the bathroom. Taking his own advice, he climbed out of the men's room window and into his girlfriend's waiting car.

After twenty-two months living as a fugitive in Alaska and San Francisco, Salvador turned himself in. This added time to his sentence, of course, but back in Ptown the story of his escape proved a boffo hit in the bars.

The same kind of adulatory folk-hero stories swirled around another Ptown icon, John "Jingles" Yingling. It was the *daring* of these guys. Yingling, the young hippie entrepreneur who had started Spiritus Pizza and was destined to become one of modern Provincetown's biggest-hearted philanthropists, a real street-side Damon Runyon, had gotten involved in a dope deal, which led to his being stopped at the Mashpee rotary late one night by the State Police. When they searched his truck and found it loaded with marijuana, one of the cops demanded, "What'd'ya think you're doing?" Squinting back into the light from the officer's flashlight, Yingling gave the response that would make him famous in the Ptown bars: "What's it look like, man?"

Adding to the legend, the forty-six-foot sloop that had brought in the dope was named *Al Lado de Ultima*—Spanish for "the ultimate high."

The thing was, the sheer chutzpah of locals like Jingles was breath-taking. Almost without fail, when one of these guys returned home from jail, he was treated like royalty.

Richard Dickey, the Fishermen's Co-Op manager, returned nearly a broken man after eighteen months in a rat-infested Jamaican jail: "I thought I'd be ostracized for life, but everybody had their arms around me, tears in their eyes, 'So glad to see ya' and all that shit, like I was a goddamned folk hero."

Joe Taves, the accountant who built a career in Boston before returning to Provincetown, remembers how his childhood friends would come to him. "I had a guy come into my office who'd just done a big one, and he brought in over three million in cash in a suitcase. He was sitting there, laughing, 'What am I gonna do now?' I said, 'I'll make one suggestion: Take one million of this and put it somewhere where you're not going to look at it for thirty years. Because when you get caught, you're going to have it for when you get out of jail. And you *will* get caught.'"

Taves, a broad-shouldered bear of a man with a deep, rumbling laugh, was a trusted figure, but no one heeded his advice. "I told some of these guys, 'You're morons. You need to go to Boston and get the best drug lawyer there is, give him fifty grand in advance, so that when you get busted you can pick up the phone and call him at two o'clock in the morning and say, "Guess what?" He's going to tell you, "Shut your mouth, I'll take it from here." When he shows up, you'll be out of court. They'll bail you out, and you'll be off and running.' But nobody did it. These guys are outlaws. They want the fifty grand in their pocket. Also, what happened to a lot of them is that they started getting caught up in their own product, and from pot they went on to harder drugs and then they lost it all."

The Portuguese, being family-oriented, were tribal when it came to out-siders. They might gossip about neighbors, but they didn't put them in jail, and that probably did more to foil law enforcement than anything else. The town's population was an interconnected web. It was no coin-cidence that in Ptown, "Cuz" was a common greeting.

During Joey Lisbon's heyday, one of his close friends was Ptown policeman Ferdinand "Freddie" DeSousa. Their history stretched back twenty years to when Freddie arrived from Portugal in 1961. Lisbon helped the newcomer learn English and protected him from the taunts of classmates. Freddie didn't forget that, or the many times he'd been invited to share the fish and kale soup at the Lisbon dinner table.

DeSousa had many other friends among the waterfront crowd, old classmates, or guys who were just part of the scene and had colorful nicknames like "Stretch," and "Cagey," and "Crowbar." Not all were smugglers, but all lived on the edge.

As a group, they saw the world in black-and-white: They were on the inside, everyone else was out. Their bond had been forged over many years, over generations, and they wanted things to stay the way they'd always been.

"I got no problem telling you, I knew all these guys' backgrounds," DeSousa acknowledges, "and we all got along because they knew that I had a job to do, and they weren't doing things that forced my hand."

If there was bribery in Ptown during the go-go seventies—and almost irrefutably there was, revolving around the town's leading gay nightclub, the Back Room at the Crown & Anchor Hotel complex—it appears doubtful that it touched DeSousa, who was investigated by town agencies in the late nineties and found to be completely clean. Later, in 1999, he was drummed out of the Provincetown P.D. after being accused of improper advances toward a female fellow officer. DeSousa denied any wrongdoing and considers himself a sacrificial lamb to the new, politically correct Provincetown.

Freddie's relationship with his friends was governed by something simpler than money—*the code*: live and let live. His friends never put him on the line by offering cash, and even at their all-night parties, nobody put drugs in his face. If they forgot themselves and did, it was understood when Freddie pushed the coke away and grabbed for the bourbon instead. What made it all the more interesting was that DeSousa's wife, Dolores, was one of the most vocal law-and-order advocates on the town's Board of Selectmen.

Freddie admits that he went to a lot of parties where he "saw things" but looked the other way. He explained his attitude toward his friends' business activities years later:

"Say you come to me, saying, 'Freddie, I'm moving my car from Point A to B. I have no plates, I don't even have a driver's license.' I tell you, 'Do what you have to do, I'm not going to be in the fucking area, okay?' That's the way it worked. What I don't know about, I don't know about. And if I don't know about it, I'm not going to be in the area."

Joe Lisbon knew the nights his friend was on duty and tried to schedule his runs accordingly.

"Even though I was a cop, he trusted me," DeSousa acknowledges. "He told me a lot of things, and I held my honesty with them."

"Held my honesty . . ." You don't have to be a philologist to see that this wasn't so much an expression of moral intelligence as an assertion of a camaraderie that was class-bound, class-originated, and most of all had to do with an intensely private shared history. Given how the Portuguese cop saw New York in the faces of the rich summer visitors year after year, DeSousa's tolerance, indeed his appreciation of guys on the "wrong" side of the law, was something tribal. If Lisbon was a dope dealer, so what? Like many blacks and Jews, the Portuguese have always seen themselves as the damned of the earth since, traditionally, it was the Yankees who had all the money, the best houses and boats, the power and control; and so if second- and third-generation kids were bringing in dope and getting away with it, so what? For DeSousa and others there was a certain satisfaction here—even if you were a cop.

All this was no different from the same sense of community that drove Freddie to help non-English-speaking locals get their driver's licenses by, say, phoning contacts at the Hyannis Motor Vehicles Registry to put in "the fix." Likewise, DeSousa and most of his colleagues on the police force were known to cut local kids slack when it came to traffic violations, even when they'd find an open liquor bottle or a couple of joints in the car. To a large extent, it was a kind of blood-and-soil nationalism, though hippie wash-ashores stood a chance of getting preferred treatment, too; even gays and artists, so long as they weren't out of control or stupid.

If you weren't born in town, you had to work harder at making the grade, certainly, but in the final analysis the key thing was you had to have a connection to Ptown's essential *apartness*. You had to have put in the time, done winters in town and endured the weather. You had to understand the difference between tourists and townies before you could be a member of the club.

Joe Lisbon's younger brother, Bobbie, who served on the police force for ten years before succumbing to a fatal illness, reportedly tipped off his friends at Spiritus Pizza about an impending coke raid, acting on information he'd picked up from visiting State Police. Another time, the well-liked Caroline Tacke, the tall, blond doper who worked at the Crown & Anchor's Back Room, had a fire in her apartment. Bobbie Lisbon got there ahead of the firemen and found Carolyn shrieking, "I've got some freakin' stuff in there, man." He ducked into her apartment and found her syringes and narcotics; then, acting on instinct, he opened her bureau drawer and found a .38 Special and several boxes of shells. All these went into his pocket. Back outside, he told her, "For Christ's sake, Tacke, you know how much shit you had in there? This is getting out of hand."

"Interpretive" law enforcement was a way of life in Ptown.

DeSousa once found himself racing eastward on Bradford Street and then Route 6A, trying to keep up with the teenage son of a local housepainter who'd taken the family jeep out onto the sand flats and was pretending he was doing speed runs on the Bonneville Salt Flats, going fifty miles per hour and throwing up great sheets of spray as he roared through one tidal pool after another. Soon the boy passed over the line into neighboring Truro. The Truro cops, listening in on their radios, began to give chase. Since they were coming from the opposite direction, it was they who finally nabbed the pot-stoned driver when he ran out of beach along Beach Point, near the Tides Motel. When DeSousa arrived, the boy was already in handcuffs. DeSousa insisted on "jurisdictionality"—a term that even today he probably couldn't explain—and he soon drove the kid back into town, where he told him to get his dad and go back to retrieve their Wagoneer before the tide came in.

Raul Matta, the man known to steal art for Reggie Cabral, once threw a safe out of a second-floor window of Town Hall. The cops, who in those days had their headquarters in the basement of the building, were down below, yelling, "Raul, stop. We know it's you."

A local heroin addict, told about an antique stained-glass window up in the eaves of the old West End Cold Storage plant, decided to steal it. "It was a beautiful window, facing Commercial Street, and he was a thieving fool," says Chris Cummings, a fisherman. "He took it while the cold storage was still operating, with people all around and still working.

He went up into the rafters, wrestled it down. His plan was to sell it back for the reward money. Never went to jail, though. It was covered up by the cops."

The key to getting by in this drug-soaked culture was a sense of proportion. One young man in town who worked as a bartender was dealing dope but simply could not get himself arrested. The guy drove a succession of snazzy four-wheel-drive trucks, zipped around the bay in loud powerboats, dressed well and ate out often, even though it was assumed by all in the know—including, presumably, Chief Meads and his detectives—that the man was not only selling drugs but bringing loads into his house directly off the beach at the East End. His secret was not his stealth, however, nor even the fact that he was Portuguese. It seems clear the he got away with it simply because he was cool enough to suspend his activities during the summer months, when the well-to-do out-of-towners (academics from Harvard) renting the property next door might pressure the cops or, worse, alert the D.A.'s office in Barnstable.

The police, it appeared, appreciated this: The man recognized that there was a line you didn't cross, and on that basis everyone got along just fine.

Without question, Chief Meads knew how to take the long view of things, and the town was smart enough in those days to give him a free hand.

As one of Meads's colleagues, a representative of the Barnstable County District Attorney's Office, put it: "The guy was just awesome, maybe *the* best cop on the Cape. . . . If you needed something, he'd just get right down to it. He knew exactly where to go, how to take the shortcut, you know? . . . And Meads could do stuff like that because people respected him, and they were afraid of him. This guy had a set of nuts they had to carry in a wheelbarrow. But that's the only way he could control Provincetown."

There was a definite comic aspect to much of what was going on, and to this day people still talk about Guy Egan, one of the biggest operators in town, who made millions, then went on to buy a half-million-dollar house in Truro and a kilo of cocaine. He spent the first year of his retirement freebasing the coke and stuffing rolls of hundred-dollar bills into Maxwell House coffee cans, which he buried around his secluded property. When the yearlong binge was over, Guy was broke—and the coffee cans? For years he dug around his house but ended up recovering only about half of them. The problem was he couldn't remember where he'd buried them all. More recently, there have been reports of locals sneaking onto the property at night with metal detectors.

The Old Colony is one of three remaining straight bars in Provincetown, and when you walk into the men's room with its bare pipes and leaky faucets, you can't help but notice that someone has painted two fishing boats on the door to the crapper, the *Cap'n Bill* and the *Menco*. To most people these boats mean nothing. But, according to local bar talk, as unreliable as that may be, the two vessels are a part of Ptown iconography as the most legendary dope-smuggling boats of the seventies and eighties.

The *Menco* was in fact Guy Egan's boat, and it was famed for having outfoxed the Coast Guard several times. Egan, a city boy from Marshfield who'd come to Provincetown for a weekend jaunt in the mid-sixties, fell in love with boats and mastered seamanship almost overnight, then slid into the dope business. Downtown in the bars, people liked him: He was tough and carried himself with an air of quiet self-assurance that told you he could handle whatever came along. Drinking in the bar one afternoon, before making a scheduled night run out to a mother ship several miles offshore, someone warned him that the Coast Guard had been tipped off, that they planned to nail him when he came back in with his load. Egan quickly recruited three other boats and they devised a different plan. The *Menco* went out that night, just as the Coast Guard thought it would. But instead of going out to the mother ship, it meandered around Cape Cod Bay. The Coast Guard was tracking its every move on radar, but while the seaborne cops were occupied with the *Menco*, the three other boats went to the mother ship and brought in the load.

An excellent mechanic, Egan had a liking for airplanes and, in addition to a float plane, one of his favorite toys was a rare World War II fighter, a two-seater Messerschmitt 108 that he kept parked at the local airport. The problem was that the plane still had its original Luftwaffe markings, including swastikas and insignia attesting to its many "kills." During high season, commuters, many of them New York Jews, wrote outraged letters to the *Advocate*, demanding the plane's removal.

The aircraft remained parked beside the main terminal until later that fall, when Egan finally sold it for reasons that none of his friends was ever able to determine.

Egan's specialty eventually became cocaine, largely because that's where the money was, and his fleet of airplanes expanded to include a serviceable Cessna that he used to fly from airport to airport, making pickups and deliveries. He never gave up running pot, however, and by the early eighties he was under surveillance by the DEA and local law enforcement, much the same way as Lisbon, with whom he occasionally joined forces. Yet he kept slipping through the noose, despite his excesses and the fact that everyone in town knew what he was up to.

His key strategy seemed to be to hide in plain sight. For years the hub of his activities was the Provincetown Fishermen's Co-Op, which he'd helped to found in the early seventies with other local fishermen. On the surface, this was a model institution, designed to give the small operators a greater slice of the pie than they'd been getting from George Colley or Colley's predecessors, the Finkle brothers, who ran Provincetown's fish buying as a near monopoly throughout the fifties. The Co-Op was located in a large wooden building at the end of the pier behind Colley's Seafood Packers and proved more successful than anyone had dared to hope. During the first year alone they forced Colley to raise his prices and to stop paying bonuses to captains, an age-old practice that reduced deckhands' shares.

"We just killed him," said Richard Dickey, who was one of the directors, along with Frankie Reis and Gayle Charles, a Yale graduate. The charismatic six-foot Egan was so appreciated in his role as the Co-Op's president that there was a movement along the waterfront to draft him for town selectman.

But Egan also used the Co-Op's headquarters as his private dope drop and to launder the dope money. For years some fish buyers in New Bedford had been writing inflated purchase orders that helped smugglers, some of them from Provincetown, to "wash" their ill-gotten monies; here at home, some of the Co-Op's members were Egan's partners in smuggling, and they were the ones receiving the payment checks.

"We knew they were off-loading there but could never prove it," says Detective Melia, stressing that the authorities weren't the only ones to know what was happening. "Every fisherman in town knew what was going on," said a close friend.

"Everybody" included the whale-watch boat operators, the fuel dock attendants, even the kids flipping burgers at the "Foot Long" hot dog stands on the pier. The IRS knew, too. But try as they might, the tax men were powerless to do anything except scare a number of older fishermen (who had nothing to do with the dope business) by swooping down to audit all the boats in the harbor.

"There were three big ports on the Cape—Sandwich, Falmouth, and Ptown," Melia points out, "and Ptown was the biggest. I mean, these guys had *balls*! They acted like they owned the place."

CHAPTER 20

TONY AND
THE COLOMBIANS

After work, Tony Jackett often stops by the Old Colony to get a quick beer before going home. He misses fishing, he says, but then he'll catch himself and become philosophical. He enjoys his job as shellfish warden; it's teaching him "a lot about the environment." Tony's his own boss, out there patrolling the tidal flats, and that matters to him. As he talks, he breaks into one of his broad grins. "You know, despite all the changes in Ptown, it's really the same as always. I mean, where else could someone be a dope smuggler and then work for the town in law enforcement?"

In 1985 Tony Jackett was working full-time on his boat, usually taking her out by himself so he wouldn't have to split the *Josephine G*'s meager earnings with a crew. If not quite Hemingway's old man of the sea, he was still the single, solitary fisherman, leaving the town pier early, coming back at dusk, trying to hack it one trip to the next.

No longer a rickety wooden contraption but a broad thoroughfare of stanchions and poured concrete, the pier runs about four hundred yards out from the populous downtown tourist area. The Dolphin Whale Watch fleet is docked on one side, and the fishermen dock their boats on the other. At the very end, next to two large, rusting metal buildings and several refrigerator trucks, where the local wholesaler buys the fishermen's catch, stands the harbormaster's shack.

Jackett was used to tourists coming down to the pier, asking him questions as he worked around his boat, mending nets and cleaning fish. "It was part of the charm of having the boat, the tourist thing," Tony remembers.

In the fall of 1984, Tony was approached by two young white men, looking, in their shorts, sneakers, and backpacks, like typical vacationers. They weren't. The two brothers wanted to know if Jackett would be interested in running a boatload of pot up from Colombia.

Tony politely declined the offer and returned to his nets. The brothers were back the next day, repeating the offer. Tony again declined. When they appeared for a third time, he decided to ask for details.

By the mid-eighties, Provincetown's fishing fleet was half the size it had been ten years earlier. The mammoth "factory ships," which had started to appear off the Cape during the late fifties, ships that hailed from all over the globe—Japan, the Soviet Union, Finland—worked twenty-four hours a day servicing fleets of draggers that scoured the local fishing grounds in well-coordinated shifts, taking vast quantities of fish without regard to size or species. Over the course of a decade, they had succeeded in wiping out the breeding grounds for all fish populations.

Fishermen and other concerned citizens had responded by lobbying Congress to extend the U.S. sovereign fishing grounds from three miles offshore to twelve miles; Congressman Gerry Studds of Massachusetts, back then the only openly gay member of Congress, worked tirelessly to push the bill through, but it didn't pass until the mid-seventies. Too late. Where once Cape Cod fishermen caught cod measuring six feet, they now hauled in cod less than twelve inches in length.

The life of the fisherman had changed. Tony, like many boat owners, had problems. He fell behind on the payments for his home mortgage, and when he asked the Seamen's Bank for more time, they refused because he was in arrears on a second mortgage he'd taken out the year before. There was another reason for the bank's refusal: Tony wasn't the fisherman his father was. His wife knew it, his father knew it, and so did much of the rest of the town, including the people at the bank. When he once came across a mother lode of fish that made him $3,000 in a single week, instead of returning to the rich fishing grounds, he took off the next two days to celebrate.

"It was crazy," fumed his father. Like most old-timers, Anthony made it a practice to leave the pier by four A.M. and not come back until after sunset, sometimes fishing six and seven days a week. "When the fish're running, you don't back off, you keep at it. Tony didn't want to know anything about that. He had all the talent but not the gumption."

With all the debts he had hanging over his head, running a load of pot from Colombia suddenly seemed like an attractive proposition. "I looked at it this way," says the former choirboy and star of Ptown High class of '68, "I was taking a chance. You go through periods in your life and certain opportunities come along. I had kids and a family, my house was on the block. I didn't think it was an immoral act. It was illegal, yes, but I was willing to take the risk."

Without the money, he faced losing not just the house but his boat. "You can call it romantic, but fishing was in my blood," he explains. "It would have been very difficult for me to give that up."

Just one dope run, and if he succeeded he could save his house and buy a new dragger. But it didn't quite work out that way.

Looking back on it today, Jackett is the first to acknowledge that the deal was incredibly disorganized from the start. But he began to consider the brothers' proposal: Their people would fly Tony to Colombia and put him aboard a sixty-foot boat loaded with pot. He would then bring the boat north.

For six weeks Tony sat around, waiting for the airline ticket to Colombia. He wasn't going out fishing, and he was losing money. The letters from Seamen's Bank started getting nastier.

The delay was giving Tony cold feet. When he talked it over with his good friend Frank "Skip" Albanese, Jr., twenty-eight, who'd scalloped with him the year before, Skip volunteered to pilot the boat up north in Tony's place.

They proposed the change of plan to the two brothers: Skip would run the boat, while Tony would arrange to off-load the marijuana. The brothers agreed and said that they would put up front money for both the boat and the dope.

"You take a chance up here, they take a chance down there" was how the brothers put it, discussing a deal involving forty thousand pounds of marijuana, with a street value of $20 million. "We'll give you the pot. If it makes it up, we all make money."

The brothers soon disappeared from the scene and were replaced by their boss, a hard-drinking, loud-mouthed Irishman from Fall River, who Tony started calling "the Redneck." Tony, Skip, and the Irishman soon went up to Maine to look for places where they might safely land their cargo. The first night there, in their motel in Ellis near Acadia National Park on Mount Desert, Jackett decided he wanted no part of what was happening. There were a number of things about the meeting that "just didn't feel right," not the least of which was that he'd overheard the Irishman trying to cut him out of the deal now that he had his skipper—namely, Albanese. In fact, the proprietor of the Holiday Inn where they were all staying had also been listening to the Redneck's bragging and called the cops, who promptly notified the DEA, and they put the Irishman and his Maine contacts under tight surveillance.

The would-be smugglers were unaware that the DEA was now in on the deal, but it was something they'd learn in the coming months.

The operation began to gain momentum. In March 1985, Skip was supplied with a phony passport and whisked off to Colombia. Shortly after he arrived, he was taken to the boat, which was already loaded. Less than twenty-four hours after starting the journey north, the transmission went, leaving him dead in the water. Skip managed to bring the crippled vessel back to Barranquilla by jury-rigging a sail; later he would joke that he was the only dope smuggler in history to ever *land* a load of marijuana on Colombian shores.

Until the Colombians could find a replacement boat, Skip, who didn't speak a word of Spanish, was stranded in Barranquilla. Since he was traveling with false documents, he was stuck inside the apartment the Colombians found for him. But the Colombian bosses loved him; he was *muy hombre* for having gotten the crippled boat back into port. To make his confinement more pleasurable, they sent up the best-looking hookers, the best dope, and an endless stream of videos. Starting to go stir crazy, Skip decided to get his teeth fixed while waiting and asked for a dentist. Soon, he had had his entire mouth done. He was also in contact with Tony, whom he called because he needed a new off-load site. He also wanted Tony to send him an American, someone he could talk to and use to run errands since the Colombians, whatever their awe, weren't letting the passportless Albanese out of the apartment. Tony, who would later comment that the dental work was "the only worthwhile thing Skip got out of the whole deal," was now back in, once again a part of the smuggle.

While the Colombians searched Miami for another boat, and Skip improved his smile, Jackett had jettisoned the idea of a Maine landing completely. Even though he was unaware that the Maine group was under surveillance, he wanted nothing to do with the boozing Irishman with his "big mouth." In addition, the delay with the boat made it possible that the delivery would be made in the summer, a time when Mount Desert is crammed with tourists. Looking for another spot, he spoke to a contact in Provincetown and settled on one along the Neponset River, south of Boston. Under the new plan, Skip would bring the boat into Boston Harbor, rendezvous with a tugboat at Buoy Number 13 in the middle of the channel, and get a tow upriver to the new, secluded unloading spot.

What Tony didn't realize was that the spot he'd chosen was "owned" by a group headed by Jerry Angiullo, allegedly the second-most powerful figure in the New England Mafia, whom authorities believe got a piece of everything that came in and out of the Boston waterfront.

Meanwhile, the Colombians stole a boat in Miami and brought it to Barranquilla, where it was loaded with the marijuana. Overloaded, in fact. The boat was supposed to carry fifteen tons, but somebody, presumably Skip, added an additional ten thousand pounds to make a little extra money on the side. Funds that should have gone for fuel and critical radio equipment were siphoned off to pay for the extra pot.

There were approximately eight hundred bales in the hold, each weighing fifty to sixty pounds, each wrapped in thick black plastic sheeting. Because of the addition to the cargo, transferring these bales into the new boat took the better part of three days.

When he met his new crew, Skip discovered that they were not experienced seamen. He would be making his way north with five hard-looking Colombian peasants, each carrying a little suitcase that housed an Uzi machine pistol.

It was around this time that Skip called Tony with an idea: The new boat looked strikingly similar to the local Provincetown dragger the *Divino Criador*. Skip suggested that they paint the new boat the same color, a light blue, and give it the same name and registration numbers. That way, when Skip reached Boston, the vessel wouldn't call attention to itself. The boat, still loaded with its twenty-ton cargo, was hauled up out of the water and the crew of Colombians put down their Uzis long enough to pick up paintbrushes.

When Skip finally got under way in the *Divino Criador* look-alike, it was already August, almost six months behind schedule. The Colombians continued to paint as the boat cruised northward through the Caribbean, skirting Cuba completely. A direct course through the Windward Passage that lies between Guantanamo Bay and Haiti was out of the question; it is covered by the biggest NOAA radar in South American waters. Instead, Skip took the Mona Passage, where the Windward Islands curve around the Leeward Isles near the eastern tip of the Dominican Republic, west of Puerto Rico. From there his course called for a big arc to the east, out into open waters past Bermuda, then a vectorlike shot almost due north before coming back to the west again in the area of the Georges Bank, the favorite fishing grounds of Cape fishermen. From "the Georges," Skip would be in a position to steam north along the backside of the Cape or, alternatively, go up through the Cape Cod Canal for the last leg into Boston.

The weather held, even though the delay had put them into the beginning of the hurricane season. Skip was the only one aboard who could run the boat and use the Loran navigational system. The Colombians, who, having finished the paint job, spent a great deal of time cleaning their guns, posed no threat so long as the boat was out of sight of land. With the autopilot switched to "on," Skip slept three- and four-hour stretches before coming topside to check his coordinates, use the radio, or change the channels on the Loran. The boat's engine was running fine, pushing them along at a steady six knots. It took them less than two weeks to arrive within striking distance of Boston.

Meanwhile, Tony made a pretense of taking the *Josephine* G out day after day, largely to keep himself from going nuts. The arrangements were beginning to unravel. Skip had told him that while he was laying over in Colombia, the two brothers who had set up the deal had called him and suggested they cut Tony out.

Tony would have been better off if Skip had agreed. The tugboat operator who was supposed to meet the *"Divino Criador"* in Boston Harbor was a DEA informant.

Every evening Tony loaded his pockets with quarters and went to one of several pay phones to call both Colombia and Boston, trying to stay abreast of what was happening.

Seamen's was going ahead with the foreclosure on Tony's house. Tony, in arrears for $2,100, tried to get them to reschedule his payments, but the bank wanted to clear the account. Seamen's president, Robert "Bobby" Silva, said Tony wasn't working his boat hard enough, and the bank's loan board figured Silva knew what he was talking about. Seamen's had been started by Yankees in the mid-nineteenth century, but in the late forties the Silva family, owners of the local insurance agency, managed to take over and impose a new conservatism that has been the bank's trademark ever since. What makes the institution special is that it never sells off any of its mortgages, thus retaining control of collateralized properties like businesses and fishing boats. Because it retains its "paper," it can also give loans on the basis of "character"—who you are and how well you are liked.

"It's called the bubba bank," explains a local business type. "If you've been in town for a while and you've been successful, they'll treat you right." If not, it's a different story.

For years, Bobby Silva had made it a practice to drive out onto the pier every morning en route to work to see who was working and who wasn't. Over the previous year, Tony's vessel had often been idle. Tony didn't go to the Knights of Columbus on Friday nights. He didn't drink at the VFW like most locals. No one could remember when he was last at Mass at St. Peter's.

At least the bank wasn't yet aware of his attempt to make money smuggling dope.

Susan, Tony's wife, was. His involvement with the *"Divino Criador"* made her want "to kill him."

"I felt that we were just trapped," she says. "I knew what was happening, because he told me, and the thing was so crazy. Tony could have fished harder. There was always an excuse—something was wrong with the boat, the price of fish was too low, there was a big swell up."

If only he'd agreed to stay home at night baby-sitting, Susan says, she would have gladly worked waiting tables. But he wouldn't have it. "He'd come home from the Surf Club or the Old Colony," she recalls, "fall into bed, then not get up the next morning."

To stave off foreclosure on the house, Tony filed a Chapter 13 "reorganization" plan. He was trying to buy time while Skip steamed north. The forty thousand pounds of Colombian Gold were only a couple of days away from Boston, and he stood to net $2 million if they got through.

As in most small towns, in Ptown gossip is king. It washes over everything, there are eddies of it, whorls and torrents, loops and rivulets. So it wasn't surprising that rumors were circulating around the Old Colony and Surf Club that a big load was about to come in.

Skip was encountering an unprecedented number of Coast Guard craft; it was the third week of August and both the U.S. Navy and Coast Guard were conducting joint training exercises in the offshore waters up and down the Eastern seaboard. He'd cut his swath to the east, then come back in through the so-called South Channel. Reaching Nantucket, his nerves had just about had it and the faux *Divino Criador* was getting seriously low on fuel. When the opportunity presented itself, he pulled alongside a local dragger in the calm seas and asked if he could use the radio-phone, explaining that his own equipment was on the fritz. When he reached Tony, he told him, "I'm going to Boston tonight."

Around eight P.M. Skip found Buoy Number 13. No one was there to meet him. After two hours, a Coast Guard vessel appeared, dimly visible in the darkness, so Skip cast off and let his boat drift quietly out into the channel. Soon he got spooked again, when another Coast Guard boat, a buoy tender, put its spotlight on him. He moved on. The rendezvous was off. "Fuck it," Skip told himself. "I'm going to Ptown."

In Maine, the two brothers, unaware that they'd been cut out of the loop, were waiting for the boat to arrive at the original rendezvous, east of Otter Creek in Acadia National Park. The DEA was waiting, too.

Early the next morning, Tony got a call from his contact in Boston. "Where the hell's the boat?"

Tony didn't have a clue. As he sat there alone on the deck of his about-to-be-foreclosed-on house in the Truro woods, the phone rang again. It was Skip. He wasn't in Boston, he was in Ptown. He'd brought the boat inside the harbor, dropped anchor in the cove at the far West End, jumped overboard, and come across the breakwater on foot. He was calling from the pay phone at the Provincetown Inn.

Tony looked at his watch. It was now early afternoon, one-thirty, August 20. He drove into town to meet his partner, careful to stay under the speed limit. Skip had told him that the boat still had all five Colombians aboard but not enough fuel to make it back to Boston. It had to be unloaded immediately. If any local fishermen came by and saw "Divino Criador" painted in fresh paint on the transom of a dragger full of Colombians, the plan, or what was left of it, would blow up in their faces.

They were running on pure adrenaline now, both of them, and after a quick beer in the Inn restaurant, Tony took off to find recruits to help with the unloading. He started at the Surf Club, then hit the Old Colony, then the Fo'c'sle, looking for friends with small skiffs or whalers. There were more than enough volunteers, including James McNulty, the twenty-three-year-old son of the town manager.

By the time Tony had made the rounds, he had a small regatta, six or seven boats in all. He left the pier in the *Josephine G*, the other boats in his wake, but he couldn't find the *"Divino Criador."* Skip had promised to meet them to the east, where the bay rounds the bluffs of North Truro, but he wasn't there.

The procession of boats crisscrossed Ptown's broad, expansive harbor, then went out five miles or so around Long Point toward Hatch's Harbor. It was a beautiful day, with recreational boats everywhere, and Provincetown's whale-watch fleet was crowded to the gunwales with tourist families with their waving children. After two hours, Tony led his flotilla back around Wood End into the harbor, where they steamed east again; after the better part of an hour, they finally found the dragger, almost completely out of fuel. One of Skip's friends announced that he knew of a barn in Truro where they could store the bales. Later that night Tony and the men could wait on the beach while Skip came in as close as he could on the high tide. They'd off-load the marijuana into pickups, then stash it in the barn.

Things didn't go as planned. Two of the locals Tony had rounded up in the bars had stayed with Skip, but none of them could see Tony's group waiting on the beach. The vessel continued searching the shoreline, but Skip was too low on fuel to continue. With the *Divino Criador* dead in the water, a small lobster boat they had alongside was now used to transport forty-three bales onto the beach at Herring Cove, ten miles away. Skip figured the trip was doomed and wanted to guarantee himself and his helpers some payoff for their labors. Already he'd committed to the contingency plan he and Tony had talked about earlier.

It was almost dawn. When Tony, who'd been on the beach all night, saw the glow of sunrise, he went home. As he stepped through the door, he heard the phone ringing. It was Skip. "Come out to Herring Cove Beach." Tony ran to his car and again drove the ten miles into town. When he got out to Herring Cove, he saw a massive pile of bales on the beach, but no *"Divino Criador."* Just the piles of pot and the five Colombians, each still clinging to his attaché case. It was seven A.M., completely light. Herring Cove is traditionally the gayest beach in America, certainly the equal of Fire Island, and in August it's completely packed by late morning. The smugglers didn't have much time. They hid the bales as best they could in the tall grass behind the first dunes, then Tony turned his attention to the five Colombians.

He had no idea how they might react if the police were to confront them. "We didn't want *anything* to happen," he remembers. "I mean, who the hell knew where these guys were coming from? Who knew what they were likely to do?"

Indeed, neither Tony nor Skip knew who was behind the operation in the first place, except that it was some vague "Colombians." Even in Barranquilla, Skip hadn't been introduced to the operation's kingpins. But then, neither Skip nor Tony had really wanted to know who was behind it. Now they weren't so sure; they were out in the open, all alone.

Tony chauffeured the five men back to his house in Truro. Susan dealt with the situation by getting dressed and making a grocery list, behaving as if it were the most natural thing in the world to have five Colombians with attaché cases containing machine guns sitting around the kitchen in the early morning hours, waiting for her to get them breakfast. One of the Colombians took out his Uzi and started cleaning it on the kitchen table. "He opened up the attaché case, and there it was, in separate pieces, like a musical instrument," recalls Tony. "It was like putting together a clarinet."

Susan, who had loudly opposed Tony's involvement, was genuinely, deeply pissed. The men stank. They were dirty. "I couldn't believe it," she says later. "Tony was so happy, so personable I could have smashed his face. I didn't know he was going to bring them home. He just walked in the house, happy-go-lucky, 'This is my wife, my son . . .'"

The Jacketts' oldest child, Braunwyn, then twelve, had wandered downstairs to see what was happening, and her mother ordered her back to her room. As she climbed the stairs, one of the Latinos looked up from his Uzi and stared at her. The other Jackett kids were clustered at the top landing of the stairs, fascinated, and refused to budge.

Tony now learned that Skip had unloaded only a fraction of the weed and had then carried out their backup plan—scuttling the boat filled with tons of pot in about five fathoms of water off Great Island, Wellfleet.

"The idea was to sink the boat and then go back and have divers get the load later. You can dry the stuff out, you know," Tony explains. "The water doesn't ruin it. The stuff's still good."

In retrospect, it was a harebrained notion, but it was the only one they'd been able to come up with. Now, while Susan wrote out the grocery list, Tony felt pretty sure that they'd gotten rid of the most glaring piece of evidence—the boat. The bales hidden in the dunes at Herring Cove were safe enough for the time being, and the Colombians were reasonably happy, hungry but smiling, and it looked like they weren't going to cause any trouble.

There was, however, one problem. The *"Divino Criador"* hadn't sunk. Skip had opened the petcocks, the water had rushed in, but the air in the empty fuel tanks had kept the boat afloat. It was dark when Skip had left the vessel, and it was only when it grew light that the stern of the boat was visible, poking up out of the water at a forty-five-degree angle, bobbing in the open sea like some huge light blue buoy. The name "Divino Criador" stared out plain as daylight.

Tony had just returned from the A&P with the Colombians' breakfast when the phone rang. It was a quarter to nine. He picked up the receiver. It was his mother-in-law. She sounded agitated. "Oh darling, who owns the *Divino Criador*?"

Tony knew something had gone very wrong. "It belongs to Fasche," he said, using the real skipper's nickname.

"Oh dear, I hope he's all right. They just found the boat sunk, down off Wellfleet," his mother-in-law said. "The Coast Guard is sending divers to see if there are any survivors."

Tony hung up the phone and turned to Skip, who was beside him in the kitchen. "They found the fuckin' boat. We've got to get these guys out of here."

The news that the phony *Divino Criador* had sunk was spreading all over Provincetown. Families were calling families in the centuries-old ritual. "Who's on the crew?" "Who's perished?"

The next time the phone rang, it was the Maine connection, still expecting the boat to land on Mount Desert, still wondering where the load was. Tony said the Coast Guard had found the boat, and he needed to get rid of the Colombians. It was arranged that someone would meet Tony in New Bedford, and the Colombians, without getting a bite of breakfast, were swept into the car. With the Uzis stashed in the trunk, Tony started driving to New Bedford.

They were in two of Tony's cars, his Ford and the bright orange Impala he'd gotten from his brother Tommy, with all the windows rolled down since the Colombians, who hadn't had time to shower, simply reeked of the pot with which they'd shared the belowdecks space of the *"Divino Criador"* for the past two weeks. They stopped at the Eastham Deli, just across Route 6 from the Eastham police station, and bought a half-dozen submarine sandwiches and two six-packs of Coke. The Colombians were finally getting something to eat.

At Buzzard's Bay, at the foot of the Cape, traffic slowed to a stop-and-go crawl. Tony found himself abreast of a very big State Trooper, who was directing traffic from the side of the road.

"I started to sweat a little with the carload of Colombians and the Uzis in the trunk," says Tony. "If this guy'd had any sense of smell at all, he'd have smelled the pot and busted us 'cause I mean, these guys really *stank*. We didn't know—at any second he could have gotten a call on his radio."

Luckily, the call never came through, and the cop waved them on. In a little more than an hour, they dropped the Colombians in New Bedford, where someone was to pick them up and drive them to New York. Skip, who had been without sleep for several days, was too exhausted to drive, so they left his Ford at a rest area and started back to the Cape in Tony's Impala. As they reached Sagamore Bridge, which spans the Cape Cod Canal, they saw a roadblock. There were a dozen or more squad cars, and the police were stopping every vehicle headed off-Cape.

As they drove by, Tony realized that if they'd left his house fifteen minutes later they'd now be in jail.

Back in Wellfleet, the Coast Guard had already sent divers down. Ermelinda Soares, the wife of the captain of the real *Divino Criador,* was frantic. After an hour, she managed to get her husband on the radio. Francisco Soares had been fishing off the Race Point since about two A.M.; he assured his wife and the authorities both that he was safe, and that the *Divino Criador*—the real *Divino Criador*—was still floating.

The Coast Guard divers had already opened the hatch on the submerged boat. Instead of bodies, they found marijuana, tons and tons of it. By five o'clock it was all over the news. Soares appeared on TV, a hot-blooded Portuguese gone mad, saying he had no idea how the media could have reported his boat was sunk, let alone transporting marijuana. When he was finally informed that the boat wasn't *his* boat, but someone else had used his boat's name, he flew into a rage and accused the news crew of "not getting your facts straight." His performance was televised around the state.

Tony was thinking of other things. The operation was in chaos, the Cape was crawling with dozens of DEA agents and State Police, and the bales they'd hidden in the dunes were hardly under deep cover. In fact, they'd already been discovered. At ten-thirty P.M., when the adrenaline-crazed gang went back to recover their meager bales, they stumbled into a stakeout. When the police fired their guns in the air and ordered everyone to freeze, all the suspects scattered. It was a scene worthy of Mack Sennett: police spotlights sweeping the dunes parachute flares drifting lazily down bathing everything in an eerie green glow, the smugglers stumbling over the uneven sandy terrain, trying to get away. Six were caught. Another later turned himself in, and yet another was arrested at home several hours later.

The next day the bay was dappled with bales of pot that had worked loose from the boat's hold and floated to the surface. People grabbed boats and hurried out to snag as many as they could, joking that they were going "bale-watching." T-shirts suddenly appeared throughout the downtown area, bearing a picture of a marijuana leaf with the logo "Save the Bales." Still smarting from Soares's tirade on the evening news, the Coast Guard sent patrol boats out into the bay to recover what remained of the floating bales and also to excavate those that remained aboard the *"Divino Criador."* These they transported to the West End Coast Guard complex, where the soaked, plastic-wrapped, and very pungent bales were guarded by cops with shotguns, creating a wonderful photo-op for the local press. Not long after, what remained of those forty thousand pounds of Colombian Gold was professionally incinerated, an act that gave rise to a chorus of lament at the Old Colony and reminded the older generation of the way the Coast Guard used to display seized contraband on the pier during Prohibition, before smashing the liquor bottles with ax handles.

The detective from the State Police Drug Task Force wanted the public to know that unloading the boat hadn't been easy. "It took us three days," he said. *"Three days!* We have a freakin' boat that was underwater with—you know, seven hundred, eight hundred bales of marijuana, and when it's water-soaked and diesel-soaked, each one come out weighing about a hundred twenty, a hundred fifty pounds. We probably had ten to fifteen divers from the Environmental Police. . . . We thought about blowing the boat up, but that would have caused too much of a navigation problem."

Jimmy Meads, Ptown's chief of police, was ecstatic. "I was six inches off my seat!" Meads told reporters. According to the chief, the bales in the dunes were very well hidden—no one could have seen them on foot. It was "a stroke of luck" that Ranger Martha Lyons, on routine horseback patrol, happened to be riding by and spotted them. Meads credited the arrests to "superior police work," never mind the startling incompetence of the smugglers. Another example of excellent detective work, he pointed out, was that someone had turned in a Colombian passport they'd found on the beach, so it was now "fairly obvious" that the shipment had come up "from Latin America." Likewise, authorities also had a wallet, and although they weren't giving out the name just yet, the police were, in fact, pursuing Skip, who'd dropped his billfold on the beach after the scuttling. Meanwhile, a desperate Colombian was calling Tony from New York, asking whether anyone had found his passport, which he needed in order to get back to Barranquilla. Tony was apologetic but explained that he had problems of his own to deal with.

Two days after the discovery of the boat, the cops arrived at Tony's house with a search warrant. It was eleven-thirty P.M. and Susan was in her nightgown, the kids were asleep, and Tony was at the Old Colony, hanging out. The raiding party consisted of several Truro cops, State Police, and DEA personnel. They went through the house, starting in the basement and working upward, filling large plastic garbage bags with evidence, which they carefully labeled and tagged. Susan, in her bathrobe, sat watching them from the living room couch.

Tony strolled in shortly after one A.M. Later, senior police officials said that he gave no indication of being surprised. The officers sat him down at the kitchen table and told him what they had: the phony numbers off the boat, Skip's wallet, the Colombian passport, and "an informant" who could place Tony in Maine and Boston. There was all the recovered grass, some twenty tons' worth, and in Tony's bedroom closet they'd found charts covered with Skip's handwriting, indicating navigation coordinates as well as the Neponset drop-off point.

What Tony was looking at if convicted, the agents explained, was a minimum of fifteen years in prison. And his conviction was almost certain.

Tony listened carefully. He remained, as always, an incredibly resilient man.

"I was the one who talked to him," recalls Detective Robert Melia, head of the Cape and Islands Drug Task Force, "and he was mostly concerned about his family—'I can protect them but if shit starts happening, I'll need you to be there' is what he said. He also didn't want the police to tear the house apart because of his kids. He knew he'd screwed up, and he was willing to pay the fiddler. He just wanted us to go gentle."

There was no crying, no begging, no coming apart, and Tony didn't have to consult lawyers to know what to do. As he recalled the scene later:

"I put my head down and thought, 'Jesus, Skip's already told me he's never gonna do time,' so I knew he was going to talk. And the DEA guys made it clear that they'd settle for just one of us. What was I gonna do? This was serious."

Like almost every dope smuggler who gets busted, Tony talked in exchange for leniency. Even so, his world fell apart. Susan was enraged; she'd had enough. Her privacy had been violated, her children terrified, and the incident detonated a time bomb of resentments.

"While he was still talking with the police, I went up to bed, and it wasn't long before they came back upstairs to look for something. I was under the covers. I wasn't afraid, just pissed off at Tony. All the years of his bullshit, he didn't care about me. He was just glad he wasn't going to jail."

In the days that followed, she found herself unable to tell her mother, which was no small matter since ordinarily the two talked on the phone several times a day, gossiping, chattering on, the way many Ptown Portuguese housewives have done for years. But now, no more, despite everyone in town knowing what had happened—Tony's involvement, the sheer magnitude of the thing. Her denial and embarrassment were typical of Susan.

When she married Tony in 1971, she had actually believed she was marrying a rock-solid Portuguese, an industrious old-school type. It wasn't until five or six years later, after the *Josephine G*, that it began to dawn on her that her man was a hopeless romantic and dreamer—"a little boy," as she'd started to let herself speak of him to her girlfriends. He had "no structure." He was "unpredictable," "immature."

"He never, *ever* worked the boat hard enough, and he always had excuses when he'd been out at the bars the night before," she said. "I don't know how much dope he was doing but, thank God, he wasn't buying it with our money, since we didn't have any money. Back then I was getting most of our stuff from the Sears catalog—me, who thought she was going to be Little Miss Betty Crocker."

The night of Tony's arrest was only a prelude. Throughout the autumn of 1985, Susan and Tony fought, sometimes loudly and almost always about money. One night Tony, demanding that Susan take a job, yelled at her, "Your days of doing nothing are over." Susan responded by trying to break a chair over his head; when he took the chair away, she tried to gouge his face with the shattered bulb of a nearby wall lamp. That night he slept on the boat.

"I was so angry that he could say such a thing," she explains. "It was just more of his bullshit. Like he'd always said that if he ran his boat the way I ran the house and raised the kids, he probably could've been a highliner. It was ridiculous, but I was supposed to believe him."

She pauses, recalling how he'd squirm this way and that to avoid dealing with their troubles.

"He asked me to take over and do his books once, even though I never studied bookkeeping in school," she continues, "and I said show me how, and I'll do it. But it was always, 'Tomorrow, I'm too tired.' Then one time I said to him, 'You know, you need to clean up that desk; show me what bills I can pay and what I can't pay.' He went over to the desk with a big paper bag, put everything into the bag, and then threw the bag into the closet and said, 'There, it's clean.' So I stopped doing the bills, and he stopped giving me money."

Down at the pier, if the boat needed a part, he'd buy the part but not pay the mortgage. The financial pressures got worse when renovations to the house went over budget, and for Susan what made everything harder was that Tony was always willing to talk, to admit that he needed "to change." The two of them talked endlessly, sometimes late into the night after the kids had finished with the TV and gone to bed.

It was only a stopgap. Nothing changed.

"We could always talk," Susan says, "that's why, with all the problems we had, we stayed together. Tony is a good man. He never abused me, he loved the kids. But he's never been able to deal with everyday things in a way that makes sense. With him, everything is always going to 'get better.' "

Over the winter of 1985-86, the wound was reopened every time he went into Boston to testify before the grand jury, which was part of the deal he'd made with the Barnstable County D.A.'s Office. Sometimes he told Susan he'd be going, sometimes not. She knew anyway just by looking into his closet and seeing what clothes were missing. Strangely, even though he was testifying within the hallowed walls of the federal courthouse, he might don an ocher-colored scarf to wear with his black roll-neck fisherman's sweater, or even jeans with the old Barleycorn sport coat that he'd picked up at a Truro yard sale. Robert Melia, the State Police detective who'd been in charge of the raid on the house back in August, accompanied him on these trips, and the two talked at length, driving up fog-shrouded Route 3 before daybreak to get into Boston on time. It didn't matter that Melia was on the opposite side of the law. The chunky six-foot-two cop had come to like Tony and more: As Melia saw it, on some basic level, Tony's infraction had even been justified.

"I felt bad for him, knowing the situation—that he was going to lose his boat because of the fishing industry going south. And he had a ton of kids, too. I knew exactly where he was coming from, and I'll tell ya, there's no doubt in my mind that if I was in the same situation, I'd have done the same thing.

"Probably half the boats in Provincetown were dirty," he adds, "close to half, anyway, and a lot of it had to do with the economics at the time. You know, for one hour, two hours' work, you could make two hundred and fifty thousand dollars."

Tony "never begged," he says. "When we talked to him about testifying, his main concern was his family. He said he could hack it, but we had to be there to protect them if that became necessary. And the other thing," he adds with a grin, "if I had just half his looks—I mean this guy could've been a movie star! I'm bringing him in and out of the courthouse, every goddamn morning, the girls there, some of the secretaries that worked on our side, they're all going 'Who is that guy?' They all wanted t' go to bed with him."

In the months Tony was working off his debt to Uncle Sam, he picked up the shards of his life and went back to fishing. The *Josephine G* was a strong boat, but her tired diesel needed work. Sometimes friends let him charge parts to their businesses (or to their bosses' businesses), which allowed him to make repairs on a stopgap basis, but even so there was less margin for error than before. He couldn't overwork the boat's engine because if it blew, he had no way of coming up with the ten grand to replace it. The Fates were not with Tony Jackett. His smuggling adventure had triggered some sort of karmic recalibration, and whenever things could go wrong, they did. Again, and again.

Not long after he got going in March, for example, he was out alone, taking risks by skimming his funnel-shaped net alongside a submerged wreck, as close as he dared, because that's where you often got the best tow. It was almost time to head home, but he wanted to get in one last drag. "I had less than a hundred feet of clearance, and there were a lot of fish. But then the tide pushed me inside, closer to the wreck, and suddenly the boat stopped. A lot of times you can just take her out of gear, let it fall back and get untangled. I tried this and then tried coming at it from a different angle."

Nothing worked. The tide was against him, so he had no choice; he had to cut the gear away. It was early spring, and he'd lost his net. He scoured the town for new gear and eventually Kenny Macara, a well-to-do boat owner and someone he'd played high school basketball with, helped by lending him another one. Still, his problems weren't over.

Several months later, he snagged his borrowed net on a wreck and couldn't bear to cut the gear away. Instead, he pulled up the wreck, which was nearly as big as his own boat, intending to drag it into shallow water. The *Josephine G* was listing wildly. The water was brown, not green-blue in color, because it was so rough, and Tony knew that if the steering failed he was going to be in serious trouble. Soon the swells were massive and with the wind accelerating to fifty knots out of the southwest, he was taking the seas broadside. He raced to get around Long Point and inside the harbor. As he rounded the point, Aaron Avellar, captain of the Dolphin Fleet, saw him: Avellar was at the helm of one of his whale-watch boats, which he was about to put on the mooring for safekeeping against the growing storm, but when he saw Jackett he came to help. Whale-watch boats are big 100- to 110-foot vessels, but the experienced captain maneuvered alongside the beleaguered *Josephine* G.

"I remember Aaron took the boat out of gear, because he was coming down on top of me and my whole superstructure almost went when the seas banged us together. The wind was just howling and when his first mate threw me a line he missed and almost went overboard. Then they made another pass. On the second time around I got the line okay. . . ."

Pal Bob Giovinno was along as crew, and later he remarked that it wasn't only Tony's seamanship but the *Josephine* G that "saved us. We beat the hell out of her and she stood up. The wind was so strong that when Aaron's man threw us a line it just got blown back in his face. Tony was in the pilothouse, and he couldn't take his hands off the wheel. I was on the radio, the whole town was listening in to make sure we were all right; even though we were on the inside, they wanted us to just keep talking. At one point, I remember, I looked up and a whole sea was coming at us. I did one of those," he smiles, raising his arm to protect his face. "Any other boat might have sunk."

It was during this period that Tony's involvement with the *"Divino Criador"* came back to haunt him. He had known before he gave his grand jury testimony that there might be reprisals from the Colombians. Bob Melia had never minimized the possible dangers. But Tony, who'd always been able to shrug things off, had felt that Melia would protect him.

Rocky Rego recalls that it was a sunny afternoon in June when Tony approached him at Lopes Square at the foot of the wharf and asked, " 'Rocky, can you help? There're two of them sitting in the black car.' I says, 'All right, I'll go down. You stay here.'

"So I go around the corner. There were two guys from Boston sitting inside a black GTO parked kitty-corner to the Chamber of Commerce office. . . ." Rocky recalls that he tapped on the window of the car and asked, "What's your problem?"

The men looked Rocky up and down and then the driver, a man with a ponytail, asked him, "Who're you?"

"Rocky Rego. What's the problem?"

"Well, you've got a guy here we got to talk to," the man said.

"Who's that?" Rego snapped.

"This guy Tony."

"You got the wrong guy. He ain't saying nothing about nobody."

"You sure?"

"Yeah," Rego said. "Talk to Joey Lisbon before you do anything. You know Joey Lisbon, don't you?"

"Oh, yeah, we know Joe."

"You don't believe me, talk t' him first."

Eventually the two torpedoes left.

This was as close as anyone had come to getting seriously hurt in connection with a dope deal in Ptown, and Tony found he couldn't sleep unless he had a load on. More and more he stayed out at night, drinking beer and cognac shooters. The fights with Susan continued, even though she no longer waited up for him.

A month and half after the close call at the wharf Tony was ready to throw in the towel with Seamen's. Susan was heartbroken at losing the place. "I raised six kids in that house. It was my home. I didn't want to sell it," she recalls. "I packed all winter. I packed and I wept."

CHAPTER 21

COMING OUT

When Jay Critchley told his wife, Alva, that he was gay, they both wept, as well, then they entered counseling. The two discussed the situation into the early morning hours while their son slept in the next room. But Jay couldn't get past the need to explore his new sexuality. After two months, at Alva's insistence, they separated.

It was August 1976, the height of the tourist season. Because of the lack of available housing, Jay took his tent to the campground in North Truro. He told himself he could "change." At that point, he still had not had a sexual experience with a man.

"I was angry that it was happening," he recalls, "completely traumatized. I didn't want to be gay, and I had no idea what I was going to do with my life. I can't tell you how scared I was."

The strictness of his Catholic upbringing made him feel he'd been thrown into "an abyss, about to die." When he tried to have sex with a man, he froze. "I could hardly breathe," he says. "I was in a state of complete terror."

He went to visit a nun he'd known for years at a Benedictine nunnery in Bethlehem, Connecticut. He journeyed to San Francisco to visit his college-roommate-turned-dope-smoking-guru, who, Jay decided, was a fraud. He made his way north from the Bay Area to a cloister on Shaw Island, Washington, founded by his cousin Mary Therese after she had been transferred from Connecticut.

Nothing worked. His life had changed, and he had to accept it.

"I realized there was no way I was going to reconcile being Catholic and being gay," he says. "I mean, they just don't match, at least not in any traditional sense. So it was, 'Okay, I just move on.' "

It was at the Drop-In Center that Jay encountered his first boyfriend, Dr. Doug Kibler, one of the resident physicians who had been hired the year before. Doug was a quiet bearded man who played the piano and introduced Jay to classical music. But that first winter apart from Alva, it wasn't Doug whom Jay moved in with, but Louis Postel, the man who put out the local poetry magazine, *Provincetown Poets*. Postel, who was straight, had a room available in his house in the East End, a drafty, ramshackle mess with a kerosene stove in the kitchen that stank. But the people who telephoned at all hours or came by to drop off manuscripts more than compensated: poets Mary Oliver, Alan Dugan, and Marge Piercy; Beatnik gadabout Gregory Corso, and painter Candy Jernigan, the magazine's art director who married Philip Glass, the brilliant modernist composer. Alan Bernheimer was another visitor, a tall ascetic Yalie, who knew modern literature inside and out, worked at the local newspaper, and was Louis's coeditor on the poetry magazine. Another visitor was E. J. "Terry" Kahn IV, the son of the *New Yorker* writer E. J. Kahn, who'd spent summers in Truro ever since he was a kid; a recent Harvard grad, Kahn was Bernheimer's boss and editor at the *Advocate*, Ptown's century-old weekly, just as he was involved with the Drop-In Center. He also DJ'd part-time at Piggy's, the hottest dance bar in town. Chris Busa was another of Postel's pals, along with Roger Skillings, the young writing coordinator at the Fine Arts Work Center.

Mainly, there was Lou Postel himself. Jay, with his organizational background, was helping the poetic, often rhapsodic Postel with the development of his magazine, telling him he had to hold meetings, answer his mail, and get his files organized. The relationship was something to behold, a model of symbiosis.

"Jay was just terrific," Postel recalls years later, pointing out that his new roommate rarely joined him and his pals for their nightly disco romps but rather stayed home or spent time with his young son, Russell. This only served to give Jay more stature. For all the brio of the Postel crowd, most of its members were starting to feel they were in some

postmodernist haze, cut off and disconnected, basically on the periphery. For them, Jay was "the adult."

"Culturally, we were very skeptical about any institution," says
Postel. "Jay was a grown man—he had a family, a real job, and people
reported to him as their boss. My friends and I were thinking about the
cultural revolution we were creating by stomping around together to
rock 'n' roll."

Of Jay's difficulties with Alva and his guilt at leaving the marriage,
Postel says, "I didn't quite know what to do with it. I'd certainly known
people in Provincetown who'd experimented. But I didn't know
whether this was something Jay was trying on because he wasn't happy,
or whether it would be something more permanent."

The two also talked about Russell. Once, Postel remembers, when
Jay was buying presents for his son, Postel cautioned him against spoil-
ing the boy. "He said, 'Well, that's okay. So what?' And I thought, God,
how wonderful. You know, he didn't recoil. There was a kind of a joie de
vivre there."

One afternoon Postel came upon his roommate looking at a piece
of abstract art that hung on the wall. "I think it was a repro of a Kline,"
says Postel, "and Jay said, 'What do you see there? I mean, what *is* that?'
I realized that he didn't get it. I said to him, 'You know, Jay, this is about
weight, structure, and blackness.' He nodded but still didn't understand.
'It's about itself, Jay. It doesn't *have* to have any reference.' Jay looked
at me and, you know, all was revealed. That whole spring was a series of
epiphanies, like something had shifted dramatically for him."

Jay's emergence, or what he later called "coming out as an artist," was
like a chick pecking its way out of the eggshell, slow and innocent, and
perhaps it was this same essential innocence or simply the need for companionship that moved Jay to ask Lou to accompany him to his therapy
sessions, the co-counseling that Patti Cozzi had recommended six
months earlier.

"This was the kind of peer therapy where you didn't have to go to
a professional—one person played therapist and the other person was
the patient. It was a 'client-counselor' kind of thing. You kind of held
hands and looked each other in the eye with a lot of trust."

All winter Jay had no trouble balancing his straight and gay friends.
It had never been an issue, really, and in April he moved out of Lou's

place with the announcement that he and Doug were going to live together. "Jay was one of the gentlest, kindest people. I mean, I felt totally comfortable with him," says Postel, but "I thought he needed someone to stand up to him, and I didn't know how he was going to grow with Doug, especially in the art world. I didn't see a lot of passion there either."

Doug and Jay bought a small cottage together. The price was $38,000, and Jay was able to come up with his half-share of the down payment because his parents, "for some reason or another," sent him the money. Going in on the house, he comments today, was "the smartest thing I ever did. . . . I could never be in town now if I hadn't done it."

The move was decisive not only in defining Jay's sexuality but in giving him roots in Provincetown. The property was located in the West End behind Bradford Street, a couple blocks off Shank Painter Road, on a narrow, pothole-filled, dead-end alley called Carnes Lane. There was no sidewalk, no big, shady elms. Most of the surrounding homes were in need of repair, just like Jay and Doug's place. They were occupied by second-generation townies, who, like blue-collar types everywhere, had surrounded their lots with galvanized chain-link fencing. Several of the front yards were filled with piles of weathered lobster traps, and, farther up the block toward Bradford, a motorboat had reached its permanent resting place atop a rusty trailer that jutted out into the street, half blocking the way. The area was old-time Ptown, Portuguese poor and unchic. But as Jay soon found out, the neighbors talked to each other, brought one another fish, and, if you had a problem with the plumbing, someone would pop over, wrench in hand, rather than let you ring up the Meads brothers, who even then didn't come cheap at twenty dollars an hour.

Jay's two-story Cape had an upstairs rental unit and a small outbuilding, which he would eventually use as his office and studio. Both structures needed work, especially the main house, which hadn't been reshingled in over forty years. As he and Doug settled in, Jay became friendly with the neighbors and the neighbors' kids. Even though he was gay and living openly with his partner, there were no problems.

That first summer together, Doug and Jay spent most of their time fixing up the house, but they also managed to give several small outdoor parties, late afternoon soirees attended by their Drop-In Center colleagues and their gregarious neighbors. Jay enjoyed watching the Portuguese fishermen with their sharp eyes rib the longhairs mercilessly, while, at the same time ogling the women guests, many of whom were braless under their T-shirts.

Jay made theater out of serving hors d'oeuvres and pouring cheap California champagne, and afterward he and Doug might stroll downtown to check out the A-House and the Back Room, which generally didn't get going until after eleven. They rarely danced, usually just taking a quick look inside before meandering on down Commercial Street, where they'd run into all kinds of people they knew. When they stopped at some of the galleries, Doug gave the impression that he was tagging along, just not interested. And sex, as Lou Postel had observed, was not a major part of their relationship.

"We might have been lovers for maybe a year. I was still not happy about being gay, and I was not enjoying it," says Jay, whose divorce was finalized in September of 1977.

At home, mainly the two "comforted" each other, as the relationship continued through the winter and into the spring. When the cold weather ended, they took separate bedrooms. Jay started meeting other men. Two years passed, and he found himself growing close to a group of four men from the Midwest: hairdressers Jim Rann and Paul Richards, and Don Sterton and Stephen Clover, who were involved in the arts. Clover had run a gallery in New York and "had a couple of Oldenburgs and Lichtensteins on his wall at home." Sterton had a job at the Art Association. All four had come to town together, and all four would later be diagnosed HIV positive.

Doug left for California late in the summer of 1980 to pursue a graduate degree in family practice at the University of California at Irvine. The split was amicable. In the late eighties Doug Kibler died of AIDS, leaving Jay to buy out his half-share of the Carnes Lane house from Doug's estate, where Critchley lives today.

For the first three years after his separation, Jay had visited his son, Russell, almost daily, and Alva did not interfere. In 1978, however, she married a local fisherman. She also started attending Bible classes at St. Peter's. Originally a Congregationalist, she embraced Catholicism, slowly at first, then more and more intensely. She wanted to bury her past, says Jay, "and it got crazy."

Jay had been through such religious intensity before; his younger brother Mark had joined a cult while still in high school and cut himself off from the family. In the early eighties, Alva, the born-again Catholic, became "fanatical and homophobic." She invented excuses to keep Jay from visiting. She wouldn't let him talk to Russell on the telephone, and, soon, she changed Russell's name; he was no longer a Critchley.

"I was like evil personified, satanic," Jay remembers. "My name couldn't be mentioned in front of Russell."

Jay took his ex-wife to court to claim his rights as Russell's father. Although he didn't have the money to hire a lawyer, Roslyn Garfield, an attorney who had given up a New York college teaching career to live openly in Provincetown as a lesbian, saw that the issues went beyond Jay.

"They were trying to pillory him for being gay," Garfield says. "The court made a long, drawn-out investigation into Jay's 'lifestyle' to determine his eligibility as a father. Social workers were sent to check his house. There were questionnaires and demeaning interviews. Jay's not the neatest housekeeper, you know," she adds, smiling, "and even that became an issue."

The litigation, which began in 1983, stretched on for more than two years, and during that time Alva and her husband moved first to Wellfleet, then off-Cape entirely to Wareham. While the court deliberated, Jay tried to keep his relations with his son alive with presents. When he brought Russell a plant for his birthday, "so he could watch it grow," Alva was angry that he hadn't sent socks and underwear instead.

"It was a very long, painful process, and basically all that was accomplished was to cause more trauma for Russell. In court one of the principal things she objected to was that I *danced* with Russell, and that I'd brought him flowers. These were like 'unacceptable forms of behavior' for a male father. Also, my art. I'd started doing performance pieces by then, and she brought up that I was trouncing around in a lobster-claw helmet—this was an indication of how crazy I was."

After the divorce, Jay's mother, in Connecticut, had often asked what was happening, gloating over how she'd foreseen the breakup years before. After she kept asking when he was going to remarry, Jay realized he was going to have to tell his mother her prize son was gay.

Their confrontation took place over lunch at the Red Inn at the West End, one of Ptown's nicer waterside restaurants. Mrs. Critchley had driven up from Connecticut with KC, Jay's developmentally disabled sister. Jay's father had died the year before. Their table looked out across the bay toward Long Point Lighthouse, where, in later years, swimmers would launch themselves into the water at Jay's annual Swim for Life AIDS fundraiser.

"Mother," he said, "I'm gay."

"That's disgusting," she snapped back, rising from the table. "You know, I can't believe you're doing this. This is not how you were raised."

"Well, this is who I am, and I'm trying to make sense out of it," he said.

It was 1980 and Mrs. Critchley would not set foot in town for fifteen years. Provincetown had become "the Evil Empire."

Critchley, whose emergence as a gay man was far less flamboyant than it is for many men who come out in Provincetown, continued working at the Drop-in Center. Ironically, it was at the Center that the question of whether someone was gay or straight began to become an issue.

The Center was trying to economize, and it struck a number of staffers that it was the straight employees, not the gay ones, who were being let go. When the clinic hired a new senior physician, Walter Richter, he quit in protest, or was fired, after only two months on the job. The Center, Richter claimed, had misrepresented itself both to him and to the town by not admitting that it was "an arm of Provincetown's gay community."

"I have serious concerns about the openness and decadence of Provincetown," the outraged Richter told the *Advocate*, explaining he'd been "horrified" to discover that the Center was listed in the Gay Yellow Pages, a nationwide directory of male-only service organizations.

There had definitely been a change at the Drop-In Center. In 1971 it was the happy-go-lucky free hippie clinic, mostly straight, but now, almost ten years later, it showed signs of having absorbed the gay summer population that, more and more, was coming to Provincetown.

Jay, meanwhile, continued to struggle to raise desperately needed funds from any and all outside sources, putting in ten- and twelve-hour days. He had been made the clinic's executive director at a time when the organization was facing bankruptcy, and his life revolved around the Center.

Things got worse, and by 1979 there was no hiding from the fact that the clinic was in serious trouble. Dick Pasonovitch, the chief administrator, was ill and hospitalized, and died shortly thereafter. More layoffs fueled the straight-gay infighting. But what really doomed the place was the decision to apply for a state license that would qualify the Drop-In Center for public grant monies.

This entailed significant renovations, like wheelchair access ramps, handrails, and other facilities for the handicapped. The board began the work, using what little cash they had. Then they realized that left no money to pay debts. The work was halted. Chaos ensued. Jay, Patti Cozzi, and Dr. Frank Zampiello, a recent addition to the clinic, went before the town manager for emergency funding. They went to private foundations and community-minded businessmen, like Patti's husband, Ciro, and John Yingling of Spiritus Pizza/Cafe Edwige. They even went to Stan Sorrentino. The little money they were able to raise went to cover bounced checks. There was nothing left to continue the renovations. It was "like trying to plug the dike," Jay says. Despite everyone's best efforts and the support of the *Advocate* under Terry Kahn, on January 11, 1980, Jay Critchley's birthday, the Drop-In Center, which had so embodied an era, was forced to close its doors.

Jay got a ride down to New York where he sat around his sister's Greenwich Village apartment for several weeks straight, reading detective novels. He had no idea what he was going to do.

When he returned to the Cape, like so many others, he went on unemployment and signed up for food stamps. As the weather began to break in April, he interviewed for a waiter's job at the Moors, the seasonal fishnet-and-driftwood-style restaurant at the West End, known for its lobsters, gimlets, and gay afternoon sing-alongs. Waiting tables, he figured, would get him through. He was right. The Moors, combined with renting the upstairs apartment on Carnes Lane, would sustain him in his new life as an artist for the next fourteen years.

In May of that year, urged on by his friend Stephen Clover, Jay had his first show at the Cafe Edwige. "All the pieces I'd done were sand-encrusted fruits, plates, cups, all kinds of crockery. I used different-colored sand that I'd collected and glued to these objects," Jay explains. Stephen suggested Jay find shelves and arrange them as still lifes. "He knew how to present things, which was something I'd never thought of," says Jay. "Doug had always been a little embarrassed by my sand-covered objects, like he'd thought them silly."

The work itself was an obvious throwback to the *Kinderspiel* of Jay's youth and called to mind the flotsam and jetsam he'd collected on Uncle Cliff's island. But whether Critchley really needed instruction in presentation is unlikely. Two months after the Cafe Edwige exhibit he managed to put himself on the map with "Just Visiting for the Week-end"—an old 1968 Dodge Coronet station wagon that, like his apples and coffeepots, was encrusted in sand.

But there was more. Crucial to the work's meaning was where it was displayed. Initially, the idea was to put the car in the median strip of Route 6, the four-lane highway leading in and out of town, as a "welcome offering" to summer tourists throughout the high season. When the State Highway Department nixed this, Jay, making sure he had all the neces-sary permits, parked the sand-covered wreck in the town parking lot at the foot of MacMillan Pier. MacMillan Pier was, and still is, the epicen-ter of Provincetown's tourism. With the car parked at the very front of the parking lot, it overlooked Lopes Square with its hot dog stands, whale-watch ticket booths, and the Chamber of Commerce building. Almost at once the crowds began to form. Big crowds. Passersby were befuddled and intrigued. People went out of their way to scratch the sand off the car's windows to see what was inside. Others took Polaroids. Articles appeared in the *Advocate* and the *Cape Cod Times*, speculating on what the sand-covered vehicle might mean.

Soon, with all the traffic jams, the town manager, who was a decent enough fellow but hardly Bernard Berenson, ordered the car removed. When he found there was no legal basis for this, he turned to Chief of Police Meads, who, uncharacteristically, pleaded, wheedled, and all but begged Critchley to take the vehicle off the pier. Critchley refused. Townspeople, many of them independent-minded Portuguese and lovers of the underdog, lent their support with letters to the local newspaper. Jay had already gone to his friend, attorney Roslyn Garfield, anticipating that the car was going to be "Texas-booted," and, soon, when Meads ran out of patience, Garfield was ready to swing into action. At the next selectmen's meeting, Town Hall was packed as she spoke of civil liberties and artistic expression. She reminded the town fathers that no laws had been broken, that the car was properly registered, and that this lone unshaven man was only standing up for what he believed in, and doing so in a way that was typically "Ptown." The argument was successful. The car was a symbol of the small guy. In its humor and camp, it was the work of a populist hero—and so it remained on the pier throughout the summer until that Thanksgiving, when Jay finally took it back to Carnes Lane for what he announced was its "annual oil change."

That was Critchley's first major piece. He was thirty-six years old and, whether or not he was completely clear about it, he'd found a direction. In 1982 the car was back in the same parking place with the addition of a sand-covered "Sand Family"—namely, figures of Ron and Nancy Reagan sitting complacently inside. The next year the piece was retitled "Just Visiting for the Weekend, 1983—A Fulfilling Visit," and now it had no sand on its exterior but the inside was filled with sand, as well as with seaweed, shells, plastic beer can holders, tampon applicators, and other standard beach debris. The crowds began to form as soon as the piece was put in place, and, as before, people asked, "What does it mean?"

Only now they also added, gleefully, "Wow, this Critchley's some kind of nut!" The name was out there and Critchley found he liked it that way.

Already a major undercurrent in the artist's work was the way he was confronting authority by deploying the establishment's language and symbols only to undermine them through the force of sheer absurdity. After all, if Provincetown was a tourist mecca willing to cater to vulgarity in exchange for dollars, why hide the fact? Why not flaunt it? The deconstruction process was elemental, and it is interesting to note that Critchley, like Warhol, was fascinated with advertising when he was a child—on one occasion, at the age of nine, he dressed up as a packet of Marlboro cigarettes, having spent many painstaking hours constructing this costume. Today, he uses many of the same techniques of advertising, though his ontology remains in direct opposition to the hypercapitalism that is his major target.

In 1983 he broadened his scope, meeting with the townspeople of Hadley, Massachusetts, to propose turning their defunct local Mountain Farms shopping mall into a museum of "modern archaeology"—that is, a symbol of what can happen in American culture "when people become so overrun by the freedom and mobility of the automobile that no thought [goes] into building malls, just exhilaration."

Not surprisingly, the townspeople greeted his proposal to encrust their shopping center under a layer of landfill with skepticism. But Critchley was not discouraged. He was back several months later with a modified scheme—to turn the mall into a National Historic Site to be listed in the National Register. The Mountain Farms Mall, he now asserted, was "a religious property." Shopping malls were "cultural temples," their rise in the sixties and seventies paralleled by "the decline in attendance at churches." When he tried to contact the developer, who was investing millions of dollars to rehabilitate the mall, his calls went unanswered.

That same year, he also founded Nuclear Recycling Consultants (NRC), a tongue-in-cheek consulting firm that he used as a platform to critique the nuclear power industry. With a number of nuclear plants reaching mothball age, and national awareness of the danger of nuclear energy at an all-time high, the NRC selected the controversial Three Mile Island for its first "conversion site." His plan called for commercial and residential development, "a unique mix" of living, working, shopping, and recreation facilities that included "The Meltdown Mall," made up of a wide variety of retail shops; a "Radiation Restaurant," "Cooling Tower Cabaret," "The BTU Bar," and, finally, the "Too Cheap to Meter Museum and Gallery," a hands-on educational look at the political and cultural dynamics of the nuclear age and its heritage.

Not content to leave well enough alone, with photographer Kathy Chapman he installed a billboard over Boston's Park Square that read "Live Free or Die, the National Nuclear Monument and Energy Research Institute at Seabrook." Elsewhere, in press releases, Critchley explained, "We have the opportunity to turn this boondoggle into a showcase for alternative energy development for New England and the whole country. It's about time the nation made such a commitment."

For his next NRC project, "Nuclear Resort Community at Seabrook," he was invited to speak at a luncheon for New Hampshire business leaders and interested investors. Evidently, his delivery took the day. Jay's picture appeared in a number of Boston–New Hampshire area newspapers, and on one TV show he was challenged by a local resident, asking if the artist was "seeing a psychiatrist." Imperturbable as ever, Critchley responded that he had indeed been in therapy to free his mind "for creative thinking."

Already it was apparent that his skills went beyond the conceptual. The *Boston Globe, Boston Magazine, Philadelphia Enquirer,* the *News-Journal* of Wilmington, Delaware, the *Boston Herald American,* and *Boston Phoenix,* as well the *Cape Cod Times,* the *Provincetown Advocate, Gay Community News,* and *ArtXpress* had, by now, all run features attesting to Critchley's flair for publicity and his use of the media as an integral element of his work. *Art New England* wrote:

"No other artist, except perhaps Christo or Warhol, can manipulate mainstream mass media with the panache of Critchley, who . . . has made the decision . . . to work both within and outside the art-world system in response to larger personal, social, cultural and political concerns of our era. Whether [his] proposals ever come to fruition . . . Critchley is expanding the way we understand art and the role of the artist. . . ."

Back in Provincetown after the NRC proposal, Jay, who seemed little short of schizoid in his ability to sustain multiple personalities, not to mention simultaneous work projects, turned his attention to the Center for Coastal Studies, the now world-famous marine biology and whale-care group, formed in 1975 by local Provincetown Ph.D. scientists Barbara and Stormy Mayo, and geologist Graham Giese. There, to further his knowledge of the Cape, he took courses in marine biology and coastal geology, just as he also spent hours walking the back beaches, digging in the bay flats at low tide, and wandering the dunes where his agitprop predecessor Harry "Poet of the Dunes" Kemp had lived from the early twenties until his death in 1960. Often Jay returned from these trips lugging bags of his prized sand, hunks of driftwood, bits of barnacle-encrusted metal, and bouquets of dried seaweed, all to be used in various assemblages.

This was, of course, the other side of Critchley, the more meditative or contemplative half of his being, yet even the Cape's sublime beauty couldn't blot out his problems with Alva. After stripping Russell of the name he'd been born with, she now made it all but impossible for Jay to exercise his court-granted visiting rights. This left him no alternative but to take her to court. He also started keeping a diary, a day-by-day account of the bitter visitation-rights fight that he thought he'd have to someday share with Russell to explain everything that was happening; it was a simple enough document, no more than a list of events, times, phone calls, and bits of dialogue, but he thought this would suffice. Most of all he wanted his son to know his own history, and Jay knew that when the time came he'd feel inadequate to explain it in his own voice. His guilt, he realized, went beyond anything that was normal for a parent who leaves a marriage. He was gay. His separation from Russell was the result of his refusal to lie about who he was or to "change." There were the difficulties created by Alva, of course, but whatever he might say or do couldn't alter the fact that there were moments when he told himself that what he'd done was to choose himself over others.

With his depression mounting, Jay jumped back into therapy in a way that made his past involvement look piddling. Not only was he doing two and sometimes three sessions weekly, he was reading, taking notes, talking about his counseling constantly. It was like he couldn't help himself. Things were strangely exciting. Everything was also bigger, more oppressive than in the past.

"I was crying and shaking and yawning, discharging pain," he recalls, and although there was no way he could know it, he was going to remain in therapy for the next five years. The particular type of counseling he was involved with was the same as he'd dragged Postel into—based on a role-reversal model where the two participants split the two-hour session, each taking the role of counselor to the other's client. For Jay especially, it was a way of getting outside himself. His parochial-school-bred stoicism often got in the way, but through the role-reversal process, he was making progress. After doing workshops in Boston, Vermont, and New Hampshire, he even began teaching the method in Province-town, assuming the role of mentor. If there are some artists who lie awake at night worrying about spreading themselves too thin, or getting diverted from their chosen career path, Jay was not one of them. He was doing what he had to.

By 1991 Jay had lost both Doug Kibler and Stephen Clover, the friend who'd pushed him to "come out" as an artist. He'd also established him-. self as a force in the year-round community.

Since the original "Just Visiting for the Weekend" sand car in 1981, he'd created a substantial and provocative body of work.

In 1990, at the height of the AIDS scourge, he founded the Old Glory Condom Corporation, which sought to encourage "safer sex" by marketing a line of red-white-and-blue prophylactics blessed with the design of the American flag. To promote the product, he had his product marketed nationally, as well as at numerous boutiques throughout Provincetown's downtown shopping area, where the Old Glory iconography drew huge and sustained laughs of appreciation. It so enraged the U.S. Patent Office, however, that the government refused to grant a trademark license, stating that it was "immoral and scandalous to associate the flag and sex." This was the first time, it turned out, that a stars-and-stripes design—used to hawk more than a thousand trademark products, from bathing suits to place mats—had ever been rejected as politically offensive; in response, Critchley made himself available to reporters from the *Wall Street Journal*, the *Washington Post*, the *New York Times*, and other national publications, as well as to the TV networks, and, nothing if not media-savvy, finessed a two-page feature in *People* magazine. The Center for Constitutional Rights in New York City, the legal team that won the landmark 1989 *Texas* v. *Johnson* flag-burning case before the Supreme Court, came aboard and appealed to the Trademark Office appellate board, which, after three years of deliberation, reversed the earlier decision, citing Critchley's "seriousness of purpose."

But no sooner had Critchley taken on the U.S. Commerce Department than his condom logo raised hackles at MIT's List Visual Arts Center, where it was part of an exhibit entitled "Trouble in Paradise." The show, which included the work of fourteen New England artists, made political and social commentaries about censorship, AIDS, homelessness, domestic violence, and drug abuse, but only Jay's piece caused trouble when Senator Jesse Helms of North Carolina threatened to close the exhibit by withdrawing its NEA funding. The resulting publicity, both in the Boston area and nationally, was considerable: Critch-ley's logo featured a twelve-by-nine-foot condom-shaped American flag surrounded by the motto "Worn with pride, countrywide." Jay milked it for all it was worth.

"Helms is great for art," he announced to the press after Helms was televised by CNN holding up an Old Glory logo in the Senate. "He draws attention to works that were created to draw attention. Helms is a moon-light art dealer and a part-time senator."

The MIT display had also featured a letter the artist had written to President George Bush, in which he urged Bush to consider the war on AIDS no less important than the war on drugs, the moon mission, or the Star Wars defense system. Helms, who had the reputation of a right-wing attack dog, backed off after the *Los Angeles Times* called his campaign "an intimidation focused on cutting-edge organizations that specialize in provocative artworks." The University of Maryland, the Hartford Atheneum, and the San Francisco Art Institute all displayed Critchley's piece when the MIT exhibition finally closed on its own.

In 1993 Jay became a massage therapist, which allowed him to quit the Moors, where he'd been waiting tables every summer for the past four-teen years. Now, literally in a hands-on manner, he began to treat peo-ple with AIDS, many of whom could not get out of bed.

"I was taking my table into their homes," Jay recalls, "and I think there were three particular clients I was seeing regularly who all died. I mean, generally, when someone is that sick . . . that's the thing about the AIDS support apparatus in Provincetown. It's a real buddy system. There's a constant stream of people in and out of sick peoples' houses, bringing meals, checking in. I was just one of many," he adds. "The AIDS support group pays twenty-five dollars for a session and the client paid five dollars. Depending upon how much money is available, there can be one to four sessions a month and it can include acupuncture, massage, and nutrition."

Though the ravages of the disease had hit Provincetown hardest dur-ing the eighties, by the mid- and late nineties gay men were still dying in significant numbers. During the first weeks of 1999, for example, the Provincetown AIDS Support Group lost ten clients. From February 2000 through April, there was one death a month, and during the two-and-a-half-week period from July 12 to July 30, three more men died. No one wanted to make comparisons with the horror years, no one had to. One thing to be said for the *Banner*, whenever there was another death in town the paper usually didn't shy away from telling you why.

Though Jay had often had someone who shared his house, he had only on occasion lived with a partner since Doug's departure in 1980. He wasn't unhappy or lonely. He was constantly busy—or "occupied," as he put it—making his constructions and other artworks, holding and attending meetings, reading, writing his broadsides, traveling, and giving talks.

And also, surprisingly, there was his family. He'd started talking with his mother again, and often, when he'd drive to New York, he stopped to see her in Forestville. His sister Eileen and her husband were living in Harwich, only thirty-five miles away, and he'd grown close to their daughter, Jessica Diamond, a college student who'd recently come out and had turned to Jay for support.

And then there was Russell.

In 1988, when his son was thirteen, Jay had decided to tell him he was gay. They were eating at McDonald's, and as Jay tried to explain, Russell shook his head in disbelief. This only added to the strain in their relationship.

In 1997 Jay got a phone call. Russell had been going to college part-time, struggling with a fledgling landscape business, and living with his girlfriend, Tanya. To save money, they were living with Alva and her husband. Now he needed someone "to talk to." Jay describes it as "one of the best moments of my life."

After that first visit, there was a series of dinners, long walks, and cross-country ski outings in the National Seashore. "I was helping him with some college papers," says Jay, "and helping him to buy a car. He ended up coming to my house a few times—he hadn't been there since he was five—and that was how we started to be close friends."

For the entire family, Russell's wedding on November 3, 2001, was an occasion for healing. Although chilly, the day was bright and sunny. One hundred and forty guests gathered in Buzzard's Bay for the reception. Russell and Tanya had a son, Russell Jr., who was two and a half years old, and he was there dressed in a tiny tuxedo. Two of Jay's sis-

ters, Eileen and Cece, had come up for the wedding. But more surprising, so had Jay's mother. It wasn't a Catholic ceremony, and, originally,
she had declined to attend.

For Jay, as for many gay men, family is not always a good thing.
Although some do support their gay offspring, many others are harsh
judges of the errant child. Jay found it "miraculous," the way so many
people who had been at war came together to forgive. Everyone danced;
everyone talked to everyone else—Jay to Alva; Alva to the eighty-six-
year-old Mrs. Critchley; Mrs. Critchley to Alva's parents, and to Jay, and
most of all to the bridegroom, the grandson she hadn't seen in twenty-
three years.

She was almost in tears. Jay was, too. "I always had this fantasy that
my mother would see Russell and her great-grandson in her lifetime," he
says, "and I think her decision to attend was courageous.

"For twenty-three years Russell was completely isolated from my
family, and now we've become reconnected," he says. "And not just me
and Russell, but all of us."

CHAPTER 22

P.RESERVATION

Regina Binder graduated from Vassar in 1983 with an art history degree. No one rushed to hire her, so for a while she worked for her father, dealing with suburban housewives and their complaints about misscheduled piano tuning appointments. It being the eighties, when she decided to change, she went to Wall Street and, for six years, worked for a private investment bank, wore Bonwit Teller business suits, and concealed her sexual identity. When she'd had enough, she enrolled in Columbia's Graduate School of Architecture to get a master's in historical preservation, conservation, and planning.

It was her master's thesis that brought her back to Provincetown in 1989. At the suggestion of her faculty adviser, she chose as her subject the dune shacks that dot the back shore of Cape Cod from Race Point to the Truro line. Most date from the thirties and forties, when they were slapped together from driftwood and the timbers of wrecked ships by beachcombers, fishermen, and artists, all claiming squatters' rights on what was then town lands, disused, outlying parcels belonging to Provincetown, Truro, Wellfleet, and Eastham. Few individuals had bothered to file deeds, or even thought to do so, until the federal government created the Cape Cod National Seashore in 1961, partitioning all the Cape's ocean shore from Chatham to Race Point, and, in effect, creating a federal protectorate. By then it was too late.

Ptown had given up its land to the National Parks Service to keep it as it was and avoid Atlantic City–type development, but no sooner had the new director, a bureaucrat unfamiliar with the Outer Cape, taken office than it became evident that the federals planned to destroy the dune shacks.

A number of locals, led by Hazel Hawthorne, a descendant of the painter Charles Hawthorne and one of the last of the old-time local bohemians, rose up to protest. Many of the shacks had been occupied by some of the best-known artists in America: Edmund Wilson, Eugene O'Neill, Willem de Kooning, and Jackson Pollock had all lived and worked in them, and the shacks, many consisting of nothing more than a bunk bed, a writing palette, and a sand floor, were living records of Provincetown's unique history as an arts colony. Jack Kerouac, responding to Hawthorne's solicitation of support, said that he had used them while rewriting *On the Road* in the summer of 1950, and he called them "uniquely sheltering."

Although Park officials refused to commit to any long-range policy during the sixties, seventies, and early eighties, they allowed the shacks to remain. Their policy, at the time, favored the protection of natural resources over cultural ones. Binder, who arrived on the scene in 1989, spent the next year wandering the dunes, talking to people and haunting Cape archives. Her thesis, which was accepted by Columbia in 1990, proved to be not only a historical exegesis but a management plan that she distributed to the Cape Cod Commission, the Provincetown Historical Commission, and the National Parks Service. What she proposed, in addition to the preservation of the nineteen remaining dune shacks that fit no federal listing criteria, was a fellowship program where the dwellings would once again be used by artists for the production of art, as well as the preservation of Provincetown's legacy. Painters and poets would be allowed to live in the sublimely primordial surroundings of the back-shore dunes, in exchange for lecturing on their work and the environment to students and other visitors. Meanwhile, the shacks would be maintained by an interested group of Ptowners or their previous owners, thus sparing the Parks Service their upkeep.

In 1993 Ginny continued to push her agenda by teaming up with Jay Critchley to organize the so-called C-Scape Mapping Project, a scaled-down version of the original plan. In order to receive monies to fund the project, she needed a 501(c)3, a nonprofit framework, and

Critchley had already set up such an umbrella group with his Community Compact.

Critchley had always been interested in the dune shacks. "Michael Sperber, a psychologist-consultant at the Drop-In Center, let me use the one he had a lease on in the seventies. I used to go out in the middle of the winter, sometimes even in the middle of a snowstorm.

"The idea for the C-Scape Shack came when the Seashore put out a public request for proposals to manage the shack after its last occupant died. It was the westernmost shack, originally on the barrier dune, but it had been moved back in 1978, so it wouldn't tumble into the sea. You can't see it from the beach. It's very private. Anyway, they were soliciting public organizations and I don't know exactly who suggested it, Tom Boland or me, but the idea was we should bring Ginny in and put a team together. We figured we needed to demonstrate the shack's historical integrity. That's what Ginny did.

"Prior to this I hadn't had much contact with Ginny. I knew who her mother was because of the whole Pied Piper connection. I thought it was kind of unusual; I mean, she and her twin were both gay, which is something that fascinates me. I know people in Provincetown who come from families where *everyone* is gay—three, four, five people. One of my roommates actually has three lesbian sisters.

"I remember the first time we went to see C-Scape, the four of us walked from the visitors' center. Ginny was kind of dressed up, and we were going through the brambles and everything, and she wasn't at home there. But I liked her attitude. She has a very whimsical attitude. There's always something underlying that's humorous.

"Eventually we got a lease—five years, with a one-and-a-half-year extension. The Parks Service had been trying to come up with a plan for all eighteen shacks. The big question was, after everyone dies, how will these shacks be maintained? The Parks Service has in mind a couple of artists' shacks, a couple of community shacks, and then they want to actually do private bed-and-breakfasts out there. They haven't made any decision about this, but I'm concerned about it. Ginny continues to have a role in the Compact as a consultant. I bounce ideas off her. She's very supportive."

Ginny, who had come back to Provincetown "to get myself together" after breaking up with Kathleen, had never seen it as either a political arena or a haven for artists. Her degree in preservation now allowed her to see the town as a unique opportunity to explore the issues most fundamental to her as a preservationist, namely, community preservation. Before Binder could really get involved, though, she was hired by an Italian conservation firm and spent nearly a year in Rome, restoring monuments.

To get back to Provincetown, Binder was hired as curator on the pirate ship *Whydah* project. Toiling alongside strapping divers, both onshore and aboard the project launch, she deconcreted encrusted cannon, pieces of eight, and other artifacts brought up from the eighteenth-century pirate wreck off Wellfleet's back shore, in order to show that the sunken galleon had been helmed by the famous rogue Captain Bellamy, one of many seventeenth- and eighteenth-century buccaneers drawn to the Outer Cape. At the time of Binder's involvement, the *Whydah* was the only pirate ship to have ever been authenticated.

Since the Parks Service had put bulldozing the shacks on hold, Ginny, who had gotten herself appointed to the local Historical Commission, moved on to what she saw as Provincetown's greatest problem: the spread of condos.

Few people outside of Ginny and developer Nicky Wells had noticed what was happening, but by the mid-nineties, almost all of Provincetown's freestanding artist's studios had been gobbled up and more and more of the town's 150- to 200-year-old structures, the sparse, aesthetically pure Capes and saltboxes along Commercial Street, had been developed—that is, bastardized—for summer apartments and shopfronts. There were no growth bylaws in place, which was not too surprising in a town that had no zoning regulations of any kind until 1978. The developers, local Portuguese as well as outsiders, gave off the nascent stench of greed that was at one with a total disregard for the impact of development on the community as a whole.

Binder began a campaign to limit growth by encouraging Provincetown to create a local historic district. In 1994 she also founded the Outer Cape's first preservation firm, Binder Boland & Associates, with preservationist Tom Boland and her good friend Rita Speicher, a writer who'd come to town in the early eighties.

"Incredibly, Provincetown was the only town on the lower Cape that had no historic district," she recalls. "Therefore, the town's control over its historic environment, as well as its cultural resources, was in the hands of county agents.

"We did preservation, conservation, and planning, and helped people to go through the regulatory process—to get their permits for their alterations, septics, and so forth. We also helped them to reconfigure their house according to their needs and in a sensitive way—sensitive to the history of the town and the preservation of the architecture."

She was more aware than ever of the real estate boom, a phenomenon she refers to as "I came, I saw, I bought." New homeowners with no stake in the history of the town and its people were gobbling up properties, in many cases with the intention of reselling them.

"It's amazing when you talk about poverty in Provincetown. We have the lowest median income in the whole state," says Ginny, "yet we have the highest property values. Many of the people who own houses don't work here; soon the only people who'll own property are people who make a living elsewhere."

Her years on Wall Street taught Ginny how money works, that power rarely flows down, and, in addition to meeting all the important people in town, she has learned the ins and outs of town government.

Ptown was incorporated in 1727, and since then it has been run according to a state-mandated charter rooted in a highly participatory democratic model. Once, and sometimes twice, a year there is the all-important Town Meeting. Two months prior to the meeting, any registered Provincetown voter can submit a petition to get an article put in the warrant, which is essentially the agenda for the upcoming meeting. They need only ten other signatures. The five elected selectmen then arrange the articles and write out the warrant. The warrant is closed thirty days before the meeting, and articles are discussed by the relevant town boards to formulate opinions that they'll put forth at the meeting. The warrant is, of course, published in the local newspaper, and notices are posted around town. When this phase is over, the town is ready to have its meeting.

Provincetown Town Hall is a building steeped in history. Paintings by Charles Hawthorne, E. Ambrose Webster, George Elmer Browne, and other local masters line the walls, and the burnished wood paneling has the patina of antiquity. There is something endearingly well-used and run-down about the interior. If one walks up the stairs outside, through the heavy wooden doors into the building and down a short wide hall-way, one arrives at the large auditorium where the Town Meetings take place. A small stage sits at the front with old velvet curtains pulled demurely to the side. Ornate moldings surround the high Palladian win-dows. Across the wide, expansive floor, arranged in carefully aligned rows in three sections and bisected by two aisles, sit hundreds of folding wooden chairs, dating back to the late 1940s.

Most Americans, existing in a political environment where less than fifty percent of the citizens vote in presidential elections, may have difficulty comprehending the level of community participation in Provincetown's Town Meetings. A Town Meeting lasts for a week to ten days, from seven-thirty P.M. until the point when exhaustion sets in—around eleven-thirty or midnight. Fridays are set aside for celebrations of democracy at the local bars. Between 500 and 750 people attend every night for the entire week and a half. Citizens sit in their regular seats year after year; newcomers tend to hover in the back. Those not registered to vote and out-of-towners are consigned to the gracefully curved second-floor balcony that encircles three sides of the Victorian hall.

The inhabitants of Provincetown are an impassioned and articulate people. Town clerk Stephan Nofield describes opening night: "People come a half hour early. They're excited, they love the system. It's empowering. Anyone can submit an article on virtually any topic. . . ." On the first night, many arrive early to secure their seats. Almost everyone congregates outside to talk with friends and neighbors, to clarify issues, to sway a vote or two, to argue. When it's time, the participants file in and each voter is given a numbered badge at the door to the auditorium, while nonvoters are turned away to climb the stairs to the balcony. And then article by article, the moderator begins to go through the warrant. Debates go back and forth, and most everyone has an opinion so that there are lines of waiting speakers at the two floor mikes. Some articles deal with lofty proposals to make Provincetown a nuclear-free zone; oth-ers are concerned with the more mundane but very important town san-itary system. The town Finance Committee weighs in whenever any expenditure is involved, and then, at the end of the discussion, the select-men make their opinions known. Finally, the article goes to the floor for a vote. And so it goes, night after night. The whole thing is refreshingly direct. The palaver from the floor can sometimes be messy, tedious, stupidly self-righteous, heated, often personal and rancorous, and sometimes a little alcoholic, but that is the nature of Ptown democracy.

What makes the process so exceptional is that it's not mediated. The five elected selectmen are not "representatives." Each is elected to a three-year term. The people represent *themselves* at Town Meeting and partake in a hallowed democratic tradition that traces its roots back to a document written by a group of struggling, freezing Pilgrims in Provincetown Harbor, a stone's throw from the present Town Hall. Of course the demographics of these modern Town Meetings would be utterly alien to the Pilgrims: The gay and lesbian citizenry come out in such force nowadays as to far outnumber the older Portuguese families and smattering of leftover Yankees. The late eighties was the time of the greatest schism between the gays and the straights in town—and now, according to Nofield, the divisions occur along socioeconomic lines. The monied interests want development, while other residents are more concerned with affordable housing and inclusivity.

No discussion of Ptown governance would be complete without a discussion of the myriad committees. More than 175 citizens serve on the 40 or so boards and commissions that manage everything from the Colonial cemetery to the financial affairs of a $10 million municipal corporation. For a town of only 3,500 people, this is a remarkable number of committees. Many think there are too many, and that it's all a bit self-indulgent. According to some sources, this is the arena where the gays have really consolidated their power in the last fifteen years—particularly with the zoning committee, which decides who gets to build what.

As demographics change, and the minority becomes the majority, it is natural that this would be reflected in the composition of Town Hall. And if truth be told, there are those who think the last ten years of town government have been the most competent Ptown has ever seen. In the year 2000, there were 2,832 registered voters out of a total population of 3,561. Of these, 48.8 percent (1,382) were registered Democrats; 5.7 percent (162), registered Republicans; and 45.5 percent (1,288), not surprisingly, remain independents.

Provincetown has seven regulatory boards that rule on matters of private property—the Planning Board, Board of Health, Zoning Board of Appeals, Conservation Commission, and so forth. To get a building permit, it is necessary to go before each group, submit evidence, plead your case, and hope for the best from the people making up these volunteer boards. Sometimes the application process will stretch out over several meetings and cover several months. Ginny, as part of her job, learned who controlled each board, as well as all the best strategies for working them.

She also got to know all the local electricians, plumbers, and contractors, as well as the lawyers, bankers, and real estate agents. And even though she stands only five feet three, she made her presence known at board meetings where, as a rule, she was able to charm the gruffest Portuguese and most misogynistic gays with her disarmingly tentative questions.

Yet with all her newfound expertise and connections, Binder has never been able to buy a home of her own in town. "I came, I saw, I bought nothing. I own nothing," she says. "I have tried to buy a house here for so many years, and it just keeps ratcheting out of my reach. My sister bought her house at 98 Commercial Street when she was young, when there was absolutely nothing across the street on the water—can you imagine that now? An empty lot on the beach? But I was too busy then, pursuing my education. Real smart, huh?"

Binder would love to own the house she now rents, a cottage on the waterside, just 425 square feet with one small bedroom upstairs, a single bath below. Not for nothing is the cottage called "Little Pilgrim." She was recently told by a Realtor that it would list for around $300,000, or more than $700 per square foot.

It took a while, but within a year or two word was out: Ginny Binder was more than the visiting expert. She might be tiny and Ivy League, and also gay, but none of that mattered; she was a "ballbuster," as the Portuguese say. Binder Boland got contracts from Town Hall. The firm also won commissions abroad to build the British National Mountaineering Museum in England's Lake District, oversee restoration work on castles in Luxembourg and Belgium, and, through John Sunderland, a renowned museum and exhibition designer from north Yorkshire with a specialty in multimedia, whom Ginny had met while on the *Whydah* project, the firm branched out into production of Sunderland's designs. Closer to home, Binder Boland was commissioned to restore Nantucket's historic eighteenth-century Methodist church.

In 1998, only four years after opening its doors for business, the firm snagged two major contracts in Provincetown: the Schoolhouse Center for the Arts, a multimillion-dollar complex consisting of three exhibition galleries, a mini-concert hall, and open studio space; and, on an even bigger scale, the downtown open-air bazaar known as Whaler's Wharf, which, more than anything they'd done so far, was destined to make Binder Boland a force to be reckoned with.

Smack in the center of town, Whaler's Wharf was a historic building, initially the town's sole movie theater. Later it housed a hodgepodge of artists, craftsmen, eccentrics, and hippies, who saw themselves as Ptown's answer to Calcutta's street market. Well into the mid-nineties, when many businesses of the same scope and size had disappeared, the colorful owner of the building, Dale Elmer, held the lid on rents until a raging fire on February 10, 1998, ripped through the building and the adjacent Crown & Anchor, leaving the town with a gaping hole in its center. Special Town Meetings were held, with complaints and demands from every abutter regarding the size and scope of possible renovations, and in August of 1998, Binder Boland was hired to develop a plan that incorporated what Whaler's Wharf had always been: a downtown location meant for locals, not just in tangible terms but collectively, socially. How could that sensibility be re-created in today's economic environment? the architects asked themselves. One design objective they soon came up with was an open public space with a walkway to the water, basically a common area with benches and a large vaulted rotunda. When Elmer was financially unable to follow through, he sold the plan, which had already been approved by the town's regulatory boards, to new developers.

Ginny says that despite a lawsuit from one of the abutters, Whaler's Wharf went through because "we actually read the rules and followed them. We decided that the best way to build was to see what every board and every state agency wanted out of a vacant lot in the center of town, then to follow those rules and build as conscientiously as possible."

The building emerged as a model of community awareness: Located in the downtown, high-rent district, the top floor is reserved for artists' studios that rent for $250 a month, some fifteen of them. Such rents are unheard of in today's Provincetown. Next door, the newly renovated Crown & Anchor advertises itself as the swankiest gay resort on the East

Coast. Every summer weekend the historic Back Room, now renamed the Paramount Ballroom, is filled beyond capacity with testosterone-driven circuit boys, most from out of town, doing Ecstasy at fifteen to twenty dollars a pop.

Although the debate continues, Whaler's Wharf is a commercial enterprise designed to both make money and fill a role as a "community resource." At a time when small shopfronts within a block or two of the town pier rent for close to four hundred dollars per square foot (on a par with New York's Madison Avenue, which has the most expensive shop rentals in the world), a long-term lease at Whaler's Wharf offers a real alternative for local businesses.

"It's a bizarre notion," says Binder, "but Provincetown could actually be pricing itself out of existence. There could come a time when no one *wants* to rent downtown, when the economics of running a seasonal business don't make sense anymore. I mean, how many ice-cream cones do you have to sell to make an eighty thousand dollar summer rent?" The rents aren't the only problem. In many cases town real estate taxes on the better properties *doubled* between 1998 and 2001 due to the run-up in market valuation even as the tax rate went down.

But it wasn't preservation that gave Ginny a true understanding of the clandestine nature of Ptown politics; it was one of her odd doing-what-it-takes-to-get-by jobs. During the summer of 1995, she was hired through her connections with the *Whydah* project to run the new Billy Bones Raw Bar, located in the future home of the *Whydah* Museum at the end of MacMillan Pier. In August of that summer, the bar-restaurant-marina was leased out for a bachelor party for the brother of Chris King, a successful fishmonger and one of the good ol' boys who worked out of the large warehouse at the end of Bobby Cabral's Fisherman's Pier. Unbeknownst to Binder, exotic dancers had been hired to provide entertainment, and the guest list included members of the Truro and Provincetown police departments, if not the entire departments.

"I insisted on having a rental cop present because I had never been at a bachelor party. I didn't know what they would get up to. And I wanted to make sure there would be no underage drinking and no noise violations. In Provincetown, it's customary to hire these special-duty policemen through the town police department directly, so I assumed everything would be okay.

"About nine-thirty I got a call from one of my people downstairs who said, 'Come outside, there's somebody who wants to speak to you.' So I went outside, and there was Detective Warren Tobias, who asked if I was in charge. I said, 'Yeah,' and he told me there was illegal activity going on. I said, 'There is a cop in there.' He said, 'There are lots of cops in there.' 'Then how could there be illegal activity?' I asked him. 'Isn't that the rule, you get to carry a gun because you get to stop illegal activity, whether you're on duty or off duty?' He said, 'Go in there, and stop it right now.' Okay, I ran inside and turned on the lights and said, 'Whatever you're doing, stop. This is over.' When I came back, Tobias said, 'Give me your number, I'll call you later.'"

Binder was called the following Friday, but not by the police. Instead, it was the *Banner*, trying to elicit her response to the bar's pending loss of its liquor license. This was the first Ginny had heard of the penalty. She went running to the selectmen, her colleagues, asking advice.

"The first one [was] Jane Antolini. And I said to her, 'I'm in trouble, and I don't know why.' And she said, 'Get yourself a lawyer. I can't talk to you,' and she slammed the door in my face. So I went running downstairs to Warren Alexander's office, and I was in tears. I asked Warren to call Bobby [Police Chief Bobby Anthony] for me. . . . 'Why won't anyone talk to me?' I mean, I was trying to do the right thing. He burst out laughing."

Ginny soon found that all doors were closed to her, in spite of the fact that she had previously been appointed to several influential town committees. She found herself with virtually no allies in Town Hall. She had been frozen out—and victimized. Although illegal activity had taken place, paramount being public sexual favors between the dancers and the clientele, no arrests were made and no one was called in, except for Binder, who was charged with eleven counts of mismanagement. Even her own lawyer, who was a good ol' boy himself, had abandoned her, she felt.

This wasn't directed at Binder per se but was simply another instance of the locals closing ranks, just as they'd always done. And it was not the only time Binder, or a number of others enmeshed in town business, would find themselves unsupported by town manager Keith Bergman or the Board of Selectmen, which seemed to see things through the same lens as the town manager.

"I'm an easy target, and I'm willing to be courageous and fight for things. And I'm not politically connected," she says.

The Billy Bones Raw Bar episode was traumatic, to say the least. Binder took a vacation from town for a while, resigning her chairmanship of the Historical Commission. Next, she took a job in Scotland organizing the traveling exhibit of the *Whydah* artifacts, and stayed away until February 1996.

In her absence, the town continued on its downward path.

Bergman was an anomaly, the only individual in Provincetown who walked to work, a prematurely old man, dressed in a camel overcoat and bowler, Brooks Brothers button-down shirt, and tasseled loafers. His outfit was not complete without a perky bow tie, usually red. Traditional town managers outfitted themselves like L.L. Bean floor managers with a standard uniform of chinos and a sweater; not Bergman, who was clearly bringing a new professionalism to the workplace. He had taken office in August 1989, a graduate of Vanderbilt University, where he studied political science and served as campus coordinator for the Scoop Jackson presidential campaign. The son of a postal service employee, he was married with two young daughters, and before coming to Provincetown had the job of executive secretary for the selectmen on Nantucket. He was pure ambition, certainly it seemed with respect to his salary, which the selectmen had been convinced to raise dramatically over the years.

It took several years for a number of townies, especially among the Portuguese community, to awaken to the transformation of Ptown from its eclectic, nonmainstream self into what could potentially be the "new" Nantucket under Bergman. However, what was becoming clear, aside from what to some observers of town government was an unusually high turnover of town staffers, was that the town manager's power and longevity in office stemmed not only from his ability but from his relationship with Alix Ritchie, owner of the *Provincetown Banner*. Ritchie's newspaper spoke of the town manager as "Keith-the-Cool," whose "actions and presence reveal him as one of Provincetown's strongest leaders. . . ."

To know why the relationship was so comfortable, one had to look at Ritchie. A former public relations executive for AT&T and the only child of a Bloomington, Illinois, family of significant old money, Ritchie had come to Provincetown in the early 1980s. She quickly joined the Provincetown Planning Board, the Cape Cod Commission, then the Cape Cod Economic Development Council. In the spring of 2000, her newspaper had swallowed up the *Advocate*, Provincetown's weekly ever since 1869, after a war over advertising and customers. To many locals, victory went to the richer, not the better, paper.

Ritchie appears to have come into the lion's share of her personal fortune in 1994 and, not long afterward, she began making large gifts of money to local cultural institutions. In 1999 she helped the Fine Arts Work Center buy another building, the large three-story Eddie Euler studio complex on Brewster Street; during the closing months of 2000, she was widely believed to have purchased the old Ford garage as the site for Provincetown's new umbrella theater group, the Provincetown Theater Foundation. Here, though never publicly disclosed, her contribution was rumored to be $400,000. There was no denying that Ptown needed a permanent year-round theater, especially since the loss of the Playhouse on the Wharf to fire in 1977 had left local thespians without a home. At the same time, Ritchie's efforts on behalf of the theater garnered her a seat on the group's board, just as she was put on the advisory board of the Fine Arts Work Center. Her fellow Foundation board members included David Davis, the sixtyish majordomo of the Schoolhouse Center for the Arts, and Hunter O'Hanian, who'd been hired several years earlier as the Fine Arts Work Center's new executive director to streamline operations and raise money. All three were gay and, at least by traditional Provincetown standards, all were relative newcomers, without a past that qualified them as bohemian, artist, or intellectual. O'Hanian, in fact, had been for years, before coming to Provincetown, a litigator in Boston with a firm that specialized in defending doctors and insurance companies against malpractice suits.

In the spring of 2001, Ritchie, with her partner, a local artist, also "gifted" $500,000 to the Fine Arts Work Center for low-cost housing. Ritchie's influence spread into other areas. With her seemingly limitless wealth, she (either directly or through the *Banner*) also gave to the Art Association, the Provincetown Film Festival, Campus Provincetown, HOW (Helping Our Women), and the local chapter of the National Gay and Lesbian Task Force, among many, many others.

Ritchie and Bergman seemed to share a decidedly straightforward view of the new Provincetown: It should be rich. Prosperity was everything, even in the arts, which both saw as a commercial prospect for the town, a lever to attract high-end tourism.

In addition to the support of Ritchie, Bergman had control of the town police department. In the past, the chief of police, along with his officers, had all been autonomous civil servants, answerable not to the town but to outside review by a panel of peers. This is the manner in which many police departments are run on the Cape and this is the way Jimmy Meads had run his primarily Portuguese police force through the early nineties.

In 1992, when Meads announced his retirement, Bergman had been in office two years, and there was a flurry of applications for the job. Bergman appointed Robert P. Anthony to the position on a temporary basis. Anthony raised no objection when Bergman soon sponsored a home rule petition to remove the job of Provincetown police chief from the jurisdiction of civil service, thus ceding complete control to Town Hall in the person of Keith Bergman.

The cops were no longer autonomous. "Bergman bought himself a Bobby Anthony" was how the knowledgeable old-timer cops put it. Their new chief of police could be seen day in, day out, hat in hand, entering the side entrance of Town Hall in the early morning and again in the afternoon to confer with Keith-the-Cool. The two might be lauded on a national level for their hate crimes initiative, as they were in 1997, but both, it was felt, were in service to the new Provincetown.

In July 2001, at the end of Anthony's tenure, the town sought another chief. The ad in the *Banner* read, "Town of Provincetown is accepting applications for the position of Chief of Police. *Chief reports to Town Manager* . . . Commitment to community policing, prevention of hate crimes and domestic violence essential: Keith Bergman, Town Manager."

View from Town Hill, 1898. (Courtesy of the Pilgrim Monument and Provincetown Museum)

Commercial Street,
West End, c. 1910.
(Courtesy of the
Provincetown Art
Association and Museum)

Charles Hawthorne and students, c. 1913.
(Courtesy of the Provincetown Art Association and Museum)

Wharf Theater (Lewis Wharf).
Home of the Provincetown
Players, 1915–16.
(Courtesy of Leona Rust Egan)

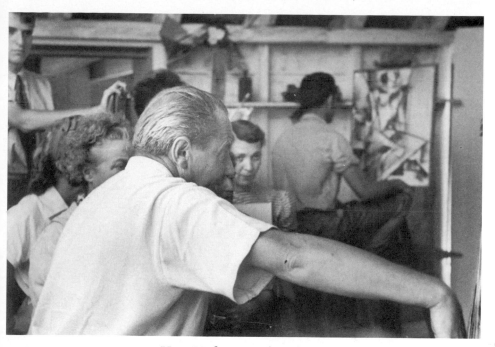

Hans Hofmann and students:
(left to right) Robert DeNiro, Beulah Stevenson, Perle Fine, 1938 or 1939.
(Photograph by Tom Milius; courtesy of the Provincetown Art Association and Museum)

Artists at work, Provincetown waterfront, 1946.
(Photo by Walter Krajicek; courtesy of the Provincetown Art Association and Museum)

Harry Kemp, poet of the dunes. (Courtesy of the Provincetown Art Association and Museum)

Forum 49. On benches *(left to right)* first row: Blanche Lazzell; second row: Morris Davidson, Fritz Pfeiffer, Perle Fine; third row: George McNeil, Adolph Gottlieb; Karl Knaths, Weldon Kees, David Heron, Giglio Dante, Kahlil Gibran (behind Knaths); fourth row: Lawrence Kupferman, Ruth Cobb, Lillian Ames, Howard Gibbs, Kenneth Campbell, Judith Rothschild; against the wall *(left to right)* sitting: Boris Margo, Minna Citron, Leo Manso, Peter Busa; standing: Fritz Bultman, John Grillo, William Freed. Paintings *(extreme left)*: Hofmann; *(extreme right)* Bultman. (Photo by Bill Witt; courtesy of *Provincetown Arts*)

Provincetown Art Association poster.
(Photo by George Yater; courtesy of the
Provincetown Art Association and Museum)

Ciro Cozzi with ex-partner Sal Del Deo *(far left)*, painter Phil Malicoat,
and leather craftsman Al Weisberg. On the beach, East End, contemplating repairs
to the Beachcombers club, late 1960s. (Collection of Ciro and Patti Cozzi)

Walter Chrysler and a member of the Velvet Underground. The rock group was in town to provide accompaniment for Warhol's *Exploding Plastic Inevitable*, a multimedia presentation, 1969. (Photo by Vincent Guadazno)

The Catholic Family of the Year in prayer: Jay Critchley, aged eight.
(Collection of Jay Critchley)

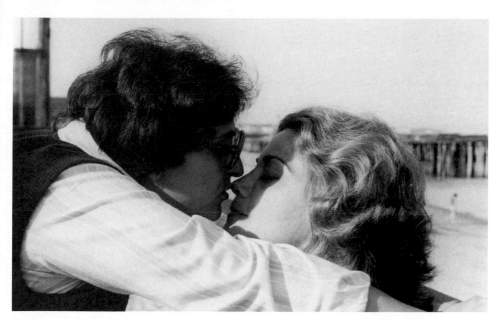

Pam Genevrino and Ginny Binder's mother, Linda Gerard, on the deck of the Pied Piper. (Collection of Linda Gerard)

Ciro Cozzi and U.S. Representative Gerry Studds, who, with almost a hundred other Provincetown residents, pitched in to build a new wing at the Art Association. At the time, Cozzi was president of the Provincetown Art Association and Museum, and Studds would shortly "come out" as the only openly gay member of Congress, 1974. (Collection of Ciro and Patti Cozzi)

A radiant Patti Cozzi at the Cozzis' annual garden party fundraiser for the Art Association, 1978. (Photo by Norma Holt)

The Provincetown Drop-In Center, summer 1979. Jay Critchley and Dr. Doug Kibler at top, surrounded by fellow staffers. (Collection of Jay Critchley)

Reggie Cabral at home with a small part of his collection: a terra-cotta sculpture by Ray Nolan; a bronze figure by Reeves Euler; a portrait of a woman by Charles Hawthorne, the founder of the Provincetown art colony; two 1963 artist's-proof lithographs by Jasper Johns; *The Birth of Venus,* a screen print by Andy Warhol, circa 1985; and a 1983 monoprint by Keith Haring.
(Photo by Ned Manter; courtesy of the Provincetown Library)

Poet Lawrence Ferlinghetti and *Provincetown Arts'* Christopher Busa at a gallery opening, 1994. (Photo by Renate Ponsold; courtesy of *Provincetown Arts*)

The Long Point Gallery group, 1991 *(left to right)* bottom row: Nora Speyer, Robert Motherwell, Judith Rothschild. Middle row: Budd Hopkins, Paul Resika, Edward Giobbi, Varujan Boghosian, Leo Manso, Sideo Frombuluti. Top row: Tony Vevers, Carmen Cicero, Sidney Simon. (Courtesy of *Provincetown Arts*)

A typical late-night crowd outside the Spiritus pizza parlor on Commercial Street in Provincetown. (Photo by Ron Schloerb; courtesy of the *Cape Cod Times*)

A drag queen leads the annual Provincetown Carnival parade, 1999. (Photo by Emilie Sommer; courtesy of the *Cape Cod Times*)

Environmentalist Jay Critchley, wearing his gown made of tampon applicators and a headdress made of feathers and lobster claws, sings "Let Freedom Ring" while performing a ceremonial dance on Race Point, 2000. Critchley organized the event to protest the start of Boston's outfall pipe, which carries sewage into Cape Cod Bay. The prayer ribbons flying above Critchley commemorate AIDS victims. (Photo by Vincent DeWitt; courtesy of the *Cape Cod Times*)

Alix Ritchie: For some, a real-life Medici; for others,
a symbol of the new monied, upwardly mobile Provincetown.
(Photo by Vincent DeWitt; courtesy of the *Cape Cod Times*)

Norman Mailer, *left*, chats with Nobel Prize–laureate Saul Bellow
at a Truro fundraiser. Painter Judith Shahn is in the background, summer 1999.
(Photo by Vincent DeWitt; courtesy of the *Cape Cod Times*)

Steeple-raising, the Schoolhouse Center for Art and Design, June, 1999. Ginny Binder and her partner Tom Boland (and half of Provincetown's East End) look on as the restoration project nears completion. (Collection of Regina Binder)

Ginny Binder, 1998. (Collection of Regina Binder)

Provincetown selectman David Atkinson, drag queen Pearline, and Jay Critchley. "Septic Graduation" ceremony, 2000. Pearline graced the ceremony with a rendition of the "Star Spangled Banner." (Collection of Jay Critchley)

The start of the Swim for Life, Long Point Beach: Jay Critchley with a bullhorn and flag about to release the hundreds of swimmers bound for Provincetown on the far side of the harbor, 1999. (Photo by Kathy Chapman; collection of Jay Critchley)

Ginny Binder writing a documentary film script for Rheged Discovery Center, an underground mixed-use retail and visitor attraction in Combria, England. (Collection of Regina Binder)

Tony Jackett at the Provincetown pier with the *Josephine G* in the background, 1992. (Photo by Gordon E. Caldwell; courtesy of the *Cape Cod Times*)

Shellfish Constable Jackett "cleaning" some of his two hundred nursery boxes containing baby clams. Provincetown harbor at low tide, summer, 2000. (Collection of Jay Critchley)

Tony Jackett's family gathered at the christening of his granddaughter, Etel Mary Amato, 1996. Top row *(left to right)*: brother Tom Jackett, son-in-law Keith Amato, Tony, sons Luke and Kyle, Kim Smith, son Beau, Susan, daughter Braunwyn Jackett Amato. Bottom row *(left to right)*: father-in-law Harold Soultz holding baby Etel, Shelley Quittugha with Nataya Quittugha, her daughter with Kim Smith. (Collection of Mr. and Mrs. Anthony R. Jackett)

C-Scape dune shack—a Provincetown retreat for art and healing, Cape Cod National Seashore (Photo by Laine Quinn; collection of Jay Critchley)

CHAPTER 23

TONY'S FAMILY

The winter of 1986 began on a positive note for Tony Jackett. His father, Anthony, had broken several ribs aboard the *Plymouth Belle*, and he had asked Tony to run the boat while he recovered. Tony jumped at the chance, even though Jackett Sr. was prepared to give him only a single "share," far less than was a fair cut for anyone filling in as captain.

Anthony had always sidestepped questions as to when he was going to step down and turn the boat over to his son. Tony told himself that maybe this was his opening. The money wasn't as important as the opportunity to prove himself to his father.

Tony had a friend take over the *Josephine G*, and he stepped in to run the family boat.

"I loved it, it was intoxicating," he explains, talking about what it meant to him to be out at sea in the larger vessel. "Fishing's about handling fear. You handle fear your whole life, preparing for the ultimate fear itself, and that's dying. And when those waves are twenty feet high, crashing into you, don't let anybody kid you—you *do* think about dying!"

A romantic in an almost Byronic mold, he enjoyed living on the edge. Throughout his whole fishing career aboard the *Josephine G*, he never once carried a life raft or even a cold-weather survival suit—the latter a piece of equipment as common aboard a Cape Cod dragger as nets and twine since it extends by several hours the time in which a man may stay alive in a frigid sea.

Soon after his father had taken back the *Plymouth Belle* after eight
months, Tony's cousin Chris Snow, attorney for Seamen's Bank, counseled him to placate Seamen's loan board by voluntarily getting rid of
the *Josephine G*. The bank had already forced the sale of the house in
Truro. Now, Snow said, it was time to make a clean break of it and sell
off the *Josephine G*, too. Seamen's was convinced Tony would never
make enough money fishing to get back on his feet.

At the bank, it was a strange and almost communal decision that
went something like, "This native son is never going to be a highliner
like his dad, the fishing stock is depleted, and we don't feel like extending ourselves. Tony Jackett needs to stop fishing, to sell his boat and find
another career so he can service his debts and get his life together." But
it was more than that, too. The bank's board members didn't understand him. He was a break with tradition, the way he didn't feel compelled to take his boat out before sunrise like his dad.

In selling his Truro house to pay his debts, Tony had walked into a
stone wall. Before the sale, he'd owed $50,000, a sum that represented
the house renovations, the back mortgage payments, and all his mis-
cellaneous debts to places like Land's End Marine, Marcey Oil, and half
a dozen other local businesses. When all these were paid off, there
wasn't enough money left to pay his tax arrears and nothing with
which to get a fresh start. Dazed, Tony rerigged the *Josephine G* to go
after scallops, which had proven a bonanza during the late seventies. But
no sooner had he changed the boat's gear over then it turned out the
scallops had gone the way of the whiting and cod. During this period,
the aging *Josephine G* sank twice, and twice Tony raised her with the
help of friends.

At home Susan and Tony continued to quarrel. From his perspective, he
needed help. As she saw things, he was staying out evenings, and when
he wasn't downtown he'd watch an hour or two of TV after dinner and
then turn in early. But she complained only when Tony reeled in at two
in the morning; otherwise, there was a listlessness, a flatness to her.
When they'd moved back to Provincetown in December 1987, Susan
had continued her work at Days' Cottages in Truro, but the next fall she
took a job at the Donut Shop on Shank Painter Road. In order to be
there in time for breakfast, she had to get up before dawn, and though

this left the family on its own each morning, it gave Susan a chance to see people she hadn't seen in years. It also meant that she was bringing in much-needed cash. Some Portuguese men would have had a hard time with this. Not Tony. The Donut Shop was a hot spot, the only early morning place in town that was open off-season, and it served as a release from all the difficulties she was faced with at home. His only complaint was that after work his wife would return to their rented house on Winslow Street bursting with gossip. Things were bad enough in Provincetown, "living in a fishbowl," as he saw it, but Susan was like a parrot, prattling on even when he'd make a show of rolling his eyes and looking up at the ceiling.

The fishing was more difficult than ever. Stocks were depleted, government quotas were in place, and during the winters of 1992 and 1993 the weather was so bad that Tony, like a lot of others, was able to go out only intermittently. In December 1994, a series appeared in the *Cape Codder* on how the fishing crisis was affecting fishermen, their families, and their communities up and down the Cape. "One Fisherman's Struggle to Survive," the first in the series, focused on Tony.

"I was thirty when I bought the boat," he was quoted, "and that was fourteen years ago, and I'm still broke. What makes me think I'm gonna have money when I'm 55? I think about getting retrained, but I can't walk away from my boat. . . . I can't leave," he said, "because I can't get ahead. The money keeps going back into the boat . . . and when I do leave I want something to show for it."

Current fishing regulations were a shambles, the story elaborated, with cod and yellowtail flounder at record lows, and haddock landings in 1993 had declined ninety-four percent from ten years earlier. To make thing tougher, Canada had been allowed to extend its coastal fishery waters out to two hundred miles, which included the richest area of the Georges Bank. Tony was only one of many affected by this, but many of the Cape's fishermen had already sold their boats and moved to places like Florida and Colorado.

The wheelhouse of Jackett's boat, the author pointed out, was decorated with a faded plastic shrine of the Virgin Mary and a poster of Robert DeNiro from the movie *Cape Fear.* The poster read, "There is nothing in the dark which can hurt you. Except fear." It also had "the cluttered look of a cellar workroom" with rusty tools lying everywhere, providing a segue to the hardship of maintaining the tired old boat over the past four years that had sucked up over $30,000. A large chunk of this money had gone toward a new engine and propeller shaft. More recently, the *Josephine G* had been laid up for nearly two weeks, losing precious days while Tony replaced the batteries and starter.

State catch quotas were crippling him more than anything, though. They stipulated where and when he could fish; for every twenty-four hours at sea, for example, he had to spend twelve at the dock, and with the shrinking fish stocks this was ruinous. "Mr. Jackett had to throw back $10,000 worth of fluke because quotas had already been reached," the sympathetic story pointed out. Tony was quoted as commenting, "What kind of sense does that make? I went home that day with something like $150 in my pocket, not enough to cover my fuel."

What he hadn't told the reporter, however, was that like other small-boat fishermen he was also cheating—staying out longer than he was allowed, exceeding his quotas, going where he wasn't supposed to. It didn't matter that getting caught meant having your boat impounded until after you'd gone to court and paid the fine; Tony's view was that it was worth the risk—you balanced it off against the extra money, especially as the bigger boats had the edge, because they could go out in bad weather.

Another take on what was happening was provided by Francis "Flyer" Santos, Provincetown's last surviving master boatbuilder, whose genealogy read like a history of Provincetown fishing.

"I've worked in a boatyard for 60 years," Santos said, "and I've seen the ups and downs of the business. There's a cycle every 30 years . . . starting with whaling, then Grand Banks salt codding, and the schooner era of fresh fish, and then trap fisheries and the ice houses.

"For a long time the draggers made a lot of money, but . . . our 30 years are way overdue with the draggers and there is no way they can survive."

Provincetown historian and selectman George Bryant added that the current crisis was unparalleled in the four-hundred-year history of Provincetown fishing, and, indeed, was changing the face of the Cape's most legendary fishing port.

"The fishermen as a political bloc are almost insignificant," he said, "and [the government] will push them right into the water. They'll treat them like trash. . . . Once they get fishing out of here, they'll never allow it back in again. Zoning bylaws and all of the governmental regulations will prohibit that."

The picture was so grim that some Ptown restaurants were already using frozen cod from Iceland and the Pacific. Flyer's Boatyard had to make the switch ten years earlier from working on commercial vessels to repairing and renting recreational craft. Even the schools were in extremis, the story suggested, since the failing fishing economy was starting to drive traditional families out of town. All things considered, it was noteworthy that the photographs of Tony in oilskins had him smiling broadly, showing a mouthful of bright Portuguese teeth, and in one he was at the controls of the *Josephine G*, posing with a dramatic, horizon-arrested stare that was definitely something off the big screen, the imagery, say, of Captain Courageous.

In 1993, the year before the *Cape Codder* series ran, Susan left the Donut Shop for a receptionist's job at the Wellfleet AIM health clinic. She also pressed Tony "to get off his ass" more strongly than she'd ever done before, saying that she'd just about had it with his excuses and was even thinking of leaving.

"She told me I had to grow up, that I had to see things as they really are—money, family, responsibility," he recalled, conceding that she was right in calling him "a cocky bastard," telling him that he wasn't fooling anyone by never complaining or letting on in public about what they were up against. It didn't mean a damn thing. The Portuguese often did this, she said. His mother had always had a tendency to cover up, and it was her pride. He could no longer be the irresponsible dreamer. It was time to get real.

And Tony, the man-child, listened. It was a watershed event in his life. He had to pull himself together or he was going to end up alone. "I was forty and she gave me an ultimatum," he says later. " 'Get real or get out.' I remember, it was late in the afternoon, a real foul fall day, and I'd been out late the night before. She said, 'I've had it with your goddamn fantasizing.' She was getting a lot of attention at the doughnut shop," he adds, "and she was putting me on notice."

•   •   •

During the winter of 1995, with Beau in his second semester at college, Tony tried to supplement his fishing income with a regular nine-to-five job, driving an oil truck for his high school buddy Mike Tasha, who owned Cape Cod Oil. He had already applied, unsuccessfully, for the position of town harbormaster, and when the oil truck job petered out, he grabbed at another town job, this one collecting rubbish. This lasted for eleven months, until the autumn of 1997, when he got the shellfish warden's job. Three years later, in July 2000, he supplemented that with the shellfish warden's job in Truro, and now, together, the two part-time positions were good for what, for Tony, was decent enough money—$35,000 yearly. It wasn't enough to make a dent in his $50,000 IRS bill, but combined with Susan's earnings, the Jacketts were now bringing in more than they'd seen in a very long time. It was certainly a far cry from Tony's selling vacuum cleaners door-to-door, as he'd done in the early eighties, soliciting other fishermen whose bankrolls were no fatter than his own.

The fact that the *Josephine G* had sunk in Pamet Harbor during Hurricane Edward, in September 1996, made giving up fishing a little easier, although Tony still took the boat out whenever he could, once he'd raised her. Then, in 1999, she sank again. He told himself he was going to refurbish the boat for real and start all over again once he had the money. In the meantime, the *Josephine G* was safe at Wright's Boat Yard in Hyannis.

With his good looks and habitual posing, you'd think Tony would have been embarrassed by picking up garbage. But he wasn't. Moving trash cans was like moving fish boxes—honest physical work that you could do badly or do well, and he never felt any indignity, as others might have.

Sometimes, when he'd stop at Chris Busa's house at three or four A.M., Busa would be up working on the next issue of *Provincetown Arts*. He'd watch Tony take that extra little bit of care to put the empty cans back inside the fence rather than just leave them flung back up on the sidewalk, rolling in the winter wind. The bookish Busa considered his friend's moves very carefully, trying to place them in the context of the time they'd spent fishing together.

"It's been one of the reasons I so came to respect him; he never felt that he'd lost his dignity. For him, it was the idea that you don't get strong, or stay strong, without daily work, and if you do the daily work you're different from people who don't do it. He never really thought about it as garbage, see. He couldn't fish, he needed a job, and he gratefully accepted this opportunity and was happy for it."

In the early eighties, when Busa was struggling to overcome a writer's block, trying to finish his Ph.D., flying into Boston once a week to see a therapist, Jackett had given him an outlet by letting him work aboard the *Josephine G*. It turned into a trade-off: Busa got to experience the physical labor of fishing, and Tony began going to gallery openings and readings at the Fine Arts Work Center.

While at sea the two talked about women the way most fishermen do. But in addition to this, they also talked about books, and Tony, Chris says, was "easy with that." He took a whole summer to get through Frank Gaspar's *Leaving Pico*, pondering the meaning of the novel in a way that was not only honest but touching. Gaspar had been a high school classmate who'd moved to Southern California, fleeing the community's "smallness"; then, in an almost Thomas Wolfe–like way, looked back over his shoulder to write his tale of the town he'd grown up in. *Pico* was a book about Portuguese Provincetown *by* a Portuguese, and Tony, reading along at a couple of pages a day, found the elements of his own history and sociology completely engrossing—the types of food at a traditional clambake, the hypocrisies of the local church, the neighbors and who came from Lisbon and who came from the islands and who was of higher status. Reading the book, he also focused on how a story is told, and he talked to Busa about how a lot of the Portuguese old-timers were very good storytellers—they knew how to joke, how to create suspense and keep your attention, how to "inject a message," he said, pointing reliably to what any academic would recognize as the key elements of the peasant oral tradition.

Busa had steered him to D. H. Lawrence, who was the subject of the editor's doctoral dissertation then in progress, and he also introduced Tony to friends, many of whom were young painters and poets like Tabitha Vevers and Mark Doty, who were then still struggling. Saturday nights, he invited him to the Beachcombers, where Tony mixed with an older, different crowd made up of year-rounders like *New Yorker* cartoonist and painter Mischa Richter and the sculptor Conrad Malicoat. Nothing fazed Tony. Provincetown was providing

him with an educational setting. He'd never gone to college, Provincetown was his college.

Another time, Busa took Tony into Boston to do a live cable TV
show on traditional Portuguese cooking. Shortly before airtime, the editor talked to the show's producer, explaining that Tony had wanted him
to come along for support, and "He wants me to ask you a few questions: Is it okay if he swears on television, because he says he thinks better when he swears, and also he believes that people listen better when
you swear."

When he went on, Tony didn't swear once, but he knew how to
command attention. "His clothes, all his jackets—what he has is *gear*,"
Busa explains. "Even when he doesn't shave and wears rags, he wants to
look good, and even though he might be stylish there has to be some
oddball element to it, like his cuffs are rolled wrong, the jacket's a little too big, or something is a little not right. The effect is he startles people . . . and he likes that. It confirms something for him.

"There he was, talking about trash fish while making a Portuguese
garlic soup, but he was coming on like someone from the north country, the tundra, the Outback, not the Cape. He looked . . . well, *different*."

He was playing against type, consciously or otherwise taking cues
from his film heroes Brando and McQueen. A self-character, a persona
was important to him as a tool, it seemed, a means not only to get attention but to interact with others.

Most of the Jacketts' six kids are now out of the house, and this, more
than the smuggling debacle and everything it left behind, tells Tony that
things have changed. Not one of the kids has gone into fishing full-time,
nor are any of them ever likely to.

Unlike Tony, his son Beau is light-skinned, with little of his father's
outdoor physicality even though he later excelled at basketball, and
a good many of the rougher kids at school saw him as the preternatural
geek. Halfway through his freshman year at Provincetown High, his
grades were solid A's. He became involved in practically every extracurricular activity open to him—the school chorus, Spanish club, and the
spring musical, which, traditionally, is attended by everyone in town. By
the end of his second year he was in the National Honor Society. By his

senior year he'd starred in productions of *Oklahoma!*, *Mame*, and *Guys and Dolls*, and was also high scorer and co-captain of the basketball team. Everyone in the school system from the school superintendent on down—the principal, even teachers whose classes he wasn't in and members of the town's school board—knew about Beau Jackett and his remarkable trajectory. He was one of those kids who seemed destined to burst all the small-town constraints and simply voyage outward. The *Cape Cod Times*, in an article at the time of his graduation, referred to him as the Cape's "Academic All-Star."

"I found this potential in myself that I never knew was there," Beau said later, "and I found it very exciting."

The contrast to Braunwyn, who was three years ahead of Beau and had graduated just as he was entering his sophomore year, was night and day. A mediocre student, she didn't care about academics and most of her attention was devoted to the horse Tony had bought her, to her friends, and to her car. She was also strikingly handsome, with the same blond hair and creamy skin as her mother's. At Adam's Pharmacy, where she worked weekends, it was a regular thing for grown men to leave a dollar tip after a glass of water so as to be able to sit at the fountain and ogle her.

Beau was "head," Braunwyn was "heart." She was also totally up front, sometimes to the point of brusqueness, and, aware of her assets, she had thought of a life in the theater. But what she wanted most all was to get out of Provincetown. The situation at home had gotten to her. At twelve, two months after the *Divino Criador* madness, she'd seen her father come reeling out of the Surf Club late one night with another woman on his arm, and then the day afterward, after Susan had backed down for the umpteenth time ("she had his bags packed at the door, but she let him apologize"), she'd dissolved in tears, overwhelmed by anger and grief.

"I was his little girl, and I just adored him. He used to take me fishing, I went on motorcycle rides with him, he bought me a car, but I'd never heard of anything until this point, so I just started to cry," she says. "My world was just crushed. I mean, this was *my father*. . . . And that's when I started not wanting to be home. I remember running away, jumping out the window, hitchhiking into town, and I wouldn't come home

at night because here he is, not coming home himself, and he's telling me
I have a curfew."

She'd started to have sex at sixteen but, she insists, "not with multiple partners." Booze and pot and occasionally some acid were part of
her rebellion, too, but she abjured heroin, which had started to be used
widely by a number of Ptown high schoolers during the early eighties.

Her real issue wasn't Tony so much as her mother, who'd failed "to
deal with his crap."

"I was mad at her for not standing up for herself and moving out—
she'd stamp her feet, throw dishes on the floor screaming, but I didn't
see her leave. I saw her go only so far and then stop."

What Susan did do was start to see a guy up-Cape, which drove Tony
to dare her to "take it further." This was when Braunwyn was a senior, in
1991. It didn't last long. But Susan had just had it.

Braunwyn's senior year represented the pinnacle of her parents' conflict, and what made it all but unbearable was Kim, who was in and out
of jail. Kim, one of Susan's two adopted Sioux children, had started doing
drugs at thirteen or fourteen. By age sixteen he stood six-two and
weighed 210. His addiction was drugs, but like many Native Americans,
he also had a drinking problem. A number of the local cops had gone out
of their way to cut him slack, but his arrests ran the gamut from DUI to
assault and battery, destruction of property, theft, and breaking-and-
entering. There were stints of three months and more in the Barnstable
County lockup. Cocaine, pot, hash, quaaludes, no one at home could
keep up with what he was doing, even though both Tony and Susan had
noted track marks on his arm.

Kim's brothers and his sister Braunwyn were deeply affected.
Braunwyn was ten when her mother first told her what was happening,
and it hit her harder than it did the other Jackett kids because Braunwyn
was so close to her mother. "When he'd be at home he was very loving.
Kim was never mean to any of us, ever, yet I remember he took all my
mother's energy, all her attention. Everything was Kim—right until the
day he died. Kim, Kim, Kim. It was draining. It was more draining than
my father."

The night of her senior prom, Braunwyn's lumbering, oversize
Sioux brother showed up at her prom party, drunk and disheveled,
weeping that he "was no good." Braunwyn had chosen an antique wed-

ding dress for the occasion, a wonderful taffeta and lace affair in which she sparkled as the evening's prom queen. Earlier, she'd made the grand entrance at Town Hall, where she and Nathanial McKean, her date, had received waves of applause, been photographed and feted, but even so, at the party afterward, she held Kim in her arms and wept along with him in front of all the other kids, unashamed and openly loyal. Of all the Jackett children Braunwyn was the toughie, the one with the mouth, but, inside, she was nothing but softness.

"I was sitting on his lap and we were hugging and he was telling me how much he loved me, my father, and our mother," she recalled years later. "He was crying because he felt like he was a disappointment. I was crying, too, and letting him know that it was okay, that we still loved him. See, I'd gone through a period where I didn't speak to him for about a year, because he was always in and out of jail. He'd broken my mother's heart. She's a strong woman but there were nights when I'd hear her going to sleep weeping. She blamed herself. 'What did I do wrong?' She had no idea about his fetal alcohol problem, and my sister's, too, Shelby. Later, we found out it was the same thing with her."

If Braunwyn was flailing and wanted out, Beau was diligence personified—the faithful son, the churchgoer, the role model for his younger brothers.

"I put a lot of pressure on myself," he recalls. "I felt I had a responsibility in the family and going after grades gave me a sense of direction. There were times when there would be just outrageous fights between my mom and dad, and I knew there had to be a better way. Braunwyn wasn't around that much, and I kind of resented that."

The better way meant preparing for college and early in his senior year, before being told that he was class salutatorian, he applied to Dartmouth, Bowdoin, and BU. For financial reasons, he wound up accepting a scholarship package from Emerson College in Boston that was to run the full four years, 1994 to 1998. Neither his father nor mother had completed college, let alone had someone else pay for it.

In Boston, even with his stipend, Beau was forced to hold down a number of part-time jobs. Other kids in the frat house where he rented a room had their own computers; that first year, Beau used the one in the school library or at Kinko's in Harvard Square, where he'd started working the late night shift on weekends. He became a devotee of Chef

Boyardee ravioli. His wardrobe consisted of two pair of chinos, three ties—two rep and one in a psychedelic floral motif that he'd received as a gift—and a single sports coat. To get home on holidays, he snagged rides to Plymouth or Hyannis with other students, then took the bus or hitched the rest of the way down-Cape; the old Chevy he'd bought the summer before had a bad rear end, and besides, he'd decided early that he didn't want to take the time to deal with parking the car in the big city.

By the start of his second year, he changed his major from speech communications to marketing and also upped his hours as a computer services attendant at Kinko's, where fellow workers, struck by his implacable earnestness, happily instructed him in advanced software. Over the previous summer, he'd sold ads at the *Advocate*, and what he'd learned about doing mock-ups led him into computer graphics; what he was doing now was an extension of that. Just as he'd impressed his teachers, Beau's bosses at Kinko's were seeing him as a long-term winner.

Although he was now only twenty, he thought constantly about the future, and, looking back, Beau admits that he became so wrapped up in his goals that "I kind of blurred everything else out." Braunwyn, for her part, had cut out for Key West two years earlier with the granddaughter of actor Kevin McCarthy, whom she'd met in Ptown; from Key West she'd gone to Seattle, then back to Key West. This used up the fall, winter, and spring of 1992–93. Returning to Provincetown for the summer of 1993, she put together a nest egg working at Spiritus Pizza and the Governor Bradford, and then took off again for Key West in October. "I am pursuing nothing," she told herself. "I am pursuing life experience, just getting to know myself."

After returning home for another summer in 1994, she took off again, now for L.A., with Keith Amato, her new boyfriend. Keith had been married, had a small child who lived with his ex-wife, was trained as a chef, and came from an affluent Manhattan family. He was a good-looking guy with an edge to him, like Braunwyn herself. In Los Angeles, they bunked with a friend of his as Braunwyn tried modeling, took waitress jobs, and at one point was doing telemarketing. To Beau, toiling away in the cold of Boston, she was impulsive and had "no direction." When an ill and pregnant Braunwyn called home for airfare to come back to the

Cape later that spring, her younger brother blew up, resentful that his parents were footing her a ticket.

His argument, of course, was he'd had to do "everything" on his own, and to a certain extent, he was right, since Tony and Susan had always held to the assumption that Beau "could take care of himself." But this didn't describe how things had started to evolve between Tony and his son while Beau was still in high school. For Beau's interview at Emerson, Tony had accompanied him on the bus to Boston and afterward taken him on a sight-seeing tour of the city. As Beau's college career unrolled, Tony brought Susan for family weekends. He telephoned. The two exchanged e-mails after Beau set his dad up with a home computer. During his senior year, when Beau delivered two seminar papers, Tony drove in from Ptown to listen to him read both of them.

For years, Tony had kept a scrapbook of stuff pertaining to all the kids—their report cards, clippings from the *Advocate, Cape Cod Times*, and *Boston Globe* reporting academic and sports feats, Boy Scout memorabilia, class photos, programs from the high school musicals. But he became more immersed still when Beau graduated in 1998 and entered Emerson's twelve-month accelerated master's program in global marketing. It was then, said the oldest Jackett son, that he realized that his father was living vicariously, participating in things that life had denied him.

"There was a certain sense of completion with himself. He felt very involved in what I was doing," says Beau, "and the more I thought about it at the time, it was clear that he was striving for something."

Over the holidays, the two had long talks about the future and the state of the world, and they discussed Beau's girlfriend, Elizabeth, a photography student who the younger Jackett thought he might want to marry. It was one of Tony's great capacities, this ability to listen, and often he'd just sit quietly as Beau explained that his life was coming to revolve more and more around Kinko's, where he'd worked his way up from attendant to weekend supervisor, to supervisor of the second shift, and most recently to assistant manager of technology for the Harvard Square store, the facility where he'd first started. Company brass was wooing him for the position of regional technology specialist, responsible for seventeen or eighteen stores in the greater Boston area once he graduated with his MBA, he explained, and as Beau saw it, the issue was whether or not to make Kinko's his career.

Amazingly, Tony-the-smuggler and third-generation Portuguese fisherman was entranced that his son was turning into a Yuppie. No one at the Old Colony could quite understand it, and only Jay Critchley, Tony's artist friend, tried to get him to explain why, especially as a Kinko's career meant that Beau could never live in Provincetown. Tony's response was that what was happening represented a break, that it was "healthy." The boy was "voyaging out," going where none of the Jacketts had ever dared to go before. To illustrate what he meant, Tony pointed to his new computer, a Compaq he'd set up in one corner of the family living room: Beau had been giving him lessons on how to use it. If, at forty-five, Tony himself had the guts to take on something so alien as this, so removed from the familiar, as represented by winches and bottom fish, say, then why shouldn't his son do the same thing?

The question wasn't rhetorical so much as it signaled Tony's bigness of spirit, not just as a father but a man. Chris Busa remembers the same kind of openness at the time he introduced Tony to the painter Robert Motherwell at the Art Association. Motherwell was diffident at meeting a fisherman, even though he'd always talked about the connection between the peasant mentality and the aristocratic one, and how, when he went to Spain, he'd liked the artisans who painted ceramics. Now, instead of his nostalgia for "the primitive source," when it came to the actual experience in the form of Tony he couldn't deal with it. Tony, however, wasn't put off by the artist's snobbery. "He's a little uncomfortable, I can see that," he'd said afterward about one of the world's most famous painters. "But that's okay. He probably has his reasons and I'm sure they're important to him."

He was always willing *not* to complain, to give the other person the benefit of the doubt.

Beau, who married his girlfriend in the fall of 2001, recently moved to suburban Fairfield, Connecticut, where Kinko's has put him in charge of digital solutions for the Manhattan metro area. Things are less clear with Braunwyn. At twenty-eight she remains as striking as ever. She's also no less headstrong, according to Tony, who wonders what's going to happen to her. In August 1995, after a final stint in California, she returned to the Cape with her husband, Keith Amato, and soon gave birth to a baby girl, Ethel, who was named after Susan's aunt, Ethelvina. They moved into the upstairs apartment in Braunwyn's grandparents' house at the East End, paying a $300-a-month rent, which made it the bargain of the decade in Ptown's superheated housing market. The arrangement lasted for five years, until the autumn of 2000, when the hot-tempered Keith got into a hassle with their equally hot-tempered neighbors and the couple moved out to take a winter rental in Truro. Unable to find an affordable summer rental when their lease was up in the spring of 2001, they moved in with Tony and Susan. With the kids gone, Braunwyn's grandfather considered putting his house up for sale: The market price for the weatherbeaten two-story waterfront property, what in other times people referred to as "a fish shack," was $875,000.

"There is no more year-round housing in Provincetown," Braunwyn complains, "and they've just made it impossible for young people. How many young people do you see coming back here to live, to work, to bust their ass to make three thousand dollars over the summer when their rent is going to be double that? It's ridiculous. I know of only a few kids who've been able to stay in town, and they've been able to do it only with the help of their families. . . . Basically, you cannot make a decent living here unless you or your family owns a business. Try living here as a young person with a child, working at the register at Land's End, say. It sucks."

It is no longer even a question of coming up with a down payment, she says. She and Keith simply can't hack a monthly mortgage, even on a "modest" Truro property they might be able to get at $300,000; the only way they could swing it would be to live in the place nine months of the year and then, like an increasing number of couples, move out and rent it to tourists for the summer. This would cut the monthly payments, plus cover taxes and insurance, but it is unacceptable to her.

"I mean, who wants to do that if you have a kid and a dog and cat?" she asks rhetorically. "Sure, you and your partner can bust your ass during the summer months—last year my cousin says she was able to save over ten thousand dollars working at Bubala's. But I'm too old for that. . . . I'm at the point where I need some stability. Do I see any way of getting that here? No. Basically, it's time to go."

Luke, two years younger than Beau, is pretty much in the same boat. At school he pulled good grades and, like his dad and brother, was high scorer on the school's championship basketball team. Recently he returned from New York, where he'd tried to break into acting, working for a Manhattan caterer on the side, and now, he's returned to waiting tables at Bubala's, where he'd worked for years before his sojourn in New York. He's not sure he'll stay there, since he's trying to figure out whether to leave town and move to Colorado with his girlfriend, then try to settle in L.A. Younger brother Kyle goes lobstering summers and works at Ciro & Sal's, training to be a chef. Like Braunwyn, last summer he lived at home.

For Tony, some of the changes in town are pretty radical, and none more daunting than what's happened with real estate. Having been forced to sell his house, he despairs of ever being able to get back in the market. Susan just sighs and says she doesn't want to talk about it.

The other thing she doesn't talk about is her adopted son, Kim. She and her son Kyle were there at his bedside when he died in a state prison hospital in early 2000 while serving a three-to-five-year sentence for burglary and assault with intent to rape. The cause of death was AIDS, contracted, presumably, from an infected shared needle. His memorial service at St. Mary's of the Harbor drew three hundred mourners, a sizable slice of traditional Provincetown. It was a blustery February day, with the sea foaming over the top of the bulkhead in front of the church, and it was typical of the town that of the many people who turned out, none had trouble speaking of Kim as a doper, a thief, and a liar, but in the same breath praised him for his warmth, generosity, and goofy good humor. A number of people cried, and among them were fishermen with hands like anvils, the toughest of the tough. Afterward in the church rectory, the service ended with simple home-made cupcakes and brownies, punch, cold cuts, and baked stuffed clams. Among those present was Beau's longtime champion, Susan Fleming, the town's gay superintendent of schools. Another was Tony's cousin Chris Landry, who wobbled up to the podium unsteadily, intro-duced himself as "a drinking man," and just kept right on talking through his bout of tears.

Tony loves his job as shellfish warden, though, and laughs that it gives him a badge that allows him to arrest clam poachers. It also allows him to experiment with aquaculture, with hydrometers and rolls of rubber tubing and the portable clam beds he's made from old wood-framed window screens, which he's incessantly lugging back and forth across the flats for his growth fields. The job, he says, "Keeps my mind alive."

Jackett still frequents the gallery openings on Friday nights, and he even dresses for these occasions, wearing a vest over a colorful T-shirt, his Levi's held up by a big handcrafted belt with a free-form Carl Tasha welded brass buckle. Usually he'll park his Jeep Cherokee at the town lot at MacMillan Pier, then walk east to the Schoolhouse Gallery and work his way back to the center of town, gallery by gallery. He's well known by many of the local artists and welcomed with open arms. Many of his artist friends are gay and are fascinated by both his good looks and unattainability. Some flirt with him shamelessly, but he seems impervious to their charms, and only laughs. It's sort of an inside joke—the gays flirt and Tony laughs. Everyone's happy.

"I'm fascinated by the gay scene. I don't get it. I mean, I don't know why a guy would want to make it with another guy, but these people have so much *energy*. There's all their bullshit, their parades and the cruising, and they want to enjoy life, and I like that. I'm even more fascinated by the women," he adds. "They're into something new, and they're out there on the edge."

Tony is probably the only local from a fishing background to venture into these waters, and he's comfortable there. He's also a long way from his smuggling days, although the story of the *"Divino Criador"* has attained cult status, and people still talk about it as the town's best shot at getting another movie after Mailer's *Tough Guys Don't Dance*, which was filmed locally in 1986. Even Robert Melia, the head narc who'd chaperoned Tony back and forth to Boston, called it "the craziest caper I ever heard of."

His marriage to Susan is, as Tony puts it, "in a funny place now," and he talks about his wife incessantly: how she has told him she doesn't care how late he stays out, although if she hears he's "going with anyone" she's leaving, no ifs, ands, or buts. He says this is fine. They are different people and have "evolved" differently. Some of Tony's friends say otherwise. Tony, they explain, is going through "some major changes" and that the next several years are going to be crucial for him. Even Braunwyn seems to sense that something is up. In company, with other people around, she'll openly tell Tony that her mother is still an extraordinary-looking woman who'd have no trouble finding herself another man.

This is the way things were up until March 31, 2001, that is. Then the bubble burst when Tony was forced to tell his wife that he'd had a child by another woman in Truro.

For two years he had been sitting on this time bomb, and his hand was forced when he got a call on his cell phone from an attorney in Orleans, explaining that she was representing Christa Worthington, the woman with his child. Tony had to face up to his responsibilities as the father, she said. Christa wanted "a fair settlement," just as she wanted Tony to simultaneously agree never to see the child again; in fact, to sign a document surrendering his rights as a parent.

The child, a girl by the name of Ava, was beautiful, of course, with Tony's wide-spaced, liquid eyes, chiseled lips, and a bit of his Mediterranean color, even though her mother was straight Mainline WASP, Vassar-educated, and the daughter of a Boston attorney. She was in her mid-forties, an heiress, and her extended family of grandparents, aunts, uncles, and cousins had been major landowners in Truro for three, some said four, generations. She was also a freelance fashion journalist with credits that included *Women's Wear Daily, Elle, Cosmopolitan*, and the *New York Times*, which wasn't irrelevant to later events, since, according to Tony, after swearing to him that all she wanted was sex, "a straightforward, uncomplicated relationship" that wouldn't interfere with his marriage, she had told him that she was infertile and had authored several magazine pieces on her frustrations as a wanna-be mother, just as she'd also discussed her condition on a women's afternoon TV show. Tony, believing her, had not bothered to use contraceptives. Five months after he'd first slept with her during the summer of 1998, at her cottage overlooking the Pamet River, he'd been confronted with her pregnancy.

"It was all incredibly stupid on my part," he told friends, unsure of what to do in the face of the lawyer's demands. He had told the lawyer that his wife was in Florida and wouldn't be back for a week, and under no circumstances was he going to sign anything until he'd told his family.

Over the next several days, he talked to Jay Critchley, Chris Busa, and a few others. Chris was especially attentive. He'd been through a divorce two years before that still continued to plague him, most recently June 2000, when a fully armored SWAT squad had taken him to Barnstable County Jail, kicking and screaming, after he refused a Sheriff's Department summons to pay "more money." His advice to Tony now was to refuse to take a DNA test and to reject Christa's demands for child support. "She has far more money than you do," he railed in solidarity. "It's outrageous, just tell her to fuck herself. What's she going to do? Get blood from a stone? The motive isn't money, anyway, so much as vindictiveness."

Jay was more temperate. He offered a bed in the little cottage where he kept his office. With his training as a lay therapist, he also let Tony talk, which is exactly what Tony did—talk, then talk more. Day by day, as he waited for Susan to come home, he grew more anxious and the color seemed to seep from his face. He let his beard grow. He contemplated leaving a letter on the kitchen table for his wife when she returned. He considered telling Braunwyn first, the idea being that she'd intercede and serve as a buffer. He even thought about moving his stuff out of the house ahead of time, as a show of contrition, hoping that Susan would ask him to stay.

All in all, he spoke of what was happening, the situation he'd created, as "life altering."

"I always had that feeling of guilt," he says of his past attractions to women, "and I never wanted to hurt my wife. But I wanted to have my cake and eat it, too. I got away with it for a long time. But I always felt that when it came to where I had to go sneaky and lie and it was getting too complicated, it would just end. This one didn't, though, so in so many ways I think, 'Here you are, you've been so successful, and you've had all these little romances, and now you deserve to get fucking burned.' "

Christa, he was convinced, might be so bitter and angry "that she wants to fuck me good." He wasn't sure, though. Maybe it was the lawyer pushing her. He didn't know what she wanted, yet she had the power to wreck his family.

He refused to go to pieces, however, even as the days went by and it got closer to Friday, when he was scheduled to pick up his wife at the Hyannis bus station. He braced himself. He phoned his pal Jennifer

Liese, the former DNA Gallery director and Chris Busa's coeditor at
Provincetown Arts who had moved to New York, to get "a woman's
view." He talked with Busa and with Jay, telling both of them the same
thing: that whatever happened he was ready "to go with it."

"If it means taking a high profile and going to court, then there's the
story," he says. "I don't have to hide anything. Sooner or later it'll be public knowledge anyway. I'm not going to do like what Clinton did; I think
Clinton one day will probably be regarded as one of our greatest pres-
idents, and they tried to take him down. But it would have been better
if he said, 'Yeah, I got a blow job.' So that's how I want to handle it."

It was the adulterer's, perhaps any man's, ultimate nightmare. There
seemed no way out. He was trapped, and to make matters worse, as he
braced himself for Susan's return, Beau phoned to say that he and his
wife would be coming up from Connecticut over the weekend. Then,
the next morning, there was another call from the lawyer in Orleans,
who, Tony found out, had a young child and had gone through a bitter
divorce herself, something that Busa jumped on. Tony told her she
could send the document to the post office box he kept in North
Truro, but that he still wasn't ready to sign anything.

"My romances have always been something of a little game—you
know that little game?" he said to Jay, not giving a fig that Jay was gay and
supposedly *different*. "You see somebody, who's that? You have this little eye contact, you talk to them. It's a little game. And then there's other
times when you're proud of yourself that you've been able to not cross
the line. And there's still other times where you're feeling vulnerable and
once you cross the line—

"Look, I've had my way with women, I don't know what it is. I don't
necessarily go pursuing them. I genuinely love women, but when I'm
having these nice little rendezvous, I'm not looking to get laid. You
know, I've been married thirty years. I love my wife, I love the relationship, and now this Christa is trying to convey to me the idea that I'm not
being 'European' enough. She thinks that I'm not being sophisticated
enough. 'What's the big deal? Why are you so paranoid about being
open about it?' "

Ruefully, he spoke of how Susan had never complained at the time
Kim was dying, blind and emaciated, and how she'd worked to get her
son home from jail before it was too late, and then in the end held her-

self responsible for how it all turned out. He also confessed to having used Kim to justify his own behavior and to keep his wife at arm's length—shutting her up, in fact—not just in connection with Christa but his other affairs; he'd manipulated her, bribed her, twisted her arm, telling her how much he'd put up with over the years with Kim's arrests and other troubles. Basically he'd threatened her when she was at her most vulnerable.

Here his self-honesty was searing: He loathed himself, saw himself as the father of chaos.

"This is how I'd get myself out of messes. Does that make sense to you?" he asked Jay. "I'm being so noble that, 'Yes, he can come live with us and disrupt my fucking life,' because I got this fucking thing hanging over my head at some point in time down the road. Yet when I've looked at my wife over the past two years, searching for ways to tell her— You know, when she says bye-bye, it's going to hit me right in the gut. She was magnificent with Kim. Very strong, and in the meantime I went and got this girl pregnant."

What transpired after Susan came home will never be known. Tony disappeared for almost a week and called no one. His friends, though worried, gave him his space. When he finally surfaced, he did so with Susan, the two of them almost ostentatiously arm in arm as a couple. Both looked ashen, as though they had survived an airplane crash and might never be the same again. Slowly things began to happen, though.

Tony had already been to see his cousin, the lawyer Chris Snow, before talking to Susan and the kids, but when Snow's contact with the Orleans lawyer proved inconclusive, Braunwyn took over. Unannounced, she marched up the hill to Christa's cottage overlooking the Pamet, stormed through the door, and loudly demanded, "Why're you trying to destroy my family?" Christa cried and didn't kick her out. A day or two later, Susan paid a visit because, as she put it, she "had to see the baby." Next, Christa began appearing in public with the child. Then she started coming to the Jacketts' house, where she'd stay all afternoon, the kid on the floor, playing with Etel's hand-me-down toys, with Tony in attendance.

"When Tony first told me, I went to Harold, my father, crying," says Susan. " 'Tony's had an affair. There's a child.'

" 'Is that all?' Harold replied. 'I thought one of your kids died. Move on.'

"So that's what we've done, moved on. I had a choice to make. I love Tony. He can be absolute dumb-nuts, but the two of us have bonded again. We even have a little car seat for the baby and take her around with us.

"We're happy, like it's really been a wake-up call. I picture myself having a conversation with Jesus. What would he say? 'Kick her in the teeth'? I mean, that's not how you deal with kids. I raised two adopted children from the time they were six months, I loved them like they were my own. You don't have to give birth to a child to love it.

"I never wanted to go to college or take courses, and maybe my beauty got in the way for me. Because what I love most is taking care of a child. Some people are like that, and I think that's what I was really meant to do in life. I mean, Kim could be very difficult, but I truly loved that child.

"The baby doesn't know Tony's her father. We're 'friends.' We asked Christa to come here for Thanksgiving, but she had to go somewhere else. But the baby was here. With Braunwyn and Luke and Kyle, all of us, including Beau and his wife. We were joking about her ears, which are Tony's ears—too big, and a little pointy. Christa thought this was funny, too, when she came to pick her up.

"Then at Anthony's [Jackett Sr.] Christmas party, all the kids were there. Even Tony's sister was there, which was another breakthrough. Like she finally forgave her father for leaving his first wife."

In April, the night Tony confessed about Ava, he left the house and went to stay at Jay Critchley's. After he and Susan decided to make a go of it, they entered counseling together. Susan also laid down the new rules: no drinking, no going into town alone, no walking around in public with his shirt unbuttoned to the waist, pirate-style. As Tony was telling friends, "I'm one argument away from a divorce." He also regretfully turned down Jay's request for help with the 2001 Swim for Life, saying, "My wife doesn't want me running around town, that's what my wife'll get."

Tony, for his part, says he wants to keep the child because it gives him "a second chance." "I can make up for a lot of my fuck-ups," he says.

●   ●   ●

Three women and Tony Jackett—it was an irony that even Tony had to appreciate. Susan had made him shave, made him take her with him into town whenever he wanted to go out at night, and even stop drinking. As a couple they were alive again, because she'd also made him come back to her bed.

It had all caught up to him in a way he had never imagined; it was so fantastical, in fact, that perhaps no one could have imagined: "It's probably been like this for a long time, but it's dawned on me that women are running my life," he joked self-derisively a month or so after the big disclosure. "With one, I'm on probation, walking on eggshells. With the other, I'm kissing her ass. And the other one's on my living room floor, taking over my house."

His mother, he told Jay, was "up there watching." She had died in 1997, still angry at his father, still doting on her firstborn son, and now Tony said he missed her terribly.

"Shit, could I use her now. What was so special was that with her I could do no wrong. I was her boy, and if she was here I'd know *exactly* what to do," he laughed.

There was also Anthony's response to what had taken place. Tony's dad was spotted chatting with one of his old buddies in the A&P near the vegetable bins a week or so after word spread throughout the town. Now everybody knew, but months before, the friend, who lived in Truro, had heard a rumor about Tony's new offspring and mentioned it to Jackett Sr., who'd dismissed it out of hand. Now the two old fishermen were smiling. It was bizarre. Jackett Sr. was trying to be adult about it, but inwardly, you could tell, he was pleased with his son for what had happened. Tony was a chip off the old block, even at the age of fifty.

But it may not have been just the child, or Anthony's pride in his son's potency. Tony and his father are on more stable ground now, and their long-standing rift seems to have healed. In fact, Tony was talking with Anthony not long ago when suddenly the older Jackett turned to him and made a startling confession.

"I'd have done it, too, if I'd had the balls," said the old captain of his son's smuggling run.

The remark came completely out of the blue and struck Tony hard. The two had been taking a walk in the East End, it was late March and the street pleasantly empty, and Tony looked at his father.

Anthony, who has a squinty, beady look even when he's relaxed, didn't break stride. They continued walking. After a moment, the older Jackett nodded and, still looking straight ahead, he let his weathered fisherman's face break into a smile in response to his son's grateful grin.

CHAPTER 24

THE SWIM FOR LIFE

It was 1998, the eleventh Swim for Life. Two boats had just taken the first load of participants over to Long Point, and just under two hundred remained. Jay Critchley was in the middle of it all, having last-minute consultations with people and providing encouragement to the swimmers, many of whom were already in their wet suits or slathered in Vaseline. The weather was good, though the water was a bit choppy. Stormy Mayo, from the Center for Coastal Studies, made his way through the crowd at the Boatslip, approaching Jay, who was resplendent in a homemade hat with two massive lobster claws sticking out like surreal antennae. Mayo had news and it wasn't good.

"There's a right whale in the harbor," he told Jay. "The Swim's got to be stopped. Someone could get hurt. It's all tangled up in a net. . . ."

Later Jay would say that there was a higher chance of an alien spacecraft landing in the harbor. There were, after all, only three hundred right whales in the entire world; the odds that one would be here, in Ptown Harbor, on this of all days, were infinitesimal. But there it was. Stormy and Jay conferred some more, and then Jay went back outside and made an announcement. "We're going to have to stop the Swim! There's a right whale in the harbor!"

There was a great moan of disbelief and frustration. "How bizarre!" people said to one another. "It must be a sign!" others said. An impromptu powwow was held, and finally it was decided that a buoy would be set up halfway out to Long Point: The swimmers would leave from the Boatslip instead of Long Point, swim out and round the buoy, then come back to the beach. The distance would be the same as if they'd come across from the other side of the bay.

And so they did.

But that was two years ago and right now Jay Critchley is looking for his notebook. He shuffles through the piles of papers on his small dining room table, and then moves on to look through the piles on the kitchen counter and the upended television. "I know it's here somewhere."

It's four days before the 2000 Swim for Life, and Jay is working the phones like a veteran, smoothly disengaging from one conversation and then dialing up another. Time is precious, and every phone call, even the purely social ones, are handled with graceful efficiency. Jay is a very social person.

"You're swimming!" he says into the phone in that medium falsetto of his, smiling. "I'm excited!"

And Jay is excited. He paces the room, trailing the phone cord. He deals with a swimmer's questions, says good-bye and, pressing the call waiting button, he's on to the next person. As he talks, he continues wandering around the living room, still looking for his notebook.

With the Swim for Life only four days away, he's also taking time tomorrow to conduct a ceremony at Race Point to protest Boston's new sewage outfall pipe. He hadn't anticipated this since the Boston Municipal Sewage Authority made its announcement only the week before and now it's jammed his schedule.

The Swim for Life is a monumental feat of organizing—over two hundred volunteers act as greeters, huggers, cashiers; they register the swimmers, cook the food, accompany them in kayaks and motorboats, pick up trash at the Boatslip. There is a group of volunteer paramedics, there are volunteer musicians and drag queens. There is the U.S. Coast Guard, the Provincetown harbormaster, the town Rescue Squad, and innumerable others. And Jay Critchley is the man responsible for all this.

He's found his notebook and is ticking off items to Jackie Freitas, who is one of his key helpers for the swim. Jackie, stocky, middle-aged, with short salt-and-pepper hair, is the volunteer coordinator. She has been involved in the Swim for many years. Like Jay, Jackie is gay but totally uncomplicated about it, like so many other longtime Ptown year-rounders.

"Dr. Lennie Alberts—did you call him? He was there last year, so see if he's coming. Rick Ferri will be doing wet suits, right? Jeremy Soya is a nurse—he'll come. He works at the Crown and Anchor. Give him a call to confirm. Pasquale Natale is going to work on registration down on the beach. He doesn't know it yet. . . ."

The list goes on and on. They're sitting at Jay's kitchen table. The radio is on, quietly playing classical music. The house is in disarray. Piles of boxes filled with Swim for Life T-shirts fill most of the living room, stacked one atop the other three and four feet high. Papers and books are strewn around, a strand of Christmas lights shaped like jalapeño peppers encircles the window, and a naked Barbie Doll is pinned behind a framed postcard of "P-town Inc.," one of Jay's other projects. A well-worn Persian rug covers the living room floor, and half a car tire hangs like a big black doughnut on one of the walls—another of Jay's pieces, "The Blessed Virgin Rubber Goddess." The neighbors' cats are mewling out side the screen door.

Jay has always had a weakness for Catholic iconography, and a small bust of Jesus hangs on another wall. Below it is a framed text:

> *I believe in the sun*
> *Even when it's not shining*
> *I believe in love*
> *Even when I do not feel it*
> *I believe in God*
> *Even when he is silent*

It is almost like a sampler, the kind of thing you find hanging on the walls of farmhouses in the Midwest. It might at first strike the visitor as sentimental, but on closer examination one sees that behind the text there is the faint photo of a muscular nude man behind a stained-glass mountainscape. It is not Jesus Christ. "It's corny, isn't it?" Jay says, laughing. But one gets the idea that both the quote and the nude man are a sincere bit of camp.

There is no time to discuss it, though, bizarre as the "it" may be. His meeting with Jackie Freitas has come to an end, and he walks outside to his "office" in the tiny little shed that lies kitty-corner behind the main house. There, an earnest young woman with short hair and an athletic build is in front of a computer, working on a spreadsheet. The Swim for Life has raised about three-quarters of a million dollars since its inception, and every year the total goes up. Last year they raised over $80,000. Database management is a crucial component of the operation. Every person who's ever done the Swim for Life is in the computer, as are all the donors and most of the volunteers. Taped above the computer screen is a small sign that reads "Tongue for Rent."

In the back area of the office space is a huge bundle of prayer ribbons hanging from a hook. They come in every color, and over the years some have grown tattered, but this only adds to their presence. These are the ribbons on which people can write messages not only to loved ones who've died of AIDS but to those still alive and struggling whom they wish to honor. There are thousands of them. "Dear Leo," reads one, "we think of you every day. We miss you. Love, Mike and Tim."

After the meetings, Jay sets about creating a ceremony for tomorrow's protest. The authorities in Boston are going to open a valve that will send millions of gallons of treated sewer water into Massachusetts Bay. Many environmentalists fear the consequences for the marine life around the Cape. Jay is a master publicist and launches his projects with a barrage of press releases. The most recent one reads:

FOR IMMEDIATE RELEASE

MRS. TAMPON LIBERTY RETURNS; NO WITH THE FLOW CEREMONY IN PROVINCETOWN TO WITNESS AND LAMENT THE 9.5-MILE BOSTON SEWAGE OUTFALL PIPE TURN-ON; CELEBRATES THE HUMAN CONNECTION WITH CAPE COD'S HEALTHY AND HEALING MARINE ECOLOGY . . .

ALTERNATIVE CEREMONY AT RACE POINT BEACH IN PROVINCETOWN— WEDNESDAY, SEPTEMBER 6, 11:00 A.M.—COINCIDING WITH THE OFFICIAL STATE AND MWRA CEREMONY ON DEER ISLAND, BOSTON.

Miss Tampon Liberty returns! reads another flyer. *With the spigot about to be opened to the controversial flow of 360 million gallons of waste water per day of questionable quality from the toilets of 43 communities in the Boston region, concerned citizens and activists will gather with artist Jay Critchley, A.K.A Miss Tampon Liberty, to reaffirm their vigilance for the health of the surrounding waters of Cape Cod and Massachusetts Bay.*

The news release goes on, *They're still dumping—first tampon applicators, now waste water!" states Provincetown artist Jay Critchley. "This is a momentous and tragic occasion and a threat to our interdependence with all species. We all have a stake in the healthy and fruitful waters that sustain us here," he continued, mindful of the hundreds of swimmers expected at the Provincetown Harbor Swim for Life on September 9. This annual festival was conceived in 1988 to both honor the clean and healing waters of the Provincetown Harbor environment and to raise funds for much needed AIDS services. . . .*

The ceremony is a manifestation of Jay's holistic vision of the world. "Ritual has always been therapeutic for me, since I was a little boy washing the feet of priests, lighting votive candles, chanting," he explains.

For Jay, the natural environment is intimately connected with the human, and his work tries to encompass them both. Later in the day, NPR calls and over the phone interviews Jay about the outflow pipe. Then Fox TV shows up on his doorstep with a camera crew. They gingerly step around the Septic Space—another of Jay's artworks where he's converted a disused cesspool in the backyard into an underground living space—and conduct the interview in Jay's chaotic garden. The media love him because he knows what makes good news. For the cameras he always has some wildly telegenic getup, and for the print media he always has something witty and provocative to say. After they leave, Jay sits down with his book on Cape Cod marine life. He wants to use some of the information for the ceremony tomorrow but doesn't know how yet.

The next day he is up early preparing for the ceremony. Two friends have shown up, Jim and Zac. Zac has known Jay for fifteen years and has helped out on his projects before. Jim, on the other hand, is from Washington, D.C., and has never met Jay. Zac is Latino, while Jim is African-American. Jay can be a little imperious when he's in a hurry and quickly sets the two men to work. In no time at all, Jim is on his knees, untying two ten-foot-high lobster-pot buoys that have been strapped to the deck handrail. He puts them in the back of his new forest-green Land Cruiser. The buoy poles are over ten feet long and stick out several feet beyond the bumper.

"I have no idea what these are for," he mutters as he struggles with the unwieldy poles. Zac is sent to get the prayer ribbons. Meanwhile Jay is inside the house in front of a mirror. He has on his lobster-claw helmet with its two monstrous claws sticking out like the horns on a Viking headpiece, the pinecone nestling between them covered with silver glitter; seagull feathers dangle from the sides. He is trying on various sunglasses, not preening, but you can tell he cares. After settling on a pair with bright red frames, he gets out his plastic tampon applicator gown, a full-length creation made from ten thousand tampon applicators found on Cape Cod beaches. He calls Jim over to help him slip a plastic bag over the gown to carry it to the beach. Jim is a little shocked by the gown, but gamely agrees, saying, "This has got to be the strangest thing I've ever done. . . ." The prayer ribbons, which are affixed to a long length of rope, are brought out, carefully bundled up, and put in the back of the Land Cruiser. A videocamera, a small music stand, and various other paraphernalia, all in a shoulder bag, also go in the back of the truck. Jay sets his hat on the backseat of his own car, an old, beat-up Toyota. He carries a sheaf of notes with him, which he stuffs in a bag, and the two vehicles are off to Race Point.

It is a brilliant crisp fall day. The night before had been very cold, a harbinger of the chilly days ahead. Today, though, the sun is shining and a cool, strong clean breeze is blowing. Once at Race Point, Jay assigns the two men the task of taking the buoys onto the beach. Zac hits Jay on the head with the end of one of the buoys. "Fuck!" Jay explodes, then, holding his head and his two bags, he walks down onto the beach. The water is brilliant and the wind, sweeping over the open space, has grown stronger. Jay seizes a shovel and starts digging a hole. Then he goes about fifteen feet to the left and digs another. The ends of the rope that holds all the prayer ribbons are attached to both buoy poles, which are then set in the holes. The line of prayer ribbons stretches from one pole to another and flutters in the wind. Behind them is the ocean. Jay sets up his music stand, which will serve as a podium, and then affixes a small red placard to the front of it, which says "T.A.C.K.I.—Tampon Applicator Creative Klubs International." Jim looks on in amazement. Seagulls hover nearby. Jay sets up the videocamera on the tripod, and then he says that he has to go "meditate," and he walks over to a small sand bank and sits there, occasionally bringing out small notecards and looking at them. Meanwhile an African-American woman, a reporter with WJAR, a local news station, walks up and asks, "Is this where the protest is going to be?"

"Yes, it is," Jay says, smiling.

"How many people do you expect?"

"Anywhere from ten to a hundred."

"Is it going to be worth bringing my camera crew down?" the reporter asks, half kidding.

"Miss Tampon Liberty is going to be there, in her gown made out of thousands of discarded tampon applicators." The reporter's eyebrows arch; she turns around and goes to get her camera crew.

A curious older couple approaches. "What's happening here?" they ask.

"We're having a ceremony to commemorate the outfall pipe," Jay tells them.

"Ah," says the older gentleman, who is not quite sure what an outfall pipe is. He is squinting at the T.A.C.K.I. sign on the music stand.

The couple leaves, and shortly thereafter, Jay, Zac, and Jim walk up through the thick sand toward the bathhouse at the edge of the parking lot. The two friends are going to help Jay into his tampon applicator gown. Fifteen minutes later, Jim and Zac return, and by now the crowd has grown to about forty people, many of whom are friends of Jay's from town. Race Point is an apt site for the demonstration, since it lies at the northernmost nub of the Cape, protruding out into the Atlantic toward Boston. The media have also heard of the demonstration, and they make up at least a quarter of those present. MediaOne is there with a camera crew, as well as a reporter from the *Cape Cod Times* and another from the *Boston Globe*.

Jan Kelly, an old-time Ptown institution, shows up in a jumpsuit with a seaweed motif. Out of nowhere, a young man with a bongo drum has appeared, and Jay's niece, Jessica Diamond, is there with her guitar. The bongo drummer begins to play, and up on the rise next to the bathhouse, overlooking the beach, there is Jay Critchley in his lobster-claw hat and tampon applicator gown. His arms are outstretched, and in one hand he holds incense. He is doing a little hopping dance that makes all the plastic tampon applicators clatter lightly against each other, creating a pleasant percussive sound that complements the bongos. The crowd starts to clap and whoop, and the TV cameramen scurry to detach their cameras from their tripods so as to get closer, while the newspaper photographers are already snapping away.

Jay wears a solemn look on his face and as he descends, getting nearer to the bongos, they grow louder and the smell of incense is in the air. He executes some last spins, ending up before the little music stand that says "T.A.C.K.I.," and then he starts to hop and make soft chanting noises. He does this for a time, then he raises his hand and the drums go dead. Without stopping his hopping he breaks into song to the tune of "My Country 'Tis of Thee."

"I'm Miss Tampon Liberty, still yearning to be free!"

This is the chant he's used in previous Miss Tampon Liberty ceremonies, and the setup is perfect: Behind him stretches the vast expanse of the Atlantic Ocean, the prayer ribbons are above him fluttering beautifully, and his gown is stunning. As he finishes the song, he slides into his speech.

"What is happening out here is basically a phallic penetration ejaculating into Massachusetts Bay!" he begins, and then goes on to talk about how the outfall pipe is sure to endanger the spawning and fishing grounds of Stellwagen Bank, as well as the beaches of Cape Cod. The Stellwagen Bank, he points out, is also the home of the Outer Cape's whales.

He then passes a metal bowl filled with seawater and invites everyone to touch it.

"This is the last time you will touch water from this bay that is unpolluted by the outfall pipe. This water is before the pipe—'B.P.' In several minutes when they open the outfall pipe this water will no longer exist. Perhaps someone can bottle it and sell it for money. When the pipe is open we enter a new age—'A.P.'—After the Pipe."

During the next part of the ceremony anyone who wants to speak or perform is invited to the makeshift podium, and three women come forward to read from a play by Jackie Freitas about whales. Jessica Diamond sings in a strong if oversoulful voice, accompanying herself on guitar. Others come up and speak. One woman says, "I'm appalled that there aren't hundreds and hundreds of people here." She goes on to explain that her family has lived on the Cape for three generations, and about how tightly bound Cape dwellers are to the environment. Then she begins to cry. The photographers click away.

The ceremony finishes with Jay reading off the names of animals that make their home in the Massachusetts Bay. Jan Kelly then rereads the names in Latin, signaling Jim ("This has got to be the strangest thing I've ever done"), who is standing by holding a small toilet, to flush the commode after each animal's name. Each time, the toilet makes the appropriate prerecorded sound. With each flush, too, Jay hits his metal bowl with a stick, making a melancholy toll. Initially, he has read off the names of fifty-two animals, one for each of the outflow pipes.

The next day Jay is very happy. The demonstration has made both the *Globe* and the *Cape Cod Times*. "Did you see? There's an incredible picture of me in the *Times!*" The photo shows him in his tampon applicator gown as he hops up and down; his eyes are closed, the seagull feathers awry in the wind, and the ocean sparkles in the background.

Jay formed the ecological group T.A.C.K.I. in 1984, and then, in 1985, he created his series of tampon-based mannequins. The first one was a model of Provincetown's Pilgrim Monument, entitled "TACKItown"; the second, a thirteen-foot replica of the Statue of Liberty, called "Miss Tampon Liberty," that had served as the rallying point for filing legislation at the Massachusetts State House to have plastic tampon applicators banned as environmentally dangerous. Critchley had shown up before lawmakers wearing a dress he'd fashioned out of three thousand of the "beach whistles." Capitol police had attempted to remove him but were so embarrassed they finally left him alone. Later the artist talked to the press about his gown, saying, "I like the sound the tampons make when you walk around in it. They clack against each other. I mean it's *loud*, which makes it harder for people to ignore my message."

Naturally, the antitampon bill died in committee for lack of support, but without Miss Tampon Liberty there wouldn't be the present project, namely, Cape Cod Bay's first "chastity belt." This was a proposed twenty-mile-long blockade from Race Point to Marshfield, south of Boston, meant to contain pollution, and if Christo could unfurl giant umbrellas in Japan, run a fabric fence through California, and wrap plastic around Florida islands, Jay seemed to be announcing, why couldn't he string plastic tampon applicators across the width of Cape Cod Bay? For decades Boston's sewage system had been sending debris to the Outer Cape's beaches, and now the proposed 9.5-mile sewage outfall pipe, capable of pumping hundreds of millions of gallons of pollutants into the rich fishing grounds of Stellwagen Bank, had to be stopped.

"The idea of this blockade is to use these applicators as weapons and send them back," he announces, explaining that unlike the blockade recently organized in three weeks by the Cape Cod Charter Boat Association to protest the planned septage tunnel, the twenty-mile-long flotilla could not be organized overnight. It required 52,800 tampon applicators. He had already collected 10,000 but needed volunteers to send him many more before the required number could be attained.

"But I don't want anyone sending me plastic tampon applicators that they're *using*," he stresses, tongue-in-cheek. "The whole point is to collect them off the beaches and make an environmental statement about plastics and marine pollution. . . ."

Conceptually, the idea of boomeranging the Establishment with its own evil instruments was reminiscent of Jerry Rubin's late, unforgettable stunt during the mid-sixties of showering the floor of the New York Stock Exchange with dollar bills, an event that had caught Critchley's attention when he was still in college. Another mentor, he explained to interviewers, had been Abbie Hoffman:

"I was affected by Hoffman's book *Steal This Book*—the title was a manipulation of the system and at the same time pointed out the insidiousness of it all—how the media just does what it's told," he said. "There's very little depth and substance out there, and with my work what I'm really interested in is breaking through that crust of superficiality—to try to reach below, where maybe there's a connection with people on a different level."

For Jay, it is impossible to separate his concerns for the community from his overall vision as an artist, including his work on the Swim for Life.

•   •   •

The Swim for Life is not the production of a regimented hierarchy, which may make the event all the more appropriate to Provincetown. Unlike Berkeley, Ptown has no tradition of organized politics or political demonstrations. Jay cofounded the Swim and is the primary organizer, and it's been going on for over a decade now. Every year many of the same volunteers come back. They know their roles, and they help the newcomers. Jay likes to keep meetings to a minimum; he believes they're counterproductive and provide an unhealthy arena for egos. He makes his phone calls, maintains his databases, and allocates responsibility to various trusted lieutenants. The power structure stays diffuse. "Horizontal," he calls it.

This Thursday, Jay meets with Rodney at the Crown & Anchor, where the Mermaid Brunch is scheduled to take place after the Swim. Restaurants from all over town have donated food. Bands and drag queens have volunteered their time. The meeting is over quickly. Jay's already gone over some last-minute logistics with the Boatslip, which is where the Swim is staged, and now he's off to the Unitarian Church to help set up the prayer ribbons for the Celebration of Life Concert on Friday, the night before the Swim.

Since the mid-eighties, the Universalist Meeting House has been the spiritual sanctuary where people could mourn the lives lost to AIDS. The Celebration of Life Concert was set up several years ago by local figures John Thomas and Jim Vincent in conjunction with the Swim for Life. Every year it is packed with townies and features local poets, musicians, and singers who donate their time for the event. None are "big name." Few own any of the waterfront houses with the great views. Many are committed year-rounders and that they meld so easily with the gay wash-ashores is one of the miracles of Provincetown.

The Meeting House was built in 1851 in the Greek Revival style so much in vogue at the time. Local ship's carpenters, using wood from nearby forests, did such sound work that the structure has held up well over the years, even though the steeple leans slightly to the right. The light tower on the building is lit every night in honor of the fishermen lost at sea. The pews inside are made of Cape Cod pine and imported mahogany. They are decorated with numbered medallions from carved sperm whale teeth, and every pew is covered with a worn red-velvet cushion.

The interior walls and ceiling of the sanctuary have recently been restored to their former grandeur. The newly redone trompe l'oeil painting that adorns the interior space gives the impression of marble walls and scalloped columns. It culminates in a dramatic apse framing the pulpit.

As could only happen in Ptown, the church is located exactly midway between the Backroom, the Gifford House, and the A-House, where, during the late seventies and eighties, there was more free-for-all gay cruising than anywhere else in town. The three nightclubs are each less than a block from the stately Christopher Wren–style structure, and the town's best bookshop, run by a middle-age gay couple for the past thirty years, is almost next door.

Jay is out in the long front lawn area that abuts Commercial Street, conferring with David Atkinson, a tall, well-built man with a twinkle in his eye, who describes himself as a "Libertarian nudist," hemp advocate, and tree surgeon. At Jay's "Septic Graduation" ceremony, he recently was awarded a degree in "Hempology." He also happens to be one of Provincetown's five selectmen.

"This is the last time I'm doing this, Jay. The torch has got to be passed on. Next year you do it or find someone else to do it," David says, only half kidding. They are there to hang up the prayer ribbons. They walk into the sanctuary, and David sets up his ladder just behind the elevated pulpit. He has a long rod that he uses for tree trimming and he climbs to the top rung of the ladder and then, using the rod, loops a bit of nylon fishing line over a hook in the ceiling. The fishing line is then attached to the middle of the prayer ribbon strand. The two ends are attached to the walls on either side of the pulpit: When the Celebration of Life starts, someone on the balcony pulls up on the end of the fishing line, and, as if by magic, the prayer ribbons rise twenty feet above the pulpit, meeting in two swooping arcs.

"The prayer ribbons are looking kind of tattered," David says, eyeing them.

"That's part of the concept," Jay replies softly, and the two men turn off the light and walk out into the yard. It is dusk.

Meanwhile, across town, Tony Jackett is just finishing up a long day out on the flats. The principal of a nearby prep school had called to tell Jay he had one hundred kids who wanted to help with the Swim for

Life. Jay, who had more than enough volunteers, suggested the school call Tony Jackett, the town's shellfish constable, to see if he had any projects that needed volunteers. Over the next couple of days, Jackett and the principal corresponded via e-mail.

"They wanted something that would be 'invigorating' for the kids. That was the word they used, 'invigorating,'" Jackett says, smiling. He decided that the high school students could help on a beach cleanup, picking up the bits of detritus the tides bring in, shards of plastic, bits of fishing nets, pieces of buoys, bottles. They could clean up the harbor shoreline and flats before the Swim for Life.

Several days before the Swim, two busloads of the kids, 120 in all, started out at the municipal parking lot on Johnson Street, not far from town center. One group worked its way east, the other group worked its way west. By the time they met, the tide had gone out and they were able to clean the flats.

"The kids were having a ball," Tony recalls. "Most of them had never been to Ptown before, and it was a beautiful day. Their teachers told them not to swim, but a lot got wet anyway. They were splashing and throwing water at each other, having a great time. Sometimes it would take twenty kids to move an abandoned net that didn't want to move. And when that wasn't enough we'd call over another ten kids."

A teacher, watching Tony supervise the teenagers, eyeing his deep tan, his bike and kayak, approached him. "You don't have a bad life, do you?"

Tony grinned. "Believe me, I've done my time."

On Friday at dusk the people started lining up for the Celebration of Life. It was a rich cross-section of the community, older straight couples, gay and lesbian couples of all generations, and groups of strapping young gay men, the so-called Gym Boys. Some of the people lingered at the table where the prayer ribbons were laid out, and with black markers wrote out their own messages and then quietly affixed the ribbons to the rope suspended nearby. Down the way, closer to the Meeting House, a table sold Swim for Life T-shirts, which by Saturday afternoon would be sold out. Jay flitted about, tying up the prayer ribbons, selling T-shirts, recruiting last-minute volunteers. It was an intimate crowd because Provincetown, despite the hordes of people who clog the summer streets, is a small town. Labor Day weekend was past; the tourist season was over, and on the night before the Swim for Life the year-round community was going to celebrate.

Inside the church a group of women was playing African drums. At eight o'clock, the big doors swung open and the people streamed in, making their way up the aisles to the pulse of the drums. When the crowd had settled, a plump woman, followed by her entourage, came dancing down the aisle. The group gathered around the pulpit, singing. Their voices reached a crescendo, and the long line of prayer ribbons suddenly rose in the air. It was a powerful sight, and people were visibly moved. Probably everyone in the room had lost someone to AIDS.

The celebration continued with a wild mélange of performances: an eccentric older woman in a campy cowgirl getup, yodeling while riding a small faux pony named Ricky Ricardo—or Dick, for short; drag queens and lesbian choirs; a handsome young man singing "Somewhere Over the Rainbow." There were poets who came up and read their poetry; there was Zoë Lewis and Her Rubber Band. At the end people sang together and danced and embraced their neighbors.

"Initially," recalls Jay, "I think we conceived of doing the Swim as an environmental celebration. That was the summer of eighty-eight, when a lot of New England beaches were being closed because syringes and waste were being washed ashore. Provincetown never had a problem like that since it has the highest tide change on Cape Cod, a nine- to twelve-foot difference between low and high tides. Imagine the flushing out of the harbor with that huge volume of water and energy! Once we thought about the symbolism of purification, we connected the Swim to AIDS. The first year we had sixteen swimmers and made seven thousand dollars."

Jim Rann, who has volunteered since the birth of the Swim for Life, recalls that first Swim thirteen years ago. It was on a Sunday, and he had been in the Universalist Church attending service, when suddenly in came Chuckie Vetter, dressed only in a gold lamé bathing suit and a long blond wig. Chuckie Vetter had AIDS and was battling valiantly to stay alive. He had always been a bit of a wild man and had his bouts with drug addictions, and now here he was, saying he was going to swim one and a half miles across the harbor. He had come into the sanctuary to try and rustle up some last-minute pledges. Chuckie was carrying a wrinkled old paper bag that people could put their money in, and when he'd finished his collection, he ran off to the Boatslip and presented Jay with his paper bag full of tattered wrinkled-up bills. It came out to three or four hundred dollars.

The first Swim started at the Boatslip and ended at Long Point. "I knew Chuckie wasn't going to make it," recalls Jay. "I knew he wasn't a swimmer. He had a lot of medical problems, so of course I had my eye on him." Eddie succeeded in only swimming a couple of hundred yards before he had to be pulled out. He died within the year.

"Thirteen years ago," Jay says, "Provincetown was a different place. AIDS was devastating people from the community."

Every week there were memorial services for the latest victims. When asked how many friends he's lost, Jay replies, "I can't keep track of them all. After thirty people, I stopped counting, and that was seven or eight years ago. Now I want to start counting again, because I'm afraid of forgetting."

The day of the Swim for Life, Jay woke up early and the first thing he did, even before he went to the bathroom, was to look out the window. It looked clear. He put on shorts, a shirt, and sandals, then went down to the water and put his feet in and saw the sky and felt the wind and sun. "It made it very concrete. It was a perfect day," he says. The week before, a vicious cold front had swept across the town and it looked like early winter, but now it felt like the middle of summer again.

After testing the water, Jay rode back up Pleasant Street to his house, had a breakfast of Eggbeaters and broccoli, and then went back down to the Boatslip. It was just after eight. He had created a new hat for this Swim—half a globe, with tendrils of ivy wrapped around it. He also had a large high-flyer buoy with a red lamé flag on the end. At the Boatslip, a large congregation of people was waiting for him and he said in mock exasperation, "Well, go on, then!" and in no time at all the deck was crawling with volunteers, setting up the registration table and the T-shirt stand. There was a first-aid center manned by the Rescue Squad, and big blue tarps, which would serve as colorful beacons for the swimmers, draped from the railings of the deck. The line holding the prayer ribbons was set up, and so was the finish line. More and more swimmers arrived, and an armada of small boats converged on the Boatslip beach from all over the harbor.

By nine-thirty swimmers surrounded the registration table, turning in the money they'd raised and a list of their sponsors. They were issued their bathing caps, and registration numbers were written in grease paint on their arms. Several people who were just passing through town and had heard about the Swim bustled around, trying to get the minimum pledge amount of a hundred dollars so they could participate. As it neared ten-thirty, Jay announced the opening ceremony.

Though the major awards ceremony follows the Swim, two awards were being given out early. Jim Rann, who couldn't make the closing ceremonies because he had to go to work, received the newly created volunteer award, named for David Asher, who had been a Swim for Life cheerleader for many years. Asher had died suddenly at the end of 1999 of a brain aneurysm unrelated to AIDS.

His brother and two sisters were on hand, and his fifteen-year-old nephew, Eddie Goldstein, was going to do the Swim today in his uncle's honor. Eddie had raised thousands of dollars in the last three years he'd participated. David's longtime partner, George Dunlap, was also present. "It's wonderful," he said. "It's going to keep David's spirit out there."

But for Jay the emotion of the moment wasn't centered only on Asher. As he presented the award, he flashed back twenty years to the time when Jim Rann had been a part of an inseparable group of four men—Jim, Paul Richards, Don Sterton, and Stephen Clover. Jim was the only one left.

"I met them as a group," remembers Jay, "around 1980, before AIDS even existed. I was boyfriends with Stephen Clover. He became a Baptist minister in a black Baptist church in Cambridge. He started out in the choir, the only white guy in an entirely black choir. He decided he wanted to become a minister, and, then, a few months after he was ordained, he died of AIDS. That memorial service was one of the most memorable experiences of my life. The whole choir from the Baptist church in Cambridge came to the Universalist church and sang for the memorial service. The church was packed. It was still a new experience, going to a memorial service. This black choir just blew people away. People were screaming and crying. It was incredible."

The gay community's collective memory has been seared by AIDS, and the straight community has no analogous experience of seeing its members fall one by one, except perhaps in times of war. Jay thinks for a moment. "People hadn't yet gotten burned out from going to memorial services. Five or six years into the epidemic, it grew to be too much. You couldn't go to all of them. But early on, people were still shocked. AIDS was just beginning."

The more one talks to Jay about these four men's intertwined lives the more one realizes how intimately connected he was to them. "Stephen and Don Sterton helped me out a lot when I was coming out as an artist. They helped me set up my first show at Cafe Edwige in 1981. Paul died first, then Stephen, then Don. After they died, Jim became positive. Giving Jim the David Asher Award reminded me of that time. They were inseparable."

Listening to Jay, it is difficult to ask, "How did you care for yourself in the face of this—emotionally and physically, both?" And of course, also to inquire if Jay himself is HIV positive—"Were you not infected by Clover? If not, why not? And do you have guilt feelings—like so many others in the gay community, a longing to be HIV positive so as to assuage your burden and/or simply be part of the gang?"

After giving Jim his award and locking him in a warm embrace, Jay next gave the Circle of Honor Award to Glen Cunha, who would not be at the later ceremony because he was holding a commitment ceremony with his partner, Ed Hudner. The award was a sterling silver medallion for individuals who had done the Swim for Life ten times, or raised ten thousand dollars. Glen stood there with his lover, who is also a Circle of Honor member. The commitment ceremony, which would follow the Swim, they told everyone, would commemorate their ten years together. Ten other swimmers would be among the witnesses. They asked everyone to come.

"To me, a big part of the Swim is about the relationships people make and how people's families come together for the event," says Jay, thinking about it later. "Besides Cunha and his partner, the whole Asher family was here. This year was a great year for my family. In the past, my sisters have volunteered, my brothers-in-law have volunteered, my nieces have swum before, but this year was special because my two sisters, Eileen and Anne, swam. My family's very close."

With the awards given out, there was a moment of silence for the dead. All that could be heard on the deck of the Boatslip was the fluttering of the prayer ribbons and the soft lapping of the sea. One young man, obviously a weight lifter, made a point of holding his chin up and keeping his eyes open as he let tears run down his cheeks.

With the Swim about to begin, Jay gave instructions to the swimmers and boat pilots on transporting the participants out to Long Point. A Rescue Squad worker described the symptoms of hypothermia. In the back of everyone's minds is the fear that they might not make it. There are strong currents that crisscross the bay, and the water can be frigid. Of course, in theory any swimmer in trouble would immediately be plucked from the water by an escort boat. "It's a relief when the last swimmer is in," exclaims Jay. "Safety is always foremost on my mind during the Swim."

Some swimmers jump up and down, shaking their limbs, trying to loosen up; others are stretching; still others have gone down the beach a little ways to meditate on the 1.4 miles of open water that lie ahead of them. Their rumination doesn't last very long. Big jars of Vaseline are passed around and the swimmers coat themselves in it—the Vaseline helps alleviate the chafing for those who choose to wear wet suits; for others it helps retain body heat. The idling engines of an armada of small boats make a deep, rumbling sound. The swimmers wade out and climb into the boats, a motley flotilla of fishing craft—inflatable Zodiacs, tour boats, Boston Whalers, Macos and Grady Whites, even an elegant, old-time mahogany-hulled Chris Craft. Jay will be riding with Assistant Harbormaster Don Fiset in the harbormaster's boat, and, as he climbs aboard, he puts his big buoy flag in a slot at the prow, and the boats are off to the Point.

Don Fiset is a Portuguese townie who's worked with Jay for the last two years on the Swim. He is a straight man, solidly built. In years past, when he was at Ptown High, he was known as something of a wiseacre; now, he is relentlessly good-humored. Like a lot of others, he has been profoundly affected by the changes in Ptown. If you ask him about the old days when local kids would take out after gays, he squirms and looks embarrassed. He's never read Erica Jong or Randy Shilts, but that doesn't matter. Ptown has made him grow up. "The Swim for Life does excellent work," he says. "It's a wonderful organization; it helps people who need help. They do the right thing, and it's important to support it.

"Our role," he says, "is to make sure no one's in harm's way, and we stick around until the last person is out of the water. Last year there was a woman, it was the first time she'd done the Swim, and she was determined to complete it no matter how long it took. We were there with her for three hours. Jay always says that he's there until the last person's out of the water."

With all the boats still making their way out to the Point, Tony Jackett is in his small fourteen-foot Whaler struggling to put in the last of the buoys that guide the swimmers across the bay. He's been doing it for the last three years, and this year he'll also be patrolling the 1.4-mile lane, picking up exhausted swimmers and offering help to anyone who needs it. The buoys are a homemade setup, high-flyer poles about eight or nine feet long with a buoyant bullet-shaped piece of Styrofoam in the middle and a large weight—bricks or pieces of cement—duct-taped to the bottom. On the top there are flags to guide the swimmers, but with the wind blowing around up on top and the bottom currents taking the anchor lines down below, Tony is having a hard time getting them into a straight line. Then, when Tony finally has the last buoys in, Grassy Santos, Flyer's son who runs the nearby boatyard, pulls up in his skiff and announces the whole line is off.

Without consulting the others, Grassy has moved a dozen boats to make a clear channel for the final stretch to the Boatslip; he's neglected to tell Tony, and now the channel is several hundred feet to the right of Tony's line of buoys. Tony curses as he turns his Whaler around and goes back to reset the buoys. He's cutting it close.

The swimmers are assembled along the broad yellow beach at Long Point. All are wearing bright pink fluorescent caps. An older woman lies flat on her back with her swim cap over her face. There are pretty gay boys, old men, old women, skinny people, flabby people, and curvaceous blondes. Behind them the Long Point Lighthouse is a mirage jutting out of the dune grass. Jay is, as always, striding through the crowd, wearing his bizarre hat, conferring and offering support. Swimmers are adjusting their wet suits, applying yet more Vaseline. Jay raises his bullhorn and shouts in a coquettish singsong, *"Five minutes!"*

The crowd starts cheering, psyching themselves up. They put their hands in the air and do the wave. A paunchy middle-aged gay man saunters about in a woman's leopard-skin swimsuit. There are often swimmers who choose to do the Swim completely nude but this year everyone is wearing something.

Finally, the whole group of 243 swimmers is gathered tightly at water's edge. Jay yells *"Go!"* and there is a flailing, splashing mass of arms and legs and pink swimming caps.

"Isn't it beautiful!" Jay says to no one in particular.

The swimmers are like a huge school of pink-headed minnows, or salmon beating their way upstream, seeking renewal in their traditional spawning grounds. It is an amazing sight. Across the water, the Pilgrim Monument, dedicated so long ago by Teddy Roosevelt, he of the Rough Riders and Big Stick, shimmers in the light breeze. Kayaks glide along on either side of the swimmers, shepherding them. Several swimmers wait until the chaos subsides before starting. The crowd on the beach roars out support, takes pictures and videos. And then suddenly, the beach is silent. The pink caps are one hundred meters away now, a kinetic splashing mass headed straight for Ptown. Jay climbs into the harbormaster's boat and takes off, while the huge Coast Guard launch cruises silently along the perimeter of the swimmers, its crew wearing sailor caps man their stations.

This last is a huge paradox, of course, a joke, but also quite serious— the straight coast guardsmen, some of them from faraway places like Kansas. What can they be thinking? What kind of education have these boys and girls from the prairie or the southern bayou gotten in their brief yearlong stint here in Ptown? Has the town changed their lives forever, democratized them beyond anyone's dream?

An older gentleman, who'd helped ferry swimmers over, cruises slowly back to the Boatslip and jokes, "The Coast Guard flagged me down on the way over. If they had been a little cuter, I would have asked them to take me into protective custody. . . ." Later he is more serious. A lawyer in Boston with a summer place in Ptown, it's his second year helping with the Swim. "You know, I sometimes think the cause is almost secondary," he says. "What's primary is the community building, where people come together to be greater than their individual selves. Black, white, gay, straight. It is not miraculous. It *is* a marvel."

Meanwhile, it seems like the whole town has turned out to support the swimmers. On the deck of the Boatslip, the new arrivals jostle and crane their heads, hoping for a first glimpse of the lead swimmer. It takes some time before he becomes visible. At first, all that appears is a tiny recurring splash that gradually grows in size until finally the pink cap can be made out. Right behind the swimmer are several others. The group that has broken away are those in the best condition. The main body of swimmers is still some distance out.

Down on the beach, there is an official roped-off reception area where the swimmers' finishing order and their numbers will be noted, just as they will be checked by volunteers to see if they need first aid. Hot tea is on hand, and Mylar blankets. The swimmers are still several hundred yards off when the crowd erupts, the cheerleaders on the beach jumping up and down, shaking their pompons. A man dressed only in a small black bathing suit begins to play the bagpipes.

Out on the water, the people in boats are emitting a steady stream of encouragement. There is a wide array of styles among the swimmers. Some choose to do the entire distance on their back so they don't get saltwater in their eyes. The more fit do the freestyle. Others alternate. Some of the larger individuals wear fins. Some mouth Zen. Others just do it.

Tracy Primavera, a swimmer, says later, "I felt great the whole swim. It was so quiet at times, and so beautiful. At points I'd look up and it seemed like a long way still, and after a while I started to get cold. But I could hear people's voices onshore—cheering us on."

The first swimmer is coming toward the beach. Every time he tilts his head to take a breath he can hear the cheers. In the shallow water, he stumbles to his feet and smiles. The crowd roars and a multitude of hands ushers him to the registration table, where he exchanges his number for a mug of hot tea. He has swum the 1.4 miles in thirty-four minutes and one second. His name is Brian Fehlav, and he is from Cambridge. According to Jay, he has never done the Swim before.

More swimmers are coming in; another man, and then, in quick succession, three women. The cheering hasn't diminished even though people know this isn't a race. If anything, it has grown more raucous. By the end of the first hour, a steady stream of swimmers reaches the Boatslip, and each swimmer is celebrated as if he or she was the first. Ecstatic swimmers pose for pictures on the beach. Everyone comes out of the water smiling. The prayer ribbons flutter in the light wind. The swimmers keep coming. There are 153 finishers, the most ever.

After two hours, most of the swimmers are onshore, but there is still a last group off in the distance and the Boatslip remains crowded with cheering supporters. These last three are swimming achingly slow, and in many ways their exertion speak more strongly to the crowd than those of the first-place finishers. Every stroke is a monumental effort. They meander off the course and are shepherded back. Then, finally, these last swimmers walk unsteadily out of the ocean. They are exhausted, but the joy is evident in their faces as the crowd cheers.

After months of preparation the thirteenth annual Swim for Life is over, and now Jay cruises in on the harbormaster's boat. The cheers grow louder and the cheerleaders have even composed a snappy little song in Jay's honor. They belt it out, as he climbs out of the boat and walks through the knee-deep water to shore, looking like an incongruous General Douglas MacArthur. He is beaming ear to ear as people shower him with kisses.

"God bless you, Jay!"

"Jay, it was smashing. Congratulations!" an older gay man says, embracing him warmly.

"You're so great!" a young woman yells.

Jay beams, but he's already thinking about the awards ceremony. He has to remember everyone, and there are so many people to thank! Jackie Freitas comes up to him and they have a terse conversation. Apparently, the sheet with the pledge amounts and the results of the kayaking part of the Swim has already gone to the bank, along with the cash and checks. This is a bit of a setback; now when it comes time for him to thank the kayakers, who have never participated in the Swim before, he won't be able to acknowledge how much they've raised. He tries to be philosophical, but he's a little peeved, especially as the sandals he left on the Boatslip deck have disappeared; he bought them ten years ago for five dollars, and they were close to his heart. But no matter. Jackie has also told him that the Swim for Life has raised over $100,000. Stunned by the amount of money collected, he seizes his flag and walks barefoot down Commercial Street to the Crown & Anchor.

There, out in front of the gay hotel complex, the Mermaid Brunch is in full swing. The outside deck is covered with people socializing, eating, and enjoying the sun, most of them running on high adrenaline, as they listen to Zoë Lewis and Her Rubber Band. Pearline, the town's best-known drag queen whose heart is as big as her big, flabby body, chatters with a passel of admirers. Then Jay begins the awards ceremony.

"Do you want to hear how much money we've raised?"

The crowd roars that it does.

"So far we've taken in over one hundred thousand dollars! It's just incredible. Thank you so much, and thank America for coming to Ptown!"

The multitude breaks into sustained applause. And then Jay Critchley begins to thank everybody, which takes some time: The kayak team from Esther's, he announces, has raised close to $4,000. The Provincetown General Store raised over $500 in donations from customers only a few days before the event. Five-year-old Gary Benjamin Rouse raised $25 selling his painted rocks. Eddie Goldstein, David Asher's nephew, raised $3,180. The list goes on. Jay hands out some of the awards and ribbons, then, visibly exhausted, passes the microphone to Betty Steele, the longtime town selectperson.

Even so, two hours later, Jay is still at the Crown & Anchor, supervising the cleanup. Tony Jackett comes up and congratulates his friend. "And thanks for mentioning the shellfish constable. That was very nice, Jay. I liked that," Tony jokes.

"Well, thank you, Tony Jackett, for helping out!" Jay says in his quasi-falsetto. He calls over his two sisters and his niece, Jessica. "Come on, guys, let's sing 'Minnie the Mermaid' for Tony!" And the Critchley clan break into song.

Tony has enjoyed himself at the Boatslip and the Mermaid Brunch. But at one point, as he sits there with his feet soaking in the pool, he suddenly exclaims to a friend, as if it were a revelation, "Look around! Everyone here is either gay or lesbian! I feel like the last of the Mohegans!"

The next day the headline on the Provincetown Banner reads, "Swim for Life Tops $100K Mark for 1st Time." Two days later, the money is still coming in. "It's so overwhelming," Jay says to his friend Donald. "It's going to be over one hundred twenty grand."

Donald asks what he'll do next. "I'm not doing a fucking thing," replies the exhausted Jay, then, after a brief silence, he concedes, "I just recruited two swimmers for next year. The Swim for Life never stops."

CHAPTER 25

AIDS

The AIDS epidemic hit Provincetown hard. As early as the winter of 1980, town nurse Alice Foley noted "the gay cancer." Over the next three years men were dying every week, usually as the result of Pneumocystis pneumonia.

"You'd see a friend on the street one day, then they'd be in the hospital, then they'd be gone," Jay Critchley recalls. "In the beginning it was just boom, boom, boom."

He puts the number of friends lost at more than a hundred. "There were so many memorial services that people stopped going to them," he says. "It just got to be too much."

The town government was slow to rouse itself to what was happening, but the response of the people themselves was extraordinary. The Provincetown AIDS Support Group (PASG) was founded in 1982 by two year-rounders, Preston Babbitt, an old-style seventies "political" gay with a Mohawk haircut, and Alan Wagg, the proprietor of a guest house opposite the Boatslip. Alice Foley, who had been Jay's colleague at the Drop-In Center, was the cochair.

Local artists donated paintings to what would become the annual PASG Auction and the nightclubs—the A-House, the Crown & Anchor, the Post Office Cafe, Pied Piper, and Pilgrim House—all held special PASG nights. Individually, many straight and gay women rallied to the cause, as well, overlooking their problems with "male dominance," and, later, even used the PASG as a model for a health group of their own, HOW (Helping Our Women).

"*Everybody* pitched in," recalls Len Stewart, PASG's executive director. In addition to donating money or items for the auction, people helped by plowing driveways or cooking meals for those too weak to do it for themselves. "Perhaps it's because every member of this community knows someone, knows someone well, who's living with AIDS."

The PASG now serves 362 clients Cape-wide, offers weekly support groups, transportation, meal preparation and delivery, counseling, social services including home care, and liaison services with Deaconess and Beth Israel hospitals in Boston. Back when the group was struggling, caring for single men covered with Karposi's lesions that made them look like they'd been splattered by a paintbrush, the biggest problem was trying to educate the EMTs on the Provincetown Rescue Squad to overcome their fear of the virus.

In June 1983, just before the start of the summer season, Chief Meads was observed giving out rubber gloves to the members of his police department. The beaches were barren, the restaurants all but empty, and suddenly the Boston media had itself a story. Overnight the town filled with TV cameramen, and the widespread coverage (which included sidebars on Ptown's resident homosexual congressman, Gerry Studds) served to frighten away whatever might have remained of the season's tourist trade, leaving town businessmen in a state of abject trauma. Locals became even more wary of the influx of gays.

The disease was still in its infancy, and little was known about its transmission or about how contagious it was. Restaurants received calls from customers wanting to know if the staff was gay. A local dentist moved his practice out of town. The usually fearless members of the town's Rescue Squad held meetings to decide on new guidelines. Even tourists on the whale-watch boats started asking who was grilling their hot dogs.

Jay, who'd helped Preston Babbitt organize the PASG, had just returned from a trip to Australia and New Zealand. Something had to be done to calm the town, and he came up with "The Immunity Mandala."

"I had been looking at the Maoris in New Zealand and the aborigines in Australia. So I started thinking about some kind of performance that would heal, like a purging of all the bad energy that was around."

"The Immunity Mandala" was a performance piece that drew nearly two hundred participants in the fall when it was staged on the beach in front of the Old Reliable Fish House. WOMR, Provincetown's recently organized listener-supported radio station; Police Chief James Meads; Jay's lawyer, Roslyn Garfield, and her partner, Realtor Phyllis Temple; the local Thrift Shop; and a dozen or so individuals—straight, gay, and lesbian—all supported the event. Critchley recalls:

"We created this symbol with colored sands that I'd collected, and we timed things so that after the ceremony was over the tide would come in and wash it all away—just as in many primitive ceremonials, ritual objects are used to evoke the spirits, but once the ritual is over the objects become meaningless. The circle on the beach was twelve feet in diameter. Four different color sands. While the tide took the sand, there was drumming and a dance-rhythm ritual."

And, as is always the case with Jay, there was a carefully worded program incorporating the mandala's chant that invoked the cleansing and purifying power of the town's waterfront:

"Give us the energy to fulfill the historic and spiritual mandate of our community, opening our arms to artists, writers, lesbians and gay men, and tourists from around the world, providing refuge and nurturing to all those lured to these shores," the mantra went, reproduced on the handout beneath the all but universal yin/yang/lamda sand-painting symbol.

"Give us the strength and pride shown by the women of this community, who have many times stood on this shore in vigil, in silence, waiting for their beloved fishermen, who often did not return.

"Through this mandala offering we gather together, and pray for health and wholeness, especially for those suffering from unknown and strange diseases, that each of us may continue to rejoice in hope and celebration with the life cycles around us. . . . Amen."

Jay, standing atop a lobster trap, had dedicated the ritual to the people of Provincetown, then spoken of the fear and confusion living in their midst. Among the many people involved was Jay's friend Paul Fonseca, whose brother was a principal dancer at the American Ballet Theater in New York, who'd choreographed the seven-person dance ensemble. Jim Shoulberg, who had lived in town for many years, was another. So was Ronnie Wise, a photographer and writer from Florida. The advent of protease inhibitors in the late nineties changed things and made it possible for those who are HIV positive to live with hope. But back then, prior to the birth of "the cocktail," testing positive was a death sentence. Poignantly, over the next several years all three died of AIDS.

"Ronnie was an oddball, like a real Provincetown character," Jay recalls. "Very independent, kind of a loner, and when he started getting sick he went home to live with his mother, which is what a lot of people with AIDS were doing. After he died, his mother called me up and said, 'I have his ashes, I'm coming to Provincetown on the bus from Florida. I want you and I to deal with his ashes together.'

"She was in her sixties, there was no father, so she came alone, bearing her son's ashes in a box. It was Labor Day weekend, she arrived and called me from the bus station. I mean, you just have to get the image of this lady from Florida, standing with a suitcase at the bus station on Labor Day in Provincetown with a box of her son's ashes, calling me, saying, 'Where do I go? I'm here.' So we got together and went out to Race Point, where we sat at the edge of the water and read some of Ronnie's poems, talked about him and dispersed some of the ashes. Eventually, I had to get to work and said good-bye. As I left, she was still sitting at the water's edge with her nylons on and half a box of the ashes. I figured, 'Okay, that's it.' I went to the Moors and I was setting tables, like it's around five o'clock just before people come in for dinner, and in walks this woman like an apparition—nylons down around her ankles, all frayed. No shoes. She had just been walking. She'd wandered across the dunes, wandered along the outer beach all the way from Race Point, and here she was, barefoot. She wasn't weeping, just kind of lost."

Maybe it was the memory of Ronnie's mother that made Jay decide to make International Re-Rooters Day an annual event. The ceremony allowed people to gather and say good-bye to loved ones who had fallen to AIDS, and it also brought together those many themes he held most vital: the community, the need to attack false values, the sanctity of nature, and the cleansing value of ritual.

A procession of people carrying Christmas wreaths and a discarded Christmas tree set in a makeshift model boat walked out across the cold tidal flats, singing "O Tannenbaum" and "We Three Kings," until they reached the water's edge. There, the tree, which was adorned with scrap tinsel, was set afire, Norse-style, and floated out to sea. Jay's role was that of shaman: Standing waist-deep in the freezing waters as the tide advanced, he chanted, sang, and communed with the great spirit, all the while dressed in a silver lamé suit and surplus gas mask.

"We're an uprooted people looking for connections with each other," he explained to a reporter covering the 1990 event, an old-timer from up-Cape who was having trouble keeping a straight face at the strange mix of young and old, sane and crazy people, as well as the gay-ness of the pomp and circumstance side by side with the gravity of what was happening. "And I'm sure that acknowledging loss is an important component of dealing with grief," Critchley went on. "This is a com-munity that has always experienced loss. One of the strongest images that comes to my mind when I focus on Provincetown is the image of women waiting on the beach for boats to return, waiting as a witness to determine if her husband is dead or alive. . . . In a way, we're all waiting to see what life brings. We're all witnesses."

In later years, Re-Rooters Day took on distinct and telling titles: "Oil My Lips," meant as a reminder of America's worship of cheap petroleum; "Prosperity Through Bankruptcy," celebrating the fall of Donald Trump, the S&L debacle, and the national banking crisis; and "Just Say Dough," a condemnation of the spendthrift eighties and its legions of white telegenic shoppers. Key to all of these were the objects people brought for "entombment" at sea that, taken together, mirrored the community's collective ethos: During one ceremony the tree was festooned with med-ical bills and pornography, as well as tokens of "obsessions" and "undue guilt." One woman added her recent navy discharge. A black man donated racism and white institutions.

At the end of the 1990 ceremony, as a totally hyped-up Critchley warbled his rewritten Christmas carols, longtime Provincetown art maven and nightclub proprietor Reggie Cabral turned to a woman in the crowd and asked, "Did you know Harry Kemp?" The woman replied she only knew the fabled poet of the dunes by reputation. "Harry Kemp was always doing stuff like this," Cabral said. "Provincetown always offers refuge to the socially conscious."

Not long ago, Jay approached Mark Silva, head of the local insurance company, son of the president of Seamen's Bank, and director of the

annual Portuguese Festival, with the idea of creating a combined fishermen's and AIDS memorial. Provincetown, unlike Gloucester, has
never had a monument to honor the thousands of its fishermen lost at
sea. To make the link to AIDS victims, Jay thought, could help bring the
community closer together.

"The town had talked about it forever. The only memorials we had
were the war memorials, that hideous structure on the corner of Ryder
Street next to Town Hall, and there's also the bas-relief, the *Mayflower*
memorial, that depicts the scene of the signing of the Mayflower Compact. So I went to Mark. 'It might sound a little radical . . .' I said, and
he said, 'Well, coming from you, Jay, I'd expect that.' "

Critchley suggested coordinating the fund-raising, knowing that in
Ptown, in the year 2000, there was a lot more interest in an AIDS
memorial than in a site honoring dead fishermen.

The project would take hundreds of thousands of dollars, and, if it
was to be done right, would involve a national competition, a jury, and
a review panel. "I was working with the man who set up the AIDS
memorial in Key West," Jay explains. His own idea for the monument,
not surprisingly, was to take a dragger, encrust the whole thing in sand
and put it up on a pedestal on the waterfront. "I wanted a Christmas tree
on the top encrusted with sand—a lot of them, you know, put Christmas trees on the tops of the mast. An omen, sort of a pagan ritual."

Silva, who speaks for the indigenous Portuguese community as
much as anyone in town, said that he'd have to think about it.

CHAPTER 26

CIRO'S NO MORE

The Portuguese are no longer the richest people in Provincetown, nor have they been for some time, but they retain that local citadel of finance, Seamen's Bank, which, if one were to chart such things, would have to be placed at the very top of the town's economic ladder. This is Provincetown's Chase Manhattan, Goldman Sachs, and Lazard Frères, all rolled into one. If you've been in town for a while and you've been successful, they'll treat you right.

In 1975 Seamen's still loved Ciro Cozzi, the kid from the Bronx who'd started out in 1952 making hero sandwiches. So did the two other banks in town, the First National and Cape Cod Bank and Trust. But 1975 was the year Ciro made a business decision that cost him dearly.

He was approached by the widow of Pat Patrick, the man who had owned the Flagship, Provincetown's venerable lobster-and-steak restaurant on Commercial Street, half a block east of Ciro & Sal's. The Flagship was a long, deep-set, ramshackle place built out over the water on pilings, with windows on three sides. Old buoys, driftwood, life jackets, harpoons, and other fishing gear hung from the ceiling beneath dust-encrusted fishnets. The place was relaxed, the food had always been good, and after ten o'clock, the bar, which was made of a weathered dory split lengthwise, was usually packed three deep.

Listening to Hilda Patrick's proposal that he buy the Flagship, Ciro at first said no. But Hilda, a cheroot-smoking toughie, who used to drink

with Mary Heaton Vorse, Hazel Hawthorne, and Ptown's other old-time
bohemians, persisted. She offered Ciro a great price. She told him that
only he could carry on the restaurant's tradition; he had "a responsibility" to the neighborhood. Finally, ignoring his accountant's advice not to
buy the place, he agreed. The Flagship became Ciro's Flagship, and there
was a grand opening with all the artists and beautiful women, dopers,
millionaires in paint-spattered dungarees, poetry-spouting alcoholic
divorcees, and psychoanalysts in from Wellfleet. That first season the bar
was the same screaming success it had always been. The kitchen wasn't.
Under the Patricks, the Flagship had served steak and lobster, fried
clams, fried shrimp, fried flounder, and fried scallops. Ciro, the big
shot, had the idea of turning the place into an East Coast center of
haute cuisine. He leaned toward sweetbreads. "I had these visions of
grandeur," he admits. He eventually turned the restaurant over to his
son, Peter, who had sound ideas for simplifying the menu but was
hampered by an unfortunate heroin habit. There were conflicts
between Peter and the staff. Peter would saunter into the kitchen in his
black leather jeans and tooled cowboy boots, dressed like a rock star, and
would interrupt the practiced flow of the chefs, who'd turn on him,
screaming. Ciro took back control, but the place was a money pit. To
keep it afloat, he siphoned money away from Ciro & Sal's.

"My accountant kept telling me, 'Walk away from it.' I couldn't,
though. It was a matter of pride."

Ciro convinced himself that, given time, the Flagship would make a
profit. He believed it so strongly that he started another restaurant in
Boston, then another in Orleans. He even entered into a discussion with
Norman Mailer and George Plimpton about opening a Ciro's in Manhattan, to compete with Elaine's. His credit was good, so he leveraged
himself. The late seventies and early eighties were Ptown's go-go years,
so why not?

His dream, he admits now, was to franchise the name "Ciro &
Sal's" for a national line of frozen foods, to use the Flagship as his base
of operations. In his mind's eye, he was going to do another Wolfgang
Puck and market gourmet pizzas.

It got crazier.

Ciro was shuttling back and forth between Ptown and Boston,

where he kept an apartment. The new Boylston Street restaurant had gotten rave reviews when it first opened, and Ciro played the role of *grand patron* relentlessly. His old pal and onetime waiter Varujan Boghosian, now an internationally recognized artist, recalls that Ciro was so busy socializing, he ignored the food.

"We had mushroom soup to start. It was cold. I said, 'Ciro, the soup's cold.' You'd think he'd race back to the kitchen and say, 'Hey, turn the flame up,' you know? But he didn't. We had chicken. The chicken was undercooked. I told him. . . . It was that way. He was enjoying . . . let's say his empire. He'd walk around, very generous, a bottle of wine here, a bottle of wine there."

In 1987, planning on retiring, Ciro decided to share control of the Ptown Ciro & Sal's with his daughter, Theo, after folding the Boston and Orleans start-ups. "I kind of pulled away from everything. But I kept pouring money into the restaurant. It used to be a cash cow, and I said, 'What the hell is going on?'" Over the course of seven years, he mismanaged the business and ran up a terrible track record with the banks. He owed money. He hadn't paid taxes, and he was paying exorbitant wages to the kitchen staff, thirty-three dollars an hour to someone doing prep.

When Ciro had first begun his expansion by buying the Flagship, all the local banks, including Seamen's, lined up and said, "No money down. Tell us what you need, you got a mortgage." When he was forced to sell the Flagship to two New York–area lawyers in 1989 in what was, essentially, a fire sale, the banks simply nodded and wished him the best. They were no more helpful when he needed money to save the original Ciro & Sal's.

"The banks screwed me, but it's also my own goddamn fault," he concedes. "I thought I could have it all, then things changed. It was pride. Maybe the hardest part is that they're also taking the name. I worked fifty years to build up that name. It's *my* name. What right does Larry have to use 'Ciro & Sal's'?"

"Larry" is Larry Luster, forty-five, the new owner of the restaurant with his wife, Cynthia Packard. Like so much else in Provincetown, the situation is an incestuous one. Luster, a black from Tennessee, originally came to Provincetown at age thirteen with his two brothers, and all the Luster boys had worked for the Cozzi family ever since. Larry's worked for the restaurant for thirty years. "They were nice kids. First they were in the kitchen doing prep, and then I put them on the floor. When I put them on as waiters, Al DiLauro said to me, 'Ciro, you've got to be crazy, they've never waited on tables, and they can't pronounce Italian names.' And I said, 'Look, they deserve a break.' So now I'm losing the restaurant to a Chattanooga kid that I befriended."

Another bitter pill is that the financing for the Packard-Luster buyout was being provided, Ciro speculates, by gay real estate speculators—the arrivistes, precisely the element that Ciro believes is eroding Provincetown's cultural heritage. "I can't prove it, but I know the money's coming from Bill Dougal," he says.

Ciro may be right. Bill Dougal is one of the most successful real estate agents in town, and although he denies having any role in the transaction other than acting as agent for the sale, it is a matter of record that Dougal and his partner, Rick Murray, have developed a number of properties that include Provincetown's most popular health club, MuscleBeach, for which they cannibalized another landmark restaurant, the Bonnie Doone. Most recently, they were among a group that purchased the downtown Crown & Anchor hotel complex for a reported $6 million.

At an emotional hearing in the Barnstable County Courthouse in March 1999, U.S. Bankruptcy Court Judge William C. Hinton negated Ciro's last-gasp effort to retain ownership of the restaurant property. In addition to testimony from Luster, in which he acknowledged Ciro as his "father figure," two other of Ciro's employees were there. Ciro sat alone, and, according to published reports, he wept.

CHAPTER 27

WEEKEND ENCOUNTERS

Tony Jackett is meeting a friend at the Provincetown Tennis Club. For a man of fifty-two, Tony is in remarkable shape, but he works at it. He swims in the ocean, jumps rope, does push-ups and crunches, and at home he works out with weights, a medicine ball, and a speed bag. He's uniformly bronzed, but if you look closely at his left eye, you'll see the faintest trace of clouding near the pupil—all those hours squinting across the glittering ocean can take their toll, and many fishermen suffer from glaucoma as they get older.

The tennis club, which is in the East End, shares a rambling, barn-like, two-story building off Bradford Street with the DNA Gallery. The small parking area in front is covered with crushed clamshells in the "old" style, and the fences surrounding the six courts are made of rickety two-by-fours and patched chicken wire. The club sits in the middle of the forest that separates Ptown proper from the dunes, and the woods around the courts press in on the ancient fences. It is a public club, available to anyone with the twenty dollars for an hour's worth of court time.

Tony and his younger opponent have been rallying for about forty-five minutes when Chris Busa walks past and begins hitting balls against the backboard. Chris has a long history with the tennis club. He was the club pro and taught tennis for fourteen summers between 1970 and 1984; it was Chris who started the Year-Rounders' Tennis Tournament.

"Hey, great letter in the *Banner*," Tony calls out.

"Thanks," Chris replies, hitting the ball without looking up. Chris has recently had some complicated dealings with what some longtime members of the tennis club have started to call "the new regime." Behind the phrase is the fear that the club has been taken over by people who resent the presence of heterosexuals, and Chris, a straight male with an honorary lifetime membership, thinks his presence is resented by many of the lesbian members. The conflict escalated when Chris was denied entry into the Year-Rounders' Tournament, the very one he had started, ostensibly because he was behind on his dues. The demand for payment ran counter to the privileges conferred by his lifetime membership but the women now running the club had taken it upon themselves to strip the former club pro of his honorary membership.

Chris says he discussed the situation with the club manager, who agreed that the dues could wait until the next issue of *Provincetown Arts* came out. In his letter to the *Banner*, he wrote, "People, who did not know me, for reasons they could not articulate, blindly attacked me— so gratuitous, so uncalled for, so unprovoked." His treatment by the administration, he wrote, was an obvious effort to blackball him.

Tony's friend, who knows Chris only in passing, asks, "So what's the deal—they want you out?"

Chris, without stopping his tennis, declares dryly, "They want me dead."

Maybe not dead, but within a year, Chris would discover that they definitely wanted him out. The women called the police and had him removed from the premises. Chris, in turn, filed a complaint with the Massachusetts Commission Against Discrimination, charging the club with "discrimination on the basis of gender." Later, when the women refused to drop the criminal charges of trespass and resisting arrest, the impecunious ex–tennis pro was forced to defend himself, unsuccessfully, in court.

After an hour and a half on the courts, Tony calls it quits. It's Friday, the galleries will be hopping, and he's scheduled to go to Jay Critchley's Septic Opera performance—a troop of Boston opera singers concertizing from Jay's artwork cesspool.

Tony, shirt off, body covered in a sheen of sweat, walks with his friend from the lower courts back to the clubhouse. The short dirt path leads through a gate and then through the other four courts, all of which are being used by athletic middle-aged women playing doubles. In Provincetown, it's not making a great leap to assume the women are lesbians.

"Wow. I haven't been here in a while," Tony whispers to his friend, as they quietly open the gate and begin to tiptoe down the edge of the court.

"Get off the court! We're in the middle of the game!"

A stout, middle-aged woman with her hair cut short on the sides, long in the back, is glaring at them. Tony's friend, a bit sheepish, asks, "Then how are we supposed to get out?"

"You wait until the point is finished!" the woman says in a clipped voice. And then, exasperated, "Fine. Go. The point is finished." The three other women continue to stare, and the first one adds, "Faster! Hustle! Run!"

Tony stops and turns on her. *"Relax!"* he says tersely. She continues glaring at him. Tony, an impeccably polite man, is angry and places great emphasis on every word: *"It's-just-a-game. . . ."*

Both men walk slowly past the first court. As they reach the next, they pause, taking their time to ask, "Mind if we pass?"

The women there look at them, stymied. "Go ahead then . . ."

"I am sure," Tony's friend says later, "that if we were gay women that wouldn't have happened." Tony, too, thinks that's the case, and he asks a woman who has been affiliated with the tennis club for decades. Unless there's a tournament going on, she says, club etiquette allows you to walk through the courts.

Tony returns home to shower and change. He's back in town around seven. Susan rarely goes along with him on his Friday-night jaunts. First he swings by the Bangs Street Gallery. The director of the gallery, a young woman named Amber, is a friend of Tony's son, Luke. She's already set up one table outside for hors d'oeuvres and Tony helps her bring out a second.

The gallery is showing portraits by David Armstrong, a New York photographer with strong ties to Ptown. The portraits are all of young boys—what one gallery visitor describes with a grin as highly competent gay soft porn. There is also a female painter, who has done an interesting series of portraits in a style similar to Lucian Freud's. Tony wanders through, looking at the work.

Tony knows some of the local artists well, and he talks with them before getting on his bicycle to go to the Septic Opera at Jay's house in the West End. Ninety minutes later, he's back. It's still early, only nine, and the streets are teeming. In addition to the Bangs Street Gallery, there are five or six others in the so-called East End Gallery District. An old friend of Tony's, recently resettled in town, invites him to have a drink at Ciro's and Tony agrees, but first he says, "We have to go to my friend Richard DeQuattro's show at his gallery up the street."

Richard DeQuattro is a gay artist who usually dresses in long, flowing clothes and capes of his own making. His hair is early Farrah Fawcett and he's a little over the top, as Hollywood types say. He greets Tony with an affectionate hug.

Tony remains fascinated with these men, who are so different from himself and the men he grew up with.

Then it's on to Ciro's, where the bar is nearly empty. The men order their drinks and talk quietly. A woman sitting two stools down lights a cigarette and drapes her arm over the empty seat to her left. Her cigarette is a few inches away from the two men.

"Excuse me," says Tony's friend. "Could you please put that somewhere else? Thank you. I appreciate it."

The woman, a little drunk, counters, "This is a bar. If you don't like the smoke, leave."

"I'm not asking you to put it out, just to move your cigarette to the other side."

"Leave," the woman says again.

"Look, I said *please*," he reminds her. Tony's friend has a bad temper and he knows it. He's bending over backward.

"If you don't like it, then just get out!" the woman repeats. Her companion, a woman wearing a black Nike sweatshirt, pasty-faced and muscular from long hours in the gym, gets off her stool and makes her way around to where the two men are sitting. She holds her arms like a weight lifter, ballooning out from her sides. Before she can say anything, Tony's friend waves her off. "Enough," he says. "I'm not going to argue with you about this. Just leave it, huh?"

The woman hesitates. Before she has time to say anything, Tony's friend repeats himself, "Just leave it, huh?" But the other woman, the one with the cigarette, can't let it go.

"Who the fuck do you think you are? This is *my* town!" she yells. She has pulled the gay trump card.

Tony's friend is staring straight ahead, drumming on the bar with the fingers of his right hand. He leans toward Tony and asks, "What do I do? I don't want to lose it. . . ."

"Stay cool, man."

"I'm trying, believe me."

The woman is still raving. Tony's friend, who bussed tables at Ciro's in the early sixties, is used to crazy scenes. He thinks the present situation is one of the craziest ever. Suddenly, the third person in the women's party, a gay man sitting on the far side of the two women, stands up and starts to walk out. As he passes by, he turns to Tony and apologizes, "I'm really sorry."

The bartender, Robert, comes up from downstairs lugging a case of beer. The woman calls Robert over and whispers to him briefly. He comes back to the two men. "Listen," he begins, "it's fine to have a disagreement, but you can't call her a bitch."

They didn't, they say, and Robert goes back to confer again with the woman. The two men hear her ultimatum: "I'm a regular customer here. Fuck him! It's your choice—them or me!"

Robert is nonplussed. Just then Larry Luster, the restaurant's new owner, walks in, drawn by the woman's voice, which has carried all the way downstairs to the main dining room. Tony's friend is sitting on his stool, visibly trembling with anger. Larry looks at him a little suspiciously and asks what's going on. Tony intervenes, explaining. Luster walks back down the bar to the two women and says, "This man has been a patron of Ciro & Sal's for the last thirty years. If you can't coexist, then *you* leave."

There is a moment's silence. "Fuck this shit," she suddenly yells, throwing two fifties onto the bar. Her sidekick is already on her feet.

"You can kiss my ass." She turns on Luster, knocking over her stool as she backs away from the bar, screaming that she's going to have her friends boycott him, that she's going to put him out of business. Luster says nothing. The drunk continues with her threats all the way down the stairs. They can hear her outside in the garden even, then ranting in the alleyway running alongside the building leading back to Commercial Street. Robert, who's gay and originally from New York, is shocked. "I've been a bartender in Manhattan, Boston, here, and I've *never* seen anything like this. I will not be held hostage by some drunk dyke!"

The night is ruined and the two men soon leave. The woman, they later learn, has been in town for about three years and embodies the recent monied element, the great philistine cultural shift. An heiress, she bought a house in the East End for $1.3 million or so—a place that used to be occupied by one of America's great novelists near the site where Lewis Wharf once stood, where the Provincetown Players put on their productions.

Three months earlier, at the Portuguese Festival celebrating the coming of summer and the Blessing of the Fleet, she had been kicked out by none other than the festival's director. There, too, she'd been drunk, making a name for herself in her new adopted town.

There is one final encounter for Tony's friend before the weekend ends.

"I was in front of Seamen's Bank, almost at the post office," he told Tony afterward, "stuck behind this black Saab convertible with Jersey plates. A huge fat woman was driving. Her girlfriend was sitting next to her, and they were just inching along, doing the tourist thing, not giving a shit."

The convertible's slow pace had already backed up traffic, but then the women stopped to chat with a group of other women. Someone back down the line blew a horn.

"After last night, I could see what was coming," said Tony's friend. The woman on the passenger side jumped out of the convertible and aimed herself at the nearest target: Tony's friend.

"What's your problem?" she asked.

"I wasn't the one who honked," he said, and then, unfortunately, suggested that it wasn't worth getting upset on such a beautiful day.

The fat woman at the wheel, who had heard the exchange, took offense. "Who're you to tell us what t' do?" she barked. The second one chorused, "And you don' like it, go back to New York!"

"Get fucked, you little worm!" the woman at the wheel added. Since this kind of thing was not totally unheard of in Ptown's streets, Tony's friend shrugged in an exaggerated sort of way, holding his hands up in the air, as if to say he was agreeable to anything they said.

The woman who had gotten out of the car tried again. "You asshole!"

Tony's friend gave another shrug. "I'm not from New York, but why don't you just go to Nantucket next summer. Do us a favor, skip Ptown."

"And why don't you go back to *Israel*," the woman snarled now.

Her voice was loud, louder than she realized, and the after-silence just hung in the air. Passersby and people sitting on the post office steps who had been watching were now paying attention in a different way.

Tony's friend opened his car door and got out. He had lost control.

"Shame on you! *Shame!*" he bellowed, shaking. "Here in Province-town we welcome diversity! You're our guest! And you—a lesbian, shouting anti-Semitic slurs! *Disgusting!*"

He took a breath and started again.

"*Disgusting*, you hear!"

The people who'd been listening on the sidelines started clapping. Two women in their mid-thirties, both obviously gay, joined in by boo-ing the women in the Saab, while another passerby yelled at the women to "Shut up." Loud honking came from several cars in the rear. The Saab sped off.

Later that night Tony's friend couldn't stop talking about the inci-dent. At the Old Colony, even with a few drinks in him, he remem-bered how he'd been shaking.

"Can you believe it? 'Go back to Israel'—in broad daylight, Ptown?" Tony asked of no one in particular. "I mean . . . I hate stuff like this. . . ."

None of the people who were sitting with them said anything. It was a new Provincetown, and nobody wanted to talk about it. But by the next morning, the story of the two anti-Semitic women was all over town.

CHAPTER 28

TROUBLE
IN PROVINCETOWN

Deep down, Provincetown was in mourning. AIDS, the demise of the fishing industry, and now the decay of the year-round community, bohemian and Portuguese both, had created a vacuum. Years later locals would attempt to unravel what had happened by recalling the winter of 1976, when the town lost two draggers, the *Patricia Marie* and the *Captain Bill*. The two fishing boats had gone down within several months of each other, and the entire community had turned out. Straight, gay, Portuguese or Yankee, rich or poor, it didn't matter, people kicked in for the widows of the nine drowned fishermen, put on fundraisers, baked cakes.

All of this stood in sharp contrast to what happened in 1978, only two years later, at Town Meeting. Electrician Ronnie White, who was an ex-selectman and head of the town's Rescue Squad, stood up to rail against a slate of new zoning restrictions: "Who're these people coming in and telling us how to use our property?" he yelled. "We've had this property for generations, we know how to use it, and now these people are telling me how t' build a bulkhead? When I can and can't put in a dormer? They think they know better? Who says?"

The applause had been thunderous, the moment defining. For locals the new regulations were a synecdoche for the outsiders; by the

mid-nineties the majority of the Board of Selectmen was gay and lesbian, just as gay men and lesbians controlled an overwhelming majority of the town's committees and licensing boards. For locals, this last
situation was the most aggravating, since the newcomers now had the
power that had traditionally been held by the Portuguese.

One person ideally situated to see this was Joe Taves, the town's leading CPA, whose client list included the Portuguese business establishment as well as many of the affluent summer people. The straights, Taves
recognized, were no longer the dominant force in town, and, like so
many others, he saw that it was a question of money—who had it and
what they were doing with it. More cash was floating around than anyone had ever seen before, largely because real estate was changing
hands at an unprecedented pace, and the gays were "the most savvy speculators around."

"Somebody buys something for $250,000, they throw some money
at it, and they sell it for $750,000 two years later. Then they buy some-
thing for $400,000 and sell it for a million. That's the kind of money that
was being made around here."

Taves marveled at the newcomers' aesthetic sense, pointing out
that his fellow locals had a name for it—"fairy dust."

"They have a tremendous amount of talent for this stuff. I mean,
they can take a shithole and make it beautiful. It's like they just say,
'We'll go in and sprinkle some fairy dust and make it look fantastic.'" He
laughs.

The newly factionalized environment troubled him, though, especially now that almost all the town committees were under the control
of gay men and women. Years before, if you wanted a permit and went
before someone whose name was Perry or Santos, chances were that
you'd get your permit the first time around. Now, Taves says, "down at
Town Hall we don't know anybody. . . . You hear things like such-and-
such board is controlled by lesbians, or you've got to be gay to get a
permit from some other committee. If you're Portuguese, forget about
it. You're going to get shit thrown at you unless someone on the board
likes you."

He goes on, his frustration building.

"You talk to any straight person who's had to go down there to get a
permit, and it's like, 'Oh man, you don't know what you're asking for.' I

mean, it's all negative. Negative, negative, negative. And you might want to do something very simple. . . . So you start in October. The first meeting they discuss your plans and make some suggestions. Now when do they meet again? The next month. So you go back the next month with their suggestions incorporated into your plans, and they say, 'Oh no, we don't think it's going to work.' Another month goes by, and you come back with more changes, and it's, 'Well, we're not too sure . . .' By the time you've gone through all the committees it's nine months."

The gays, he says, "are now by far the richest, most powerful people in Provincetown. Power," he adds, "can be very intoxicating. A lot of these people *love* being on these committees."

Taves has to be careful, talking about gay power, and for the moment he switches gears. He does, after all, continue to do business in Provincetown.

For the accountant, the principal fact of Provincetown life has been the shift from an economy based on fishing to one dependent on tourism, which now accounts for sixty to seventy percent of all local employment. The town's year-round population stands at less than 3,500 yet there are 48 restaurants, 16 bars, 4 pizza stands, and 3 erotica stores. In addition, the tax rolls show that there are 66 apparel boutiques, 18 jewelry shops, 8 hair salons, and no less than 13 real estate agencies.

Crowne Pointe, the latest in high-end, gay-owned guest houses, is rumored to have cost over $4.5 million. Its better suites go for $425 a night in high season, generally with a three- to five-day minimum. The Brass Key is another guest house that falls into this category. Unprecedented in Ptown, these new five-star accommodations offer three-hundred-ten-thread-count sheets, whirlpool tubs, fireplaces, PCs, and refrigerators in every room, as well as antique furnishings and gourmet cooking. The BMWs, Mercedes, and Saab convertibles lining Commercial Street during high season point to the same affluence, and if there is any question that Provincetown has thrown in with the Vineyard and the Hamptons in its commitment to expensive pleasures, there is the East End's new Dean & DeLuca–style food shop that offers fresh-baked baguettes at $3 a loaf, buttermilk crème fraîche, and handmade tortellini.

Large amounts of money pass through Provincetown—estimates

put annual tourist dollars at over $100 million. Even so, the younger set doesn't seem to get much out of this since almost 15 percent of the town's population is living below the poverty line—double the rate for Barnstable County as a whole and 60 percent higher than for the state. Although the 1990 census still has yet to be updated, the federal government's 1995 definition of the poverty level is $7,470 for a single person living alone, $10,030 for a two-person household.

Provincetown has the third-lowest per capita income in Massachusetts. Yet its waterfront properties, most of them former fish sheds and small sail lofts, start at over $1 million. In the last decade, the run-up in local real estate has been so spectacular, even in comparison with the Hamptons and the San Francisco Bay Area, as to warrant full-page articles in the Sunday *New York Times* and *USA Today*. According to *Banker and Tradesman*, an industry organ, the median price of a single-family home in 1992 was $165,000; in 1995, $190,000; by 1999 it was $335,000—making Provincetown the costliest town on Cape Cod. Currently, the average price is $379,388, as opposed to the Cape-wide average of $179,000. That's townwide, not the choicer properties. According to Bill Dougal, the town's reigning Realtor, 97 percent of all recent buyers have been gay. "That's who's coming into our office," he says. "It's Joe and Harry, Leslie and Donna. We just sold something last week to a straight couple, and it was like, What are they doing in Provincetown? I mean, straight couples are not moving into this community. They can't afford it."

Regina Binder finds it a tough balancing act, keeping her mind on her work and tracking the inequities of the town. "Provincetown," she says, "is no longer tolerant of poor people."

The problem can be traced back to the loss of year-round rental units, itself traceable to the profits that are being made from weekly rentals during high season. Typically, the new strategy is for home owners—principally out-of-town, middle-age, double-income gay couples—to charge $20,000 to $25,000 rental over the summer, which usually is sufficient to cover their mortgage and taxes, then to use their property themselves on weekends and holidays in the off-season. The rest of the time the house remains vacant.

The Town Assessor's Office estimates that over 60 percent of the housing stock is owned by nonresidents. Long-term renters find themselves scrambling for space, priced out of the market. It has grown so difficult for low-paid workers in Provincetown's service industry to survive that business owners have started importing them. In a surreal twist, some restaurants have signed agreements with foreign governments, resulting in a wholesale influx of Irish and Jamaicans; these workers are boarded in specially built dormitories on the periphery of town, take their meals at the restaurants where they are employed, and, according to some accounts, cannot return home to their native lands until they have "earned out" their work contracts.

"The fact that you have restaurateurs buying real estate to house their workforce and then docking their workers' pay for 'rent' creates a situation that amounts to indentured servitude," says Mark Baker, a highly regarded community activist who is involved with Outer Cape Health Services and the Provincetown AIDS Support Group, in addition to chairing the town's Board of Health. "And it's not just the Lobster Pot, Clem & Ursie's, and the Provincetown Inn," he says, referring to the more popular, "mixed" downtown restaurants. "Some of the most expensive gay places use Jamaicans for their cleaning staff, too."

The Brass Key and Crowne Pointe held fund-raisers for AIDS victims and supported gay charities like the National Gay & Lesbian Task Force. *They* were the marginalized, put-upon, and discriminated-against people. For the most part, the names Lincoln Steffans, Eugene V. Debs, and Upton Sinclair were meaningless to them, certainly of less weight than Madonna and the Latino disco craze Ricky Martin.

Provincetown had more and more come to be Fire Island.

"All they want to do is throw lavish dinner parties," Baker continues, "and there are *a lot* of caterers in town nowadays, as well as four interior decorating shops. We have a kitchen supply store, another niche business, which started out small and expanded to a double storefront. You know who one of the partners is? Hunter O'Hanian, the executive director of the Fine Arts Work Center! Sure, he's pure of spirit but also smart like a fox.

"There's also been a gradual upscale-ization of clothing stores. Body-Body has gotten bigger and more chic. Number 5, Louie's across from Spiritus—they just rented the place on a five-year contract. Also Daniel Cleary's store—T-shirts all the way up to three hundred, four hundred dollars, hand-sewn microsilk fabrics from Europe. Cleary just moved into a bigger space on the Shank Painter Commons. He's also started a store in Chelsea, too, and the interesting thing is that he started here and went to New York, as opposed to the other way around. That tells you everything.

"Restaurants, too. You used to be able to go to Gallerani's and get a huge meal for ten dollars. Now you're hard pressed to find an appetizer at Gallerani's for twenty. Chester's is a better example—they've developed a clientele of exactly the people who are building the multimillion-dollar homes. Their prices are extraordinary. The same goes for the Martin House, Front Street, and the Mews."

But perhaps the clearest expression of what was happening was how gay had become an identity, not a sexual preference, for a large number of the newcomers. Philosophically, this constituted an absolute: You *were*, or you *weren't*, and it didn't take an Einstein to understand that day to day, in the course of the most casual interchanges, this amounted to a local *apartheid*, something separatist and sometimes hostile. If you had any doubts, all you had to do was count the rainbow insignias that filled the town from one end to the other—jumping out at you from car bumpers, the balconies of rooming houses, the windows of real estate offices; even shops that sold T-shirts and souvenir tchotchkes boasted the banners. The new PC sentiment applauded this iconography as an expression of tolerance and oneness; others saw the flags as divisive and sanctioning antistraight behavior on the streets.

"I won't patronize businesses that fly rainbow flags," says Dr. Brian O'Malley, the town's bearded general practitioner, who had treated "all kinds" and had been a card-carrying member of SDS prior to coming to Provincetown in the early seventies. "I consider that analogous to flying a Confederate flag, to flying a Nazi flag. I'm sorry, it's exclusionism. That flag is saying to me I'm not welcome there."

John Sinaiko, filmmaker, craftsman, volunteer fireman, and expatriate New Yorker, whose mother was a major benefactor of the Art Association during the seventies, says, "It never used to matter if you were gay or straight in this town, and now it does."

Mary-Jo Avellar, the town's longest-seated selectperson, says that "For a while it seemed like there was this incredible homogenization going on among straights and gays. Now straight people are feeling kind of like, 'Gee whiz, you know, we never had any problem with you, how come all of a sudden you gay people are having problems with *us?'* "

In 1997–98, when the gay-backed Provincetown Business Guild printed a new letterhead for its stationery and press releases, it carried the slogan "Our Town." A number of people protested, including, reportedly, several of the PBG's own board members. The settlement that emerged from the ruckus involved the PBG having *two* logos. Some mailings went out with letterheads reading "Everybody's Town"; those aimed at a strictly gay audience said "Our Town." It was "ridiculous and solved nothing," editorialized the *Advocate*.

"I'm a member of a persecuted group," says one recent transplant, a onetime *Premiere* magazine editor from New York, "and this town is ours. We deserve it. Eventually straight people are going to have to leave."

Throughout the late nineties, people tried to come up with ways to deal with the new, wealthy Provincetown. Ginny Binder thought one solution to the problem of year-round rentals might be a "usage tax" on short-term rentals, which would make vacancy-ownership less attractive. Stricter growth management bylaws, more subsidized housing, and turning unused commercial space like the old A&P into cottage-industry work zones were other suggestions she made to buoy the town's economy. A meeting was held the summer of 1998 in the annex of the high school, organized by Jay Critchley. For a Monday in August, the attendance was phenomenal and included many who were seemingly in a position to implement change, like Ginny and her associate Tom Boland. A subsequent meeting, held three weeks later, was not as well attended; by the fall, most initiatives had been relegated to chance meetings in the post office or A&P.

It is not for lack of effort that the artists' stake in Provincetown is slipping. Some of the most outspoken defenders have left suddenly, in midfight, like John Perry Ryan, longtime AIDS activist and community organizer, who quietly left town with his partner, novelist John Caruso, in the late spring of 2001. Up until his unexpected departure, Ryan was a relentless defender of the Provincetown experience, helping to write the town's Hate Crimes Initiative and working on an antibias school curriculum. From his new home in central Vermont, Ryan issued the following statement: "It used to be that you could eke out a living in Provincetown and you were among the many who were doing the same thing. Now one feels almost inundated, swallowed up, suffocated by the wealth."

One of Ryan's colleagues on the antibias curriculum project and a longtime advocate for the youth of Provincetown, writer Kathe Izzo, found herself at a similar crossroads less than a year later. The single mother of three young daughters, for the previous eight years Izzo had supported herself by developing small projects aimed at helping Provincetown's young people who were in trouble. Her largest effort, the Shadow Writing Project, funded primarily by a matching grant from the Youth Initiative of the Massachusetts Cultural Council, was supported energetically by Critchley's Provincetown Community Compact, which offered administrative and accounting services as well as yearly retreats at the C-Scape dune shack. Although lucky enough to own her own home, Izzo found herself living in smaller and smaller quarters, renting out larger parts of her house each year to meet rising living costs, and refinancing like crazy until there was nothing left to refinance.

In 2002 she moved to the more affordable art colony of the upper Hudson Valley, buying a large commercial property in Hudson, New York—already filled with more than its share of expatriate Provincetown artists. She worries about her kids coming back to Ptown when they're older and finding it unrecognizable.

Although there have been a number of affordable housing projects developed to help local artists, many, albeit grateful for a place to live, find themselves skeptical of such offers. The majority of these live/work dwellings are still out of their price range. One such program recently promised to award "down payment grants" of up to $2,000 to enable creative people to purchase property, an offer so out of line with the realities of the real estate market as to be laughable if it were not so depressing. To be a working artist in today's Provincetown means exactly that, an artist who must work full-time at a job other than art.

Michael Carroll, managing director of the Schoolhouse Center and proud homeowner in the new artists' development of Hensche Lane

across from the old A&P, finds himself in just this predicament. A successful painter himself, represented by Robyn Watson in her new gallery
at Kiley Court, Carroll wonders if he will be able to make the payments
on his new "affordable" condo. Working full-time at the Schoolhouse
Center, along with other longtime, year-round artists David Foley, Larry
Collins, and David Carrino, he excitedly shows off his painting studio,
still unfinished, in the attic of his home. The pitch of the roof was mis-
drawn by designers, and so the attic affords the six-foot-two artist just
enough room to work, when he has time. Unfortunately, like most of
his peers, the main thought in his head these days is not his own work
but money and real estate, refinancing, and the possibilities of rental
income.

Many of these new housing projects call to mind the more collo-
quial urban use of that term: clustered dwellings occupied by minorities
and the fiscally challenged. Although clean and well manicured, these
new "communities" are overwhelmingly sterile, and therein lies another
irony. Developed for the most part by Ted Malone (who himself is
building a grand home overlooking the moors at the far West End) with
various collaborators such as the Fine Arts Work Center and one of their
primary benefactors, Alix Ritchie, they are spoken of by Ms. Ritchie as
a way "to keep the soul of Provincetown alive." But the soul of the town
is in those buildings that are full of quirky details and anecdotal histo-
ries, and these have become overpriced second homes.

It is the housing crisis and the inevitable loss of the "rebel class" that
Ginny Binder considers the town's biggest problem. "That's what made
Provincetown a mecca for anyone who came with nothing. The free-
dom to be."

Because of the geographical boundaries of the town—the sea on
three sides, coupled with the National Seashore—expansion and
development possibilities are nil. "You can't build here," says Ginny.
"There aren't the lots to buy, and we're also restricted in our water.
What this means is that there are real limits on sustainable economic
growth. We have to look at our population and make sure that they are
accommodated without freezing the community. We're talking about
looking at the demographics of this place, which is the poorest, lowest-
earning town on the Cape and one of the poorest in the Common-
wealth, too."

The dilemma now, what with escalating property values and their many consequences for the year-round community, is that preservation alone won't stabilize things or stem the flight of the Portuguese, artists, and other nonmillionaires.

Although respectful of town matriarch Alix Ritchie, Ginny feels that Ritchie, like Keith Bergman, the town manager, has tended to factionalize the town. "What Alix wants in Provincetown is not necessarily for everyone to be able to be here. For example, Alix would love to see a marina. She wants to see MacMillan Wharf developed for recreational boats, which is the kind way to say 'yachts.' I don't think she wants only rich people here, but many of the issues she champions, even though they're good issues, aren't ones that can be supported by people who don't have money. She's not an elitist. In fact, I'm convinced she means well, but you have to be in a certain socioeconomic realm to benefit from what she proposes, or appreciate her vision of the community."

Separatist and clustered as they sometimes tend to be, it took the local Portuguese no more than a year after the *Advocate* folded in 2000 to see who was running things. But for them and others the real indicator of what was happening was the annual Town Report, which showed that during the year 2000 there had been only a single birth in town. The previous year the figure had been four. Now the birth rate was *one* out of a year-round population of 3,500! For many—and remember, for a hundred years and more Ptown's roots had been ingrainedly Catholic—this was the most singularly horrifying fact of all, sending ripples, as it did, into every corner of the community—the schools, the manor, the church. All seemed in jeopardy, about to vanish without a trace. "We've lost the town" was the whisper on most people's lips as they wondered how much more time they actually had left.

One old-timer, the rock 'n' roller, bon vivant, and whale-boat skipper Joe Bones, coined the catchy phrase "Take back the rainbow." Bones was one of the original members of the Jug Band, a seventies group that had started out banging on pots and pans and just wailing away. Eventually the group began to gel, evolving from the old-time San Francisco Bay Blues tradition. They played seven nights a week at the Surf Club, from Memorial Day through Labor Day, and as things worked out, the gigs lasted all the way through the mid-eighties.

Bones was also one of the originators of the Dump Concerts, held at the town dump in the early afternoon. The first concert drew about two or three hundred people. There was no fancy sound equipment or pricey admission, not even a generator, just people and their dogs hanging out, soaking up the tunes, and imbibing. By the third concert, there were over a thousand people, and the police arrived, ticketing people for just about everything, even simple parking violations. The party was over.

Bones wasn't the only one protesting the changes in Provincetown. Another old-timer walked through the streets like an idiot late at night, half-boozed, chanting, "Get it straight / I ain't gay / And I ain't leaving!" Still others would drive down Commercial Street too fast, cutting it close as gays paraded along three abreast.

Those more philosophically inclined consoled themselves with thoughts that what was so precious about the Outer Cape could never change—the all-embracing harbor, the dunes, the soft morning light, the muzzy fog muffling the clank of distant buoys.

With more and more of the local powers-that-be bringing in their income from elsewhere, Provincetown is more homogenized, more mainstream, more PC. As Izzo prepares herself for her exodus from town, she is barraged with phone calls from fellow artists. "You're leaving? The town is really going to miss you!" Not "I will miss you," but *the town*, the town is what will miss Kathe Izzo and those like her. The phrasing is interesting because Izzo likens her relationship with Provincetown to that of a relationship with a dysfunctional lover.

"I fell in love with this place, crazy, head over heels in love, and I disrupted everything in my life to live here. And I took the place head-on, too. Never said no. I can't fight endlessly for a right to live here. And I'm not talking just real estate. I own my home. I'm fighting for a place, just a place to breathe. I feel abandoned."

She recalls an old friend, Mara Tracy, the owner of one of the first in the wave of home furnishing businesses in town. After a few years moving to smaller and smaller and less fashionable locations, Tracy found herself bankrupt and moved out to L.A. with virtually nothing. "I came to Provincetown with my little nest egg, with the idea of finally living the life I deserved. It turned out it was easier and less stressful to lead a corporate life than to fight it out on the streets of Provincetown. I don't miss it." In her last winter in town, Tracy came up with the idea of constructing a guerrilla memorial in the center of town, dedicated to those forced to leave their home for economic reasons. She put up notices in strategic locations, asking for contributions to the growing list of "casualties." Unfortunately, she moved without ever executing the project.

The point for so many is to find something that works. Across the street from where Ginny lives in her tiny seven-hundred-dollars-a-month cottage, her neighbor Paul Bowen, a fifty-one-year-old sculptor of uncommon ability, struggles with the same problem. Bowen is Welsh. He came to town as a Fine Arts Work Center Fellow in 1977 and was then elected as one of the youngest members of the elite Long Point Gallery. Three years ago, he volunteered to do the cover illustration for a Provincetown AIDS anthology, gratis. He lives on the sale of his sculpture and the occasional teaching stint, and with his wife, Pam Mandell, manages to get by because the Fine Arts Work Center provides him with a low-rental house bequeathed by the estate of the late painter Gerrit Hondius. Bowen's studio is at the rear of the house, in the same area where Hondius used to work. Like Binder, he is part of a new coalition of year-rounders, people brought together by the housing crisis, by the town's AIDS epidemic, by the wintertime beauty of the Outer Cape, and by their respect for one another's work. Bowen feels he owes a certain amount of his success to his connection with the older Provincetown and his membership in the Long Point Gallery. He is one of the few artists left in town still able to cultivate this connection to the historic days of Provincetown's art colony.

As early as 1974, artist and gallery owner Yeffe Kimball decried the growing pressure on the artist to conform in order to survive. "Artists need to feel welcome. They can't work when they feel unhappy," Kimball claimed on her way out of town to relocate to Sante Fe, New Mexico, after refusing to up the rent on her several Ptown apartments. Now such a statement seems naive, almost sophomoric. Nowadays, Provincetown is no less arduous a home for creative people than any other setting. Where will the Harry Kemps, the Sharon Niesp, the Ray Nolans go? Those in a position to do something about the situation shrug. They do not know who Sharon Niesp and Ray Nolan are, and some haven't heard of Harry Kemp either.

"But we're not going to give up," Binder says. "People in my position have no choice. Provincetown is our home. We know it's unique and that we're lucky to be living here. We're just going to have to find a way."

CHAPTER 29

LIFE IN
THE THEME PARK

For Jay Critchley, what's at issue in Provincetown isn't gay versus straight; it's the haves versus the have-nots.

"I never went to art school," he says. "I was a year-round person, working six nights a week at a restaurant, and I wasn't in the loop at all. I knew a few artists who lived here, but the summer artists—even now there's a real distinction between people who come for the summer and people who live here. I can remember Ellen O'Donnell, head of the Art Association, saying, 'Why are you guys always working? Why can't you come to all these events?' Well, hello? We're working. We're not like rich summer artists from New York."

This, of course, was the nub of it. Jay was on the other side, the working-class prole, and issues of money were as central to his life as they were to his work. Critchley was asking people to take a hard look at what the new money was doing to the community.

Artists in town were losing "the luxury of being poor," and, to complicate their plight, a good number of locals were bulldozing old family-owned boat sheds so they could cash in like everybody else. The very *look* of Provincetown was different. Traditionally, shingles were weathered; now everything was high-gloss. Storefronts had displaced elegant, if lopsided, bay windows, and privet hedges had been cut down to make room for wide driveways. Spidery, scaffoldlike outside stairways of treated two-by-fours serviced new one-bedroom "studios" and defiled the pure, austere lines of classic one-and-a-half Capes, just as dormers protruded from the mansard roofs of Greek Revival mansions. It was now all about numbers—the restaurants, B&B's, and other fast-turnover businesses, and all of it on a scale far beyond what any previous wave of tourism had ever wrought.

Critchley's analysis went further than architecture or even the gallery scene that had devolved, for the most part, into a vulgar collection of quick-buck outlets peddling "interior decorator art," homoerotic castings, and even mass-produced laser-painted landscapes.

Not every new arrival in town was significantly rich, of course, but the large number who were had chosen to announce themselves in very visible ways.

Critchley had begun to read periodicals like the *Gay and Lesbian Review* and the leftist *Gay Community News*, and A. L. Rowse's *Homosexuals in History*, as well as other books on gay sociology and psychology. He was using the Internet to research patterns of gay consumerism and income distribution. One thing that interested him were the changes in gay-oriented marketing ever since AT&T and Continental Airlines sponsored the New York City Gay Games in 1994, during the celebration of the twenty-fifth anniversary of Stonewall. What made gay and lesbians a market niche wasn't household income but the community's special characteristics as consumers: higher discretionary income and more disposable time, both attributable to the absence of children. Compared with the straight population, gay consumers spent significantly more on travel (with an emphasis on warm locations); on alcohol (gay culture has traditionally centered around the gay bar); on clothing, jewelry, cosmetics, and drugs (exclusive of HIV drugs); and on the growing array of financial services that cater to the special problems of managing joint ownership of assets for unmarried couples.

All of this, by the late nineties, had been accepted by Wall Street and stemmed from the extensive market research into gay and lesbian spending habits conducted by mega-companies like American Airlines, Levi-Strauss, American Express, Absolut Vodka, IKEA furniture, and Saab. The turning point, historically, had been the launch of *Out* magazine in 1992, when the editors banned all sex ads to provide a more congenial environment for conventional advertisers with dramatic results.

"The general rule of marketing, borne out by years of practical experience and research, is that if you want to sell more of something, target the people [or type of people] who are already buying it," asserts Howard Buford, president of Prime Access, Inc., an advertising and marketing agency that specializes in emerging markets, including gay and lesbian, African-American, and Latino consumers. "As consumers, gay men and lesbians have measurable preferences. . . . We can only speculate as to why that is, but it seems likely that cruise lines and resort hotels didn't create this demand but are instead, as it were, going with the flow."

The psychosexual *whys* were unimportant, and Jay refused to be daunted by the charge that he was dealing in stereotypes or even, as a few people alleged, that he was homophobic: Provincetown had become a consumer society, a place of trophy homes, show-off gardens, and fancy automobiles. Even in the wake of the AIDS crisis, hedonism ruled the day. Thanks to the Provincetown Business Guild, gay businessmen were flocking in from as far away as San Francisco and skillfully "flipping" real estate, opening restaurants, hotels, and boutiques. Few of these new arrivals were artists or writers; they were money people. Many had business interests in gay hubs like Key West, Palm Springs, and Malibu, and what they brought with them, in addition to their expertise, was an attitude that put status first.

They were also bringing *cash*, as the local Realtors were more than happy to tell you. Many of the one-million-dollar homes and guest houses were being bought outright, without mortgages. What was happening wasn't just an influx of big money but people whose funds were liquid, which gave them additional clout.

Because Ptown was small, more land was needed for homes and businesses. Developers were somehow going to find it, and one proposal made in the early nineties was to put a solid-waste disposal plant near Clapp's Pond, threatening acres of precious wetlands. Another proposal was to widen the two-mile-long route out to Race Point, where the town's airport was located; the narrow two-lane country road ran through woodland and unspoiled dunes, but this didn't matter. Although it was never fully spelled out, the underlying reason for the expansion was to accommodate fuel tankers and tourist buses, so that the tiny fifty-year-old landing strip could be turned into "an international jet airport," according to Peter Souza, the town's outspoken environmentalist.

When Souza and his gang blocked the road-widening plan, he was labeled homophobic, a charge he denied. "I'm not homophobic, I'm *wealthaphobic*," he said. "I mean, there's nothing wrong with money, but if it's going to be used to destroy our heritage and replace our way of life and our history, then screw them."

"The money, the showplaces, what was happening was all about status and cachet," says Jay. "The house up on the hill with the $30,000 sink, the cars, and everyone going, 'Oh yeah, have you been to that house? He's got a pool. He's got guys over there at three in the morning.' This wasn't unique to the gay community, obviously, but here, again, it was the imbalance. It wasn't the money alone. It was the elimination of the balance between the classes that absolutely limited creating a *real* diversity here."

Critchley decided it was time to get organized. His vehicle was the Provincetown Community Compact, a community-building and philanthropic organization dedicated to keeping Ptown intact. Provincetown, he announced with the group's formation in 1993, was "a cultural sanctuary"—a distinct legacy of "people, place and environment that nurtures the soul and the creative process." The Compact would be a catalyst, raising funds for collaborative work among the community's artists, and acting as a link between the artists themselves and arts organizations, government agencies, the local business community, and the public.

Jay set up a five-person board, hired an accountant, and arranged for volunteer legal assistance. Then he placed his annual Swim for Life under the Compact's umbrella. Funds raised by the Swim were earmarked for the PWA Coalition, the AIDS Support Group, and the Family Tree Project, which plants trees on public land in memory of those who have died of AIDS.

For the next ten years, the Compact was Critchley's war wagon. It sponsored performance events like the Operafest, Theater in the Ground, and the MusicArt Concert Series; Fall Arts Festival; the Shadow Writing Project, a once-a-week outreach tutorial for twenty to twenty-five elementary and high school students meeting in small writing groups; and, in collaboration with other local groups, the Art Archives, established for the purpose of documenting the work of Outer Cape visual artists, performers, writers, and composers who'd died of AIDS, all in all some eighty-five in number.

There were awards from the Massachusetts Cultural Council, the Cape Cod Arts Foundation, and other institutions. Even so, it was an uphill fight. By the late nineties it was tougher, not easier, to talk about the changes in town. Behind closed doors there was criticism that the Compact was a way for Critchley to line his pockets; his critics called him narcissistic, vain, opportunistic, and a media hound. Jay responded by saying that publicity was *absolutely* part of his work.

"What is it that I'm trying to say? Am I trying to say, 'I'm Jay Critchley, I'm fabulous'? Or am I saying, 'This is a serious issue here.' I mean, I'm the messenger. I'm using the stage to communicate my ideas about what I feel is important in this dialogue about the environment and everything else. I have no problem with the terms *exploiting, manipulating.* That's the way the system operates."

What bothers Jay most is the unrelenting efforts of the Provincetown Business Guild. Backed by the owners of gay and lesbian guest houses, restaurants, discos, boutiques, catering services, and health clubs, by the late nineties the group had evolved as a marketing tool with a highly sophisticated Web site. "What we thought was excess in the eighties was quaint compared to the nineties," says Jay. "The money, the way people were buying, and most of all, the lack of any opposition to that kind of excessiveness. . . ."

"What makes Provincetown so special?" a typical PBG ad might read. "While internationally known for its charm and beauty, Ptown is THE gay destination! There are no closets in this community. Show your affection! Be yourself! Come Tomorrow and Stay Forever!" One gay travel magazine asserted, "If gay people ruled the world, this is how one might imagine life to be everywhere. . . . The testosterone level in Ptown is off the charts!"

National gay tourism was, and is, a multimillion-dollar industry, and the PBG wanted Provincetown to have its share. Deciding that profits shouldn't be limited to the traditional summer season, they came up with Holly Folly. Advertised as "the World's only Gay and Lesbian Holiday Festival," it was created in 1997 as a spirited stroll for gays during Ptown's shoulder-season, when the town is at its most hospitable. Jay saw it as nothing more than a "shopping extravaganza."

"Holly Folly, the latest Yuletide attraction," he wrote in a cleverly satiric piece in the *Banner*, "fits in nicely with the town's vision of extending the tourist season year-round (tourists should now be called 'visitors' or 'guests,' and there is no more 'off-season'). This will alleviate the winter drought when people tend to their lives and write and paint and meditate. . . ."

According to the Critchley narrative, local businesses were embezzling away the soul of Provincetown. It is "the colonization of Ptown by postmodern gay consumers," he claims, pointing to the fact that Holly Folly was just one in a long line of profitable events the PBG had organized in the name of gay identity. Gay Family Week, Fantasia Fair, Leather Weekend, Gay Pride Weekend, Annual Single Men's Weekend, and Women's Week were others. Even Halloween was being billed as a "gay" extravaganza. For the millennium, the Art Association had rented itself out to promoters putting on a New Year's Eve gala, with dinner tickets going for $125 a head; the town was sold out, there was traffic gridlock downtown on New Year's Day, and Alix Ritchie, the publisher of the *Banner*, threw a laser show on the side of the 253-foot-high Pilgrim Monument.

To some, it was cheesy. But that didn't matter. Gay men and women had poured into Provincetown and the town raked in the chips.

By the late nineties, the PBG compiled a digitized mail and telephone polling operation that was being used to support candidates in local elections. The machinery had been put to work in support of a "diversity in curriculum" agenda put before the school board in 1997, then three years later it again came into play when a member of the school board, a straight man, was subjected to a voter-recall petition after he had the temerity to question the future of the schools in light of Provincetown's dwindling, single-digit birthrate.

The irony was that the new gays, many of them comfortable retirees, voted overwhelmingly to re-fund the crumbling high school to the tune of $6 million rather than accept their role in the town's changing demographics. For Critchley, pluralism and genuine diversity had been all but forgotten.

"The newer gay and lesbian property owners still have to prove something, so they focus on being gay. This whole concept of gay pride without talking to the people who live here negates the whole idea of what it means to be gay in Provincetown."

Part of Critchley's strategy was to restate his critique, then restate it again and again, to bludgeon you; although he could be shameless, he was rarely without art or humor. With *Provincetown Arts*, he created a pullout place mat "map" in advance of the millennium holiday season. Dated "Thanksgiving Day, 1999 - April Fools' Day, 2000," it carried the large logo "Provincetown Survivalist Camp Resort" and presented a vermillion-on-white outline of the Outer Cape that showed Provincetown as an island, cut off from the "mainland" at the Provincetown-Truro town line. The outlying, "offshore" cartoons that surrounded the new Ptown were ten or so in number and depicted such attractions as the Pilgrim Monument overshadowed by a new, castlelike skyscraper flying banners with the caption "Visitor Processing Center—Gaydar Testing/Credit Checks/Fashion Values"; a clearly identifiable Jay Critchley popping up out of his Theater in the Ground at Septic Space; a Pentagon-like fortress dubbed "P-Town, Inc. Gayted Corporate Compound & Heliport"; the beach at Flyer's Boatyard ("After Hours Male Bonding & Survivalist Party"); the town "Welcoming Committee" made up of seven men, a single female, and a monkey (a spoof of the Village People gay disco group). Other equally savage but accurate caricatures included the "Lobster Claw Commitment Chapel," "Gay Golden Triangle—Boatslip/Crown & Anchor/Gifford House/A-House Axis," and "Ms. Gay Target Market," represented by a silhouette figure in high heels superimposed over a standard shooting-gallery ring target, its crotch area at one with the bull's-eye.

If there was really any doubt as to what was being said here, the tongue-in-cheek place mat sought to help newcomers understand Provincetown by identifying it as "The World's Only Gayted Theme Park for Well-heeled Gay, Lesbian, and Bisexual Survivalists Fleeing Botheration from Y2K."

In a related vein, he's suggested that anyone not rich and gay in Provincetown be banished to a service-sector underworld, and that a checkpoint be established on the highway leading into town, designed to turn away undesirables not meeting strict criteria of "theme park" behavior, fashion, spending, and liquidity standards.

The astute Critchley, with an eye to capitalizing on this transformation of Ptown into what he calls a Guppie ("Gay Urban Professional") paradise, has even founded a company, P-Town Inc.–Formerly Provincetown, whose slogan reads, "You'll swear you were really there." More than any other local resident, for the past twenty years he has addressed the changes attendant to the so-called gay takeover, even as the Guppies come heavily armed in their "Reinforced Sports Futility Vehicles," their thickly padded wallets, and perhaps most of all, their smug ignorance.

The invasion mentality ("Let's take the town over") disturbs him. Critchley is well-versed in Ptown history; he understands the town's tradition of tolerance for people who are "different," and he's frustrated at the homogenizing force of the upscale gay urbanites.

"Are we going to be hiring artists to paint on the street or hiring fishermen to mend their nets so people can see what it was like to live here?" he asks.

One of his answers to this question was the so-called Alms House Project, which resulted in his arrest for trespassing after he stapled a banner and two signs to the front of the last remaining "unspoiled" house in the West End. The incident took place on November 13, 2001, at 141 Commercial Street—less than a fortnight before Thanksgiving, and not much more than a stone's throw from where the Pilgrims first stepped ashore a fortnight before celebrating their own first Thanksgiving in America. The symmetry of it all was delicious. No one appreciated it more than Jay, who, as always, kept a smile on his face.

"The place was a wreck, and what caught my attention was how the house just didn't fit in there. For most people it would be an eyesore, for me it was a very *textural* kind of icon—textural, meaning that all the other houses in the area were newly painted smooth surfaces with perfect windows and everything in place. Here you had this rough-hewn wreck—I mean it had asbestos siding and was scheduled to be torn down anyway."

The house stood on the water side of Commercial Street, the land running down to the beach, and in today's market it was worth probably $1 million. The local attorney, Chris Snow, had inherited it from his father and also owned the building next door, where his tall California-handsome wife ran an antiques shop. More shops lay to the east, between the wreck and the Provincetown Deli, and all of it was new— the general store, Joe's Coffee, several galleries and flower shops, and a beauty spa.

For Jay, it was a natural.

"I just noticed this place and so I felt, like, there was something calling me, beckoning me to make a statement."

What was beckoning him was the news that the place was going to be torn down for another piece of new, upscale real estate. Permits had been granted, and the bulldozer already signed up, "so I felt a calling to respond," Critchley says. "I didn't know what it was going to be. I just started taking notes and making observations."

This was at the end of the summer, and mulling over the possibilities when things calmed down after the annual Swim after Labor Day, he came up with the idea of the Outermost Alms Museum—as in "almshouse," or "poor house." The idea was to honor the heritage of the community that takes care of its poor, as Provincetown did at the turn of the century when there was an Overseer of the Poor, and "widows houses" were provided rent-free to the families of men lost at sea. The echo of Dickens was unmistakable. " 'Almshouse,' I love the word," he says. "To me the house symbolized the character of the town in the midst of our present sudden affluence, and also as being lost on a number of levels."

What he did that sunny November morning was to staple a red and yellow flag over the bay window of the condemned dwelling, along with two signs reading "Outermost Alms Museum." The flag was tattered; he'd had it for twenty years. It was about six feet wide and eight feet long, and he even used a stepladder so as not to lean against the side of the building. The whole operation, with the assistance of his friend Chris Silva, took about five minutes. He'd even made a point of doing his "installation" during daylight hours, not covertly after dark.

That afternoon he left for Boston on one of his periodic jaunts out of town to attend a meeting with the Volunteer Lawyers for the Arts, and a seminar about filmmaking near Newbury Street. He was gone for two days. When he came back, there was a message on his answering machine telling him to call Sergeant Souza. Chris Silva had also gotten a call from Souza, saying that the owner of the property was upset and that the policeman wanted to talk to them. Together. ASAP.

Eventually it became clear that Chris Snow was determined to file a complaint. It was slightly ridiculous, of course, not just because Jay hadn't disturbed or damaged anything, but because the old wreck was slated to be demolished a week or two after Thanksgiving. None of this mattered, though. Jay's sense was that Snow was insulted.

"He probably felt that I was personally criticizing him, because a lot of people had been on his back about the property for years, 'Why aren't you doing something about it? It's an eyesore.' He probably thinks I'm making fun of him, but it has nothing to do with him."

Roslyn Garfield's advice was to try and talk it out with Souza, who was one of the community-minded cops who'd come up under Jimmy Meads. Snow refused to withdraw his complaint, though. "I don't know what I'm going to do," Jay said matter-of-factly when told he'd have to stand trial in Orleans sometime in the spring. Grinning, he added, "I might just have to represent myself."

Here was another sweet Provincetown irony. Not only was Chris Snow Tony Jackett's cousin, but the judge most likely to hear Jay's case was Robert Welsh, Jr., the third of three Barnstable district court judges, all of them sons of Provincetown, whose control of the Outer Cape court remained unbroken after ninety-four consecutive years. The present Judge Welsh's father, Robert A. Welsh, Sr., had tried, among others, Norman Mailer, Marlon Brando, and the editorial staff and writers of the *Provincetown Review*. Now Jay Critchley, with another Welch, was faced with the responsibility of holding up the same distinguished dissident tradition.

Ptown may be the focus of much of his work, but critics in the outside world have been taking notice of Critchley's antics for some time. Recently he finished a Marshall Cogan Visiting Artist Fellowship at Harvard, where he was running a theater workshop on gender issues for the sons and daughters of the nation's elites. *The Lympdyk Diatribes*, as the Harvard production was dubbed, was a poignant, probing look at the social pressures that define gender roles and the great spiritual burden of the phallus. After the opening night performance in the basement of Adams House, Critchley, dressed in his trademark black biker's jacket, announced that he'd be taking the production on the road, and some of his new protégés, a few of them openly gay, looked at him in awe.

"But I'm not interested in followers, or having an artistic 'school,'" he told the packed crowd after the applause died down. "There are issues to confront. You must bear witness. My mother taught me that years ago, when I was still an altar boy, and it makes more sense to me now than ever before."

He laughed, giving it a bit more falsetto than usual, then bowed and grandly swept out into the wintery night for a nightcap with friends who'd driven over from the Cape.

Many would call the artist's struggle to save Provincetown a quixotic quest or misplaced nostalgia, but Critchley insists that he has always been deadly serious. "Provincetown," he says, "has become my palette.

"I've sometimes thought, 'Oh, fuck it. I just want to leave this place. Enough is enough. Like a lot of the Portuguese, I'm gonna move to Truro.' But that's very scary, a frightening thought," he adds.

One consideration is that the town is safe for him as a gay man. It's also beautiful, with a history rich in the arts, and like many other college-educated wash-ashores, he has a theory that the Cape's geology has forced him to have a special "connectedness" to the place that he wouldn't have anywhere else. He's fifty-five, he still has tremendous energy, and much of this, he's certain, derives from the ebb and pulse of the local tides, which he sees as Provincetown's essential logos.

"You really have to use cosmic imagery. I've never calculated how many tons of water move in and out of our harbor every day, but we have the greatest tidal range on the Cape. Some other places, it's three or four feet. Here it's ten or twelve. Four times a day, in and out twice a day. The energy is massive.

"And the tides also move tons of sand, too, remember. Provincetown is a sand dune, it's constantly shifting. Ten thousand years ago the glacier left glacial till, clay, rocks up to High Head, which was then the end of the Cape, and then, as the water rose, it eroded the rest of the Cape and the wind and waves built this sandbar. Provincetown."

Living on the isolated fingertip left most inhabitants unfit to live anywhere else—desocialized, capable of coexisting only with others of their own kind.

"You can't escape Provincetown no matter where you move, and the fact is that it's very hard to recover afterward," Critchley says. "People actually have little groups in L.A. and San Francisco. They get together and talk about how much they miss Provincetown and how they hope to come back. But it's not just the natural beauty they miss; what they miss most of all is how people don't judge, that's probably the bottom line—in Provincetown people will laugh at you and tease you, but you're accepted as part of the community. You have a place here. Everyone has a little niche that they fill."

The perfect example was Popeye, one of Provincetown's three or four town drunks. In his late sixties, the toothless vagrant was known to most people from his meanderings up and down Commercial Street with a shopping cart swiped from the A&P. He'd rummage through the garbage cans to collect pop bottles for the deposit money. This he did openly, each and every week, staying a couple hours ahead of the town garbage truck, and the cops never busted him. Most of the summer people didn't know about this and didn't care but many year-rounders actually presorted their trash for Popeye, who died in the summer of 2000. For Jay he was like "the Town Crier for the unspoken." He never said a lot but his presence said a lot about Provincetown, which made Popeye a symbol. Because he wasn't hassled, like other castoffs and damaged individuals, he was an expression of Ptown's gentleness, a reminder of just how much the place was removed from your ordinary stereotypical community. For Jay and others, it was "very reassuring to have that kind of idiosyncrasy in town."

"I mean, people have described Provincetown as an open ward, a ward filled with ambulatory patients," he says. "But the point is that you can be crazy here, and people will look beyond the crazy. They won't just say, 'Oh, he's nuts.' They'll deal with you. When you leave here and go somewhere else, you find you're alone."

The fact that there is only a single street with a sidewalk that runs the length of the town, and that the street runs along the water's edge in a perfectly parallel crescent has had an effect, too. Commercial Street forces people to interact. It's narrow, you bump into acquaintances whether you want to see them or not, and in all but the foulest weather it's like being in a continuous social whirl. There's no escape, no alternate route if you're walking or biking, which means you cannot hide. An affair, an illness, a bankruptcy, or a Guggenheim grant, even—the whole town will know about it within a week. Gossip is king. Secrets cannot be kept.

"I'm here because I feel comfortable here," Jay explains. "I do my work here and in fact as an artist I may have more influence here than if I were living in New York. I'm marking a place that my work emanates from organically, from the materials of the place—the sand, fish skins, the tampon applicators. I mean, I'm gathering this stuff. The world at large is moving but I haven't moved *anywhere*.

"Why it works is that Provincetown is a staging area for me. I go out to the Statute of Liberty, or to Harvard or to the artists' community AS220 in Rhode Island, I do my thing, then I come back. I can nurture a larger force here, and somehow the balance seems to work for me, so I take the place seriously.

"The other thing, I live on probably only thirty to thirty-five thousand a year, derived largely from my rental apartment, and massage work, and my work with the Compact. Provincetown is cheaper than most places, at least for eight months of the year if you're lucky enough to own your own house. I slipped under the wire, basically. I'm one of those people who came to town at a time when you could still buy a house here."

What does he see for Provincetown in the future?

"Well, I'm going to be president of this theme park, and I'm going to be very rich," he jokes. "But really, I don't know and it can get depressing. I was having a conversation with somebody recently and, like, God, the thought never crossed my mind that I would ever leave Provincetown. Where do you go? What's the next frontier? Is there one? Cyber? Virtual reality? I mean, I guess I've always assumed that I'd be this aging year-round crazy, an old-fashioned artist living in the past."

CHAPTER 30

AN AFTERWORD

At four-thirty on the afternoon of January 6 the body of Christa Worthington was found on the kitchen floor of her isolated hilltop Truro bungalow. According to police, the heiress had been dead for upwards of thirty-six hours. She had been beaten and her body showed evidence of multiple stab wounds. Her child, the two-and-a-half-year-old Ava fathered by Tony Jackett, was found in blood-smeared nightclothes, unharmed, suckling on the dead woman's breast. The back door to the Worthington cottage had been forced open, the deadbolt shattered, but nothing had been taken, including the writer's laptop computer, which was still running when neighbor Tim Arnold first came upon the scene while returning a flashlight.

Later that night, after State Police detectives had secured the property and personnel from the Medical Examiner's Office were still huddling over the body, members of the Worthington clan clustered in the home of Christa's aunt and uncle, Cindy and John Worthington, not two hundred yards from the end of Christa's driveway. This was the family "compound" the press was to talk about so avidly: behind Cindy's weathered saltbox stood the home of Jan, the oldest of Cindy's five daughters; Pam, the second oldest, lives next door, almost opposite Christa's driveway. Another Worthington daughter is farther down Depot Road toward Pamet Inlet, where Ben Affleck bought a place for his mother last summer, and Cindy's sister-in-law Diana is one road over on Pond Road. Still another Worthington, Ansel Chaplin, has a place on Depot and another on High Pamet Road. For five generations, this has been the most talked-about clan in Truro, with roots that, supposedly, go back to the *Mayflower*. During the Depression, the family, more than any other, had even gotten the town through the hard times—"Big John," the family patriarch, by employing fifty or more locals at the fish processing plant he'd revitalized at the end of Highland Road; Tiny, his wife, by hiring others to work at her Fish Net Industries clothing business, which was later featured in *Vogue*.

This was WASPitude writ big. Harvard, Connecticut's exclusive Kent School, the Episcopal church, the Cape Cod National Seashore, years of service on Truro's Board of Selectmen, not to say a circle of friends that had included Edward Hopper, the prominent artist who once painted the Depot Road house of Patricia Worthington Bartlett, still another family member. Through the 1960s an invitation to one of the Worthington's Bermuda shorts–only cocktail parties or to their Pamet Sailing Club get-togethers was the best, if not the only, ticket into Truro summertime society; sophisticated visitors like *New Yorker* writer E. J. Kahn, actor Kevin McCarthy, and "60 Minutes" second-in-command Palmer Williams, all were happy to know "Big John" and Tiny, who wore a size-ten field boot while driving ambulances during World War I.

Tonight, two of Christa's aunts, an uncle, and three of her cousins are present, along with Tony and Susan Jackett, who have been summoned to Cindy's by Truro police chief John Thomas. Ava is also present, having been changed out of the 'jammies she'd been found in. Sitting in Susan Jackett's lap as an ever-changing cast of detectives come and go, she giggles even though the room is filled with the sounds of people weeping.

Sometime around nine, Christa's father, Christopher Worthington, arrives from Boston. Toppy, as he is called familiarly, is the brother of John, Cindy's husband. Toppy served as state assistant attorney general from 1976 to 1987. More recently, he has been in private practice. Now, in response to Tony Jackett's asking him if he's "all right"—how he's holding up under the strain, and all—the slain woman's father comments, almost breezily, "Oh, the traffic wasn't too bad, not too bad at all."

Bizarre as it may seem, for many in Truro's insular community, Toppy's response would not have seemed strange. "Neither of the Worthington sons could compete with their dad, even though they tried" is how people talk about the Worthington boys, and for good reason. Big John served in both World War I and World War II, worked in the oil industry, and, as an experienced pilot, pioneered the use of single-seat "spotter" planes to harpoon tuna, just as he made pots of money brokering frozen fish.

But aside from the sons' failure to measure up, basically the family's glory days are past.

How could they not be? At the time Bill and Hillary Clinton were vacationing on nearby Martha's Vineyard, the mid-nineties saw Vice President Al Gore in Truro, just as the Clinton administration's labor secretary Robert Reich was also visiting. Fame and the media spotlight, as well as the Cape's skyrocketing real estate values, toppled the town's traditional Yankee fundaments.

By early Monday, the day after the discovery of Christa's body, most of the good people of Truro came awake to what had taken place when the press arrived like a tidal wave. The AP, the *Boston Globe, New York Times, New York Post*, and even *People*, had clots of reporters filling the town, and among the invaders were producers, producers' assistants, and a hoard of overly dressed correspondents from the Boston and Providence TV-news outlets, as well as from the evening tabloid shows. In due course, representatives of CBS's "48 Hours," ABC's "20/20," and NBC's "Dateline" would join their ranks. For now, as AOL featured "The Cape Cod Murder" on its opening Web page, the Worthingtons, with the exception of one cousin in Georgia, made a pact with each other to say absolutely nothing.

Christa's neighbor Tim Arnold and Tony were less taciturn, perhaps because they were among the main suspects. The State Police had taken charge and the two had, by now, been hauled in for questioning, as had a number of locals, including several known heroin users and Provincetown bar types. One story making the rounds was that Christa had spent Friday evening, two days before the discovery of her body, hanging out with a woman friend at the Squealing Pig in Ptown; another take, altogether unsubstantiated but not to be discounted, was that after leaving the Pig she'd gone up the street to the Bradford, Provincetown's toughest off-season bar.

Was it Jackett or Arnold? Or could she have picked up a stranger, someone no one knew about? A transient, perhaps, whom she then brought home with her back to Truro?

As the days slipped by with no arrest, a number of Truro residents began locking their doors for the first time ever. During the winter, Truro, with its year-round population of sixteen hundred, is still one of the most desolate places on the Cape; from most houses you see no lights at night, only the stars. The wind howls. Coyotes roam the woods, baying in the distance. Even during daylight hours time hangs heavy, and usually the place feels so cut off that at eleven A.M., when the mail gets sorted, many locals will hang out at the post office just to have someone to talk to. Now, with Christa's death, many townspeople had begun talking about Tony "Chop Chop" Costa, the crazed Provincetown handyman who had cut up four young vacationing women in the late sixties, then buried their limbs along a secluded fire road less than a mile from the Worthington compound. What old-timers remembered most was Costa's final words to the court before sentencing—"Keep digging."

By the second week of their investigation police abruptly shifted their attention to Boston, largely as the result of a front-page exposé in the *Globe*. Toppy, Christa's seventy-two-year-old father, it turned out, had been keeping a twenty-eight-year-old mistress for more than two years. The affair had started before Christa's mother had lost her fight with cancer in the spring of 1999. The woman was a heroin addict and a convicted prostitute who had been involved in the recent murder trial of Dr. Dirk Greineder, a Wellesley allergist who was found guilty of stabbing and bludgeoning his wife to death. She also had a live-in boyfriend with an arrest record. Christa, family members revealed to investigators, had been agitated over her father's frittering away the family fortune and had threatened to go to court to stop him. One account had it that, in November, she'd even changed her will to exclude her father in the event of her death.

Although the police continued to say nothing publicly, they had already taken notice of the senior Worthington's filing probate the day after the discovery of Christa's body, with the result that now Worthington, his hooker girlfriend, and the girlfriend's boyfriend were given polygraph tests. The results all proved "inconclusive."

Even so, the chief suspects in the case still remained Tim Arnold and Tony. Arnold, an author of children's books, was not only Christa's neighbor but her onetime boyfriend who had recently had "major" brain surgery. Whether this might induce him to murder, nobody knew. Pointing to Tony, Christa's inheritance stood at $700,000 and the sole beneficiary was the child, Ava; the Jacketts, starting the night of the discovery of Christa's body, had pledged to raise the child even if it meant a protracted custody fight. Complicating matters further, in the event of the child's death, it was Arnold, along with Worthington Sr., not Jackett, who stood to inherit a share of the estate.

There was also the question of whether Tony had actually ended his extramarital affair, and detectives weren't completely comfortable with the rosy scenario of the Jacketts joining forces "to share" Ava with the child's natural mother—over Christmas the three adults had spent time together, just as Susan and Tony had started taking the child out for regular afternoon car rides. There was something too enlightened here, something too "modern." For almost two years the shellfish warden had kept the secret of his baby, then told his wife only after his mistress had demanded child support and also Tony's forfeiture of paternity. Christa, the cops knew, was nobody's pushover. She could be brittle and demanding, not to say capricious. She'd rewritten her will and during the same period asked not one, but three different parties to be Ava's guardian in the event of her death.

Tony, for his part, was holding up remarkably well. He cooperated fully with the cops and continued talking to the press, repeating that Christa had "trapped" him, that he was "naive" and had been "duped."

"She was very 'European,' you know? She said we'd 'use' each other, no strings attached. Boy, did I get fucked," he told one reporter after another.

He spoke of her claims of infertility, how she'd written articles, attended adoption clinics, even gone on television to talk about the frustrations of not being able to have a child. In one interview with the author of this book, he explained that with the conclusion of one of their afternoon sex sessions Christa had refused a towel, then, from her bed, waved good-bye to him with both her feet up in the air as though gravity, not God, might deliver her a child.

The cops, of course, were not impressed. Tony was a Lothario. Like

Toppy and his gang, he was asked to take a lie-detector test. He complied. He passed. He still remained a suspect.

The police had also started to put together a composite, or "timeline," of Christa's past, a typical enough procedure in any homicide case. The forty-six-year-old heiress's desire to have a child, they saw, was in fact the principal reason she'd returned to the Cape eight or nine years earlier, giving up her "career for a baby." This was no small trade-off, it seemed. After Vassar, she'd gone to New York in 1977, where she'd written freelance assignments for *Cosmopolitan,* then landed a job as *Women's Wear Daily's* accessories editor. In 1983 she was sent to Paris to head *W's* office there, and while in France she was not only showered with invitations to the best parties but did a number of plum pieces on top designers Valentino, Yves Saint Laurent, Thierry Mugler, and other fashion giants. In London, she wrote for the tony *Independent.* When she returned to New York in the late eighties, she worked for *Elle, Elle Decor, Harper's Bazaar,* and the *New York Times,* and also contributed to several books. As in Europe, she went to parties where she hobnobbed with celebrities like Woody Allen, and her friends included *New York Times* theater critic Ben Brantley.

There was a darker side to all this, though. Her departure from Paris had been unpleasant—she'd been passed over for the position of permanent bureau chief at *W,* a turn of events that led to a loud and very public shouting match with *Women's Wear Daily* chairman John Fairchild in the office elevator. One close friend of Christa's, a fellow publishing exec, maintained that the reason she hadn't gotten the job was a sarcastic piece she'd penned on Valentino; he'd also spoken of tax problems that *W* was having with the URSAFF, the French employment authority, that allegedly stemmed from the company's hiring of "illegals," for which Christa was made to take the fall.

But there was still another dimension to her returning home. For years Christa had had a daydream that she was Virginia Woolf, and at other times she'd become Dorothy Parker. Coming back to Truro, she'd told close friends, would finally let her write "for real."

The problem was, after landing back on the Cape, she hadn't produced.

What she did, instead, was have the affair with Jackett and give birth to Ava. Then, over the next two years, she went to Weight Watchers, socialized with other middle-age mothers, and had her off-again, on-again affair with neighbor Tim Arnold, who claimed to adore the baby. She also let herself drift into Ptown from time to time on the weekends: On the Cape, as in Europe and New York, Christa Worthington had always gravitated toward "difficult men," sometimes more than one at a time.

As the police investigation continued into February, the media heated up when the Jacketts went to court for the second time to challenge the custody of Ava, which had been granted to Cliff and Amyra Chase, the Cohasset couple designated as guardians in Worthington's latest will. Weeks before, Tony had given a DNA sample. Now, before a hushed courtroom filled with reporters, it was confirmed that Anthony "Tony" Jackett, Jr., was the child's biological father. A representative of the Cape and Islands District Attorney's Office next rose to advise the court that to the extent that it could be a factor in granting custody, Jackett could not be ruled out as a suspect in the ongoing murder investigation. He was "only one of any number of other suspects," the D.A.'s rep cautioned; Judge Robert Scandurra listened carefully. The judge also listened to the arguments presented by Chris Snow, and to the counterarguments of the Chases' attorney, Paul Mayer—the one side pleading biology and blood; the other, the wishes of the child's murdered mother.

After two hours Scandurra finally ruled in favor of the Chases, rejecting the Jacketts' bid not only on the grounds that Tony was still a suspect but that the shellfish constable had never tried to establish paternity until after Worthington's death. The Chases' temporary custody was to remain in effect until April 8. Scandurra advised both sides to work out visitation and child-support arrangements.

Before gaveling the hearing to a close, the bearded judge also commented, "It looks like this case is headed for a trial."

Tony, who hadn't said a word throughout the two-hour proceeding, again worked the media outside in the hallway afterward. He'd already appeared on the "Today" show and, despite his attorney's advice to keep silent, talked to the *New York Times*, the *New York Times Sunday Magazine*, *Newsweek*, *New York Magazine*, the *Boston Globe*, and many other print media. Some said he'd courted the press attention. There were even rumors that in his mind's eye he was already casting the inevitable made-for-TV movie—Antonio Banderas as himself, Madonna as Susan, and Britney Spears in the role of Braunwyn. As with so much else in his life, Tony didn't care. All along, his goal had been to try to win the custody battle, and the media, he believed, might help him do it.

"I'm the father," he said, surrounded by Susan and their four children, including Beau and his wife, Elizabeth, who had driven up from Connecticut. "If we don't have her now, we'll take her home in two months. She's our child, she belongs with us. Who are these people, the Chases? *They're not Ava's family.*"

Meanwhile, Christa's killer remained at large. As this book goes to print one of the victim's cousins has "signed" to write and coproduce a Hollywood movie based on the tragedy, leaving many of the family's neighbors appalled and disgusted. A growing number of Truro residents have also resigned themselves to the painful possibility that the murderer may never be found, as was the case with the middle-age woman discovered in 1975 in the Province Lands, with her hands severed. Likewise, the same thing happened twenty years later, in September 1997, when Linda Silva, a forty-seven-year-old social worker, was shot in the back of the head not a block and a half from the Bradford bar, in a well-lit area in the heart of Provincetown. Not a single eyewitness has come forward, and that case, too, remains unsolved.

For Christa's baby-sitter, Ellen Webb, as for others, the murder of Christa Worthington was "like getting sucked back into the vortex."

Truro has been changed forever, yet now, four months after the murder and the accompanying flood of media exposure, not many locals are really all that surprised—the harsh, flat, weatherbeaten Outer Cape, this isolated landscape that has drawn painters and repelled Pilgrims, has never given up its secrets of genius any more than it has ever given up its secrets of crime. Why should it be any different now?

ACKNOWLEDGMENTS

I am grateful, above all, to the people who appear in this book for their cooperation and trust in allowing me into their lives.

Next, I thank my editor, Lisa Drew, for her faith in this project from the very start, as well as for her encouragement and advice throughout. It was she who said, several years ago, "When are you going to do your Ptown book?" Susan Dooley Carey helped immeasurably, too, more than I believe she knows. I also thank Eric Taylor and Kathe Izzo, as well as Nancy Olson Garofalo and Michelle Costantino, who transcribed my interviews with great rigor. Erin Curler, Lisa Drew's assistant at Scribner, was unflagging in her attention to detail. Elisa Rivlin, Simon & Schuster's head legal counsel, was a rare and special model of sensitivity and thoroughness in her reading of the manuscript.

David Black at the David Black Literary Agency held up his end and I thank him, too.

In Provincetown Town Hall, I am beholden to Roslyn Garfield, town moderator; Stephan J. Nofield, town clerk; Dana Faris and Richard Faust in the Provincetown Town Assessor's Office; Eric Dray of the Housing Authority; William Dougal, Finance Committee; Susan Fleming, superintendent of schools; Building Commissioner Warren G. Alexander, and Town Selectpersons Mary-Jo Avellar and David Atkinson. Without Debbie DeJonker-Berry and her staff at the Provincetown Library this project would have been dead in the water.

At the Barnstable County Second District Court in Orleans I received valuable help from Judge Robert A. Welch and his brother,

Assistant Clerk Magistrate Charles F. Welch. I thank them and their staff.

At the *Cape Cod Times*, Robin Smith Johnson and Arnold Miller provided access to news and photo files, respectively. Closer to home, Hamilton Kahn, editor of the *Provincetown Banner*, was similarly helpful.

Robyn Watson, former director of the Provincetown Art Association and Museum, generously shared her extensive knowledge of the Cape art scene with me, as did PAAM's Jim Zimmerman. Laurel Guadazno, Jeff Morris, Dick Caouett, Mike Van Bel, and Chuck Turley, director of the Pilgrim Monument & Provincetown Museum, gave me access to their archives and provided photos. Special thanks must go to George Bryant, whose store of information about the Outer Cape's history is without parallel. Likewise, thanks to Ray Elman and Christopher Busa for having created *Provincetown Arts*, which has been a helpful source of information on Provincetown's vast cultural riches.

At Shank Painter Printing, the whole gang pitched in but I must thank Eva Nogiec, especially, not only for her technical support but for constant reminders never to forget the "old days." Thanks also to Porsche Cars of North America, and especially Bob Carlson and Martin Peters, for the use of a Carrera 4—the most capable vehicle on the road today. Rain or shine, the Porsche showed its love for the Outer Cape and the Outer Cape more than went for the Porsche. All writers, indeed all lovers of great machinery, should have it so lucky.

Anthony M. Doniger, Esq., of Sugarman, Rogers, Barshak, and Cohen, was, as always, there for me when I needed his guidance.

Many friends listened to me while I was doing my research and writing: James and Denise Landis, Peter Bloch, Thomas Sanchez, Nicholas von Hoffman, Christophe Laffaille, and Olivier Royant in Paris; E. J. "Terry" and Rose Kahn, Curtis Hartman, Rhoda and Will Rossmoore, Ray and Lee Elman, Jonathan Sinaiko, Pam Worthington Franklin, Dr. Walter Richter, Charlotte and Michael Jerace. From time to time all of them must have grown weary of my writer's babblings, and I thank them all for their patience and support.

As is often the case with a nonfiction book, a number of people who helped me wish to remain anonymous. They know who they are. I thank them.

Finally, although words ultimately fail me, I must thank my parents, Leo and Blanche Manso, who first gave me my beloved childhood vacations in Provincetown without which this book would never have been written.

NOTES

12 *"A cow, two goats, five sheep"*: William Bradford, *The History of the Plimoth Plantation*, pp. 474–76. See also, Henry C. Kittredge, *Cape Cod: Its People and Their History*, Hyannis, Mass.: Parnassus Imprints edition, 1987.

14 *Fortunes were being made*: Schneider, *The Enduring Shore*, pp. 164–65; 293–97.

15 *"One may stand here"*: Thoreau, *Cape Cod*, p. 319.

19 *"The people in Provincetown"*: Mary Heaton Vorse, *Time and the Town*, p. 87. See also, Arthur N. Strahler, *A Geologist's View of Cape Cod*, pp. 3–25.

21 *"Sand is the great enemy"*: Thoreau, *Cape Cod*, p. 256.

22 *"a filmy sliver"*: Thoreau, ibid, p. 293.

27 *"It is none too easy"*: Qtd. in Marion Campbell Hawthorne, ed., *Hawthorne on Painting*, p. 44. See also, Leona Rust Egan, *Provincetown as a Stage*, and Mary Heaton Vorse, *Time and the Town*, pp. 116–26.

29 *"the thing that staggers"*: A. J. Philpot, *Boston Globe Sunday Magazine*, August 27, 1916.

31 *"Buddy-buddy-shipmate!"*: Tennessee Williams, *Letters to Donald Windham, 1940–1965*, pp. 137–38.

33 See Jennifer Leise, "Forum 49: Relating All the Arts," and Irving Sandler, "The Irascible Weldon Kees," *Provincetown Arts*, Vol. 14, 1999, pp. 38–39; 40–43.

35 *"New York got to be"*: Quoted in Irving Sandler, ibid., p. 42.

38 See Donald Cantin, "The Revenge of Roger Skillings," *Provincetown Arts*, Vol. 8, 1992, p. 137.

65 *In 1947*: John Hardy Wright, *Images of America, Provincetown, Vol. II*, p. 113.

67 *"Provincetown is a gay haven"*: Quoted in the *Advocate*, Aug. 21, 1986.

90 *"to a neighborhood"*: Mike Barnacle, *Boston Globe*, Aug. 31, 1981.

91 *"History"*: Quoted in the *Advocate*, Sept. 29, 1988.

95 *"The whole thing is"*: Quoted in the *Advocate*, Aug. 25, 1977.

95 *"If Provincetown nowadays"*: Quoted in the *Advocate*, Aug. 22, 1996.

139 *The Reverend Isaiah Lewis*: Schneider, ibid, p. 206–7. See also Henry C. Kittredge, *Mooncussers of Cape Cod*, New York: Houghton Mifflin Co., 1964.

144 Jimmy Buffett, *Tales from Margaritaville*, pp. 239–40.

191 *"Stars and Strife"*: *People*, May 24, 1993.

191 *Senator Jesse Helms*: *Advocate*, Feb. 15, 1990. See also *Washington Post*, May 21, 1992; *Wall Street Journal*, Feb. 6, 1992.

204 *During the summer of 1995*: "Billy Bones' Liquor License Suspended After 'Raw' Party," *The Cape Codder*, Sept. 22, 1995.

212 *Another take on what was*: *Sunday Cape Cod Times*, Oct. 30, 1994.

277 "The Rewards of Provincetown's Popularity," *New York Times*, Sunday, May 21, 2000, p. 35; *USA Today*, Aug. 2, 2000, p. 6B.

280 Quoted in "Housing Issue Displaces Activist Ryan," *The Provincetown Banner*, May 10, 2001, p. 22.

288 Quoted in "Understanding Gay Consumers," Howard Buford, *Gay and Lesbian Review*, Spring, 2000, pp. 26–28. See also, Charles Kaiser, *The Gay Metropolis*, p. 339.

BIBLIOGRAPHY

The following is a bibliography of some of the materials I used in my research, arranged alphabetically. Provincetown's longtime local newspaper, the *Advocate*, went out of business in the spring of 2000 but was unusually helpful, and no listing of research assets would be complete without it.

Alden, Peter, et al. *National Audubon Society Field Guide to New England*. New York: Alfred A. Knopf, 1998.

Boyle, Charles, and Louis Postel. *Provincetown Poets*, Vol. 2, No. 1. Provincetown, Mass.: Total World Services of Provincetown, 1976.

Bradford, William. *The History of the Plimoth Plantation*. Boston: Wright & Potter, 1899.

Braham, Jeanne, and Pamela Peterson. *Starry, Starry Night: Provincetown's Response to the AIDS Epidemic*. Cambridge, Mass.: Lumen Editions, 1998.

Brevda, William. *Harry Kemp: The Last Bohemian*. London and Toronto: Bucknell University Press, 1986.

Buffett, Jimmy. *Tales from Margaritaville*. New York: Ballantine Books, 1989.

Carey, Richard Adams. *Against the Tide: The Fate of the New England Fisherman*. Boston: Houghton Mifflin Company, 1999.

Controversial Century: 1850–1950: Paintings from the Collection of Walter P. Chrysler, Jr. The Chrysler Art Museum of Provincetown, Massachusetts, and National Gallery of Canada, Ottawa, undated.

Crotty, Frank. *Provincetown Profiles and Others on Cape Cod*. Barre, Mass.: Barre Gazette, 1958.

De Tocqueville, Alexis. *Democracy in America*. New York: Bantam Classic, 2000.

Drake, Gillian. *The Complete Guide to Provincetown*. Provincetown, Mass.: Shank Painter Publishing, 1992.

Days Lumberyard Studios, Provincetown 1914–71. Exhibition catalog, August 18, 1978–October 1, 1978. Provincetown Art Association and Museum, Provincetown, Massachusetts, 1978.

Egan, Leona Rust. *Provincetown as a Stage: Provincetown, the Provincetown Players, and the Discovery of Eugene O'Neill.* Orleans, Mass.: Parnassus Imprints, 1994.

Finch, Robert. *Outlands: Journeys to the Outer Edges of Cape Cod.* Boston: David R. Godine, 1986.

————, ed. *A Place Apart: A Cape Cod Reader.* New York: W.W. Norton & Company, 1993.

Garrison, Dee, ed. *Rebel Pen: The Writings of Mary Heaton Vorse.* New York: Monthly Review Press, 1985.

Gaspar, Frank X. *Leaving Pico.* Hanover, N.H.: University Press of New England, 1999.

Gelb, Arthur, and Barbara Gelb. *O'Neill: Life with Monte Cristo.* New York: Applause Books, 2000.

Hawthorne, Charles. *Hawthorne on Painting,* ed. Marion Campbell Hawthorne. New York: Dover Publications, 1938.

Huntington, Cynthia. *The Salt House: A Summer on the Dunes of Cape Cod.* Hanover, N.H.: University Press of New England, 1999.

Jacobs, Michael. *The Good & Simple Life: Artist Colonies in Europe and America.* Oxford, England: Phaidon Press Limited, 1985.

Kaiser, Charles. *The Gay Metropolis: The Landmark History of Gay Life in America Since World War II.* San Diego: Harcourt Brace, 1998.

Kidder, Tracy. *Home Town.* New York: Random House, 1999.

Kittredge, Henry. *Cape Cod: Its People and Their History.* Hyannis, Mass.: Parnassus Imprints, 1987.

————. *Mooncussers of Cape Cod.* New York: Houghton Mifflin, 1964.

Kurlansky, Mark. *Cod: A Biography of the Fish That Changed the World.* New York: Penguin Books, 1997.

Matthiessen, Peter. *Men's Lives.* New York: Vintage Books, 1988.

Miller, John, and Tim Smith, eds. *Cape Cod Stories.* San Francisco: Chronicle Books, 1996.

Miller, Neil. *Out of the Past: Gay and Lesbian History from 1869 to the Present.* New York: Vintage Books, 1995.

Moffett, Ross. *Art in Narrow Streets: The First Thirty-three Years of the Provincetown Art Association.* Provincetown, Mass.: Cape Cod Pilgrim Memorial Association, 1989.

Provincetown Art Association and Museum: The Permanent Collection. Provincetown, Mass.: Provincetown Art Association and Museum, 1999.

Sarlós, Robert Károly. *Jig Cook and the Provincetown Players.* Boston: University of Massachusetts Press, 1982.

Schneider, Paul. *The Enduring Shore: A History of Cape Cod, Martha's Vineyard, and Nantucket.* New York: Henry Holt and Company, 2000.

Stansell, Christine. *American Moderns: Bohemian New York and the Creation of a New Century.* New York: Henry Holt and Company, 2000.

Sterling, Dorothy. *The Outer Lands: A Natural History Guide to Cape Cod, Martha's Vineyard, Nantucket, Block Island and Long Island.* New York: W.W. Norton & Company, 1978.

Strahler, Arthur N. *A Geologist's View of Cape Cod.* Orleans, Mass.: Parnassus Imprints, 1966.

Thoreau, Henry David. *Cape Cod.* New York: Penguin Books, 1987.

Vorse, Mary Heaton. *Time and the Town: A Provincetown Chronicle.* New Brunswick, N.J.: Rutgers University Press, 1991.

Williams. Tennessee. *Letters to Donald Windham, 1940–1965.* Ed. Donald Windham. New York: Holt, Rinehart and Winston, 1977.

Wolfson, Victor. *Cabral.* New York: Avon Books, 1972.

Wright, John Hardy. *Images of America: Provincetown,* Vol. 1. Dover, N.H.: Arcadia, 1997.

———. *Images of America: Provincetown,* Vol. 2. Charleston, S.C.: Arcadia, 1998.

INDEX